Route and Branch

Being an account of my life: as I grappled
with it to the best of my ability!

*With my very best
'Wishes'.
Bill Clark*

Bill Clark

Head Warden of
Wandlebury Country Park
and Nature Reserve: 1973 – 1998

First published in 2013 by Milton Contact Ltd.

A CIP catalogue record for this book is available from The British Library.

ISBN 978-0-9571959-3-6

Milton Contact Ltd
3 Hall End, Milton
Cambridge, United Kingdom
CB24 6AQ

www.miltoncontact.co.uk

Dedication

To Caroline with fondest memory.
Tragically departing before this memoir could go into print.

Also for my dear wife Wendy.
Without whom I would have been an entirely
different person; and this account would certainly
never have been written.

My thanks also go to all the people who have been of so
much help to me – especially during my Wandlebury years
and since my retirement. I am afraid you are too many to
mention, but you all know who you are!

Contents

1. Early Days in Bedfordshire

With farming in the doldrums in the 1920s, father decided to try his luck in London. Working as a foreman to a street resurfacing gang, whilst near the home of the Tates, of Tate and Lyle, one of their servants caught his eye whilst running errands, and she soon stole away to meet him at every opportunity. Brought up in a Dr Barnardo's home – her mother unable to care for her – she had now been placed in 'Service' with the despotic Lady Tate, her unhappiness compounded by the harsh housekeeper. But as she explained to her new boyfriend, being now 21 she could make her own decisions, and yes, she would marry him! The deed was done as soon as possible, my father's brother Cecil, the only member of family present. When mother confessed that night ˝ that she was not yet 21, and had lied on the marriage certificate, they moved back to his parents in Bedfordshire in a hurry!

They rented a cottage on the outskirts of Colmworth and, as all the Clark clan were keen gardeners, it was soon looking a picture, with the addition of rustic arbours and arches constructed with coppiced hazel. His 'foreman's' pay on a large estate was abysmal, and the town girl was having to very quickly get to grips with rabbit skinning, bird plucking and scavenging nearby fields for left-behind potatoes, swedes and turnips. The daily choice too, of whether to light the unpredictable black leaded coal stove – after collecting wood – or the smelly paraffin one, was part of the joys of country living in the early thirties. She was

1

now pregnant and, for the first time ever, spending her days alone. She said she had never known such silence – which was probably why her first country thunderstorm sounded so terrifying, that she was still under the stairs when father came home from work. Her next unwelcome experience was a demanding tramp who made return visits, so father bought a dog – 'sight unseen' – from a local publican for half a crown.

Ben was no ordinary Irish wolfhound – neither in his huge size, nor temperament. He attacked everyone on sight, even his owner, who pushed his food to him with a clothes-prop! Apparently he had not been loose or touched by human hand since being chained to an apple tree in the garden. It transpired that the crafty publican had sold the animal on more than one occasion. However, the dog held no fears for father, who had always been able to handle unruly animals of all descriptions, and in moments Ben found himself attached to a lead and trotting off beside his cycle.

Early next morning father let him into the garden to relieve himself; but with one bound he was over the fence and off. A chase by cycle, following the sounds of barking – and shouting – revealed first a dishevelled postman pushing his bike, and then another rider, this time on a horse, desperately fending off the dog with his riding crop. Thankfully, Ben shrunk to the ground at the sound of father's voice, and after profuse apologies and explanations, he was led home. Next, side by side with father, mother had to go through an early morning tutorial of training and dominance of Ben, before father left for work. No tramp ever bothered her again. Neither would the postman call; he just stood in the road and waved her occasional letters!

By the time I was born, Ben had taken to his new life like a duck to water and next decided to be my 'Guardian Angel.' No one, including my paternal grandmother, ever approached cot or pram whilst I was in it – for Ben's constant supine manner at my side would change to instant alertness, and one more step would bring forth a warning growl. There was no problem when mother told him to move away. I could even be picked up. But he would immediately dart back when I was replaced, to check my condition and give my cheek the odd lick, before settling down again beside me. Unfortunately, eighteen months later, the owner of the cottage gave my parents a week's notice to quit and moved his mother in, 'Because she had fallen in love with the pretty garden.' Father took little interest in flower gardening ever again.

Fortunately he was renting a small meadow at the end of a lane to raise chickens and hearing of a gypsy caravan for sale, he acquired it and the rest of my first two years were spent in this idyllic place. With no room for Ben inside, a large barrel was obtained and he spent his days tethered to it on a long chain, quite happy as long as I was within his reach – for outside, I too was tethered on a long clothes line and often happily slept between Ben's paws. But as I approached my second birthday, my brother Bob was soon to arrive and we moved into a small thatched cottage. Poor mother was still having little luck. Only days after moving in, as she turned from the stove with a new enamel saucepan full of boiling water, the handle came away and tipped most of it over me playing on the floor. Although I hovered between life and death for a couple of weeks, I had recovered sufficiently to slap my brother's face when he arrived and unfortunately, Ben looked unfavourably on him too. Deciding the dog was too great a risk, he was given to a gypsy family; the last time my parents saw Ben, he was trotting behind a van among a group of children.

I must have been about four when I spent hours hanging on the fence at the end of our garden, listening to the hammering and watching the sparks and smoke emanating from the village blacksmith's workshop – I can smell the acrid fumes now as they put the hot shoes to the horses hooves. I also crept through the side hedge to run across a meadow to watch an old man with a beard – he could have been about forty – working bees in both skeps and hives. I don't recall how many times I peered through the barbed wire strands before he invited me in, but I never felt afraid as he explained what he was doing and what the bees were doing. He never wore a veil and we never got stung; although I can remember when I was about six, standing with older boys and throwing things up at bee's nests in old hollow elms on the edge of the meadow, and of them chasing and stinging us!

I cannot remember the occasion when my father came in from the garden, to find me sitting in the middle of the floor with his pocket watch in pieces around me, but my mother assured me that I was only four, repeating the story each time I tinkered with a clock. At this time mother struck up a friendship with a widow who had four children. The third oldest, a twelve year old girl, was encouraged to look after me and my brother during her free time and in return her family were given eggs and rabbits. Under Blanche's care we spent hours wandering cowslip meadows and finding the odd orchid – which even then was considered a prize – in woodlands carpeted with bluebells, primroses or wind flowers in their season; and walks along quiet lanes with white and blue violets scattered along the banks; never was anyone prouder than I, to take a large, wilting bunch of flowers to my mother, and to watch her and my 'nursemaid' arrange them in earthenware jam jars around the house. The largest glass jam jars, with a convenient rim to take a string loop for a handle, were in almost constant use: in spring it was frog spawn being carried home; a little later newts – caught with a worm dangled from a length of string; in summer the 'peeps' from cowslip flowers – for mother to make into wine; late summer, the blackberries – for jam; and last of all, hazel nuts.

All too soon it was time for school. I remember my first day, only because of my mother's repeats of it. We arrived at the tiny Colmworth School, with me in great excitement. I couldn't wait to get inside the playground and wave good-bye and, apparently, my excitement did not abate in the schoolroom, constantly interrupting and

4

wanting to know every detail about work pinned to the walls, etc. Finally, after I rushed to the window as a steam engine drove past, calling for everyone else to look too, Miss Arter told me to hold out my hand and struck it with her cane, telling me in no uncertain terms, that this would happen every time I jumped out of my seat or interrupted in future. After school, the other children gathered round my mother to give her a resume of my day. She was horrified and, dragging me by the hand, stormed into the classroom. Miss Arter apologised to my mother, saying she had found it impossible to teach the rest of the class, that it had only been a tap, and that I had responded and settled down after the initial sobbing.

Certainly I never held it against Miss Arter, for I worked my little socks off for her. She was keen on natural history, and I took in every word she had to say on the subject, regularly contributing to the 'Nature Table', and often received the chocolate 'Rollo' for the best find. I also slogged at my reading and arithmetic, determined to win the promised month's pictures from the large wall calendar; one of a pair of bullfinches and the other of goldfinches feeding on thistles – triumphantly carrying them both home to adorn our walls.

Towards the end of my second year, we had to move into a new council house to the south of the school – our old clay-daub cottage had been condemned – and soon after, Miss Arter visited my parents to inform them that, even though she had put me in a class ahead of my age group, her mother – the head teacher – thought that I was still being held back, and that I should be moved into her class. On the following Monday I not only moved into the 'Big Room', but also the 'Big Playground'.

My parents though were having difficulty meeting the rent for the new house and when one of the 'tied' farm houses became vacant, moved to Bolnhurst. Although we were now more than twice the distance from school, they thought I should stay – on my bicycle it was still within reach, though the down side for me was that a carrier was fitted on the back to carry my brother. As we still never got on very well when in close proximity, we used to have some eventful rides back and forth. Nevertheless my world could not have been happier – then catastrophe! In midsummer father had a dispute with his employer and upped and moved the family some six miles to Thurleigh.

2. A House Move and the War make for a Busy Later Childhood

Looking back, my start at that school in 1940 could not have been at a worse time – it was soon after the influx of the evacuees, and the local lads were probably finding it hard, being squeezed in both the school and their homes, and found it much easier to take it out on my brother and I. Unfortunately the evacuees joined in too.

Only three incidents stand out in my memory of those first weeks – the Colmworth school re-routed the annual day-trip coach, to pick up my brother and I for a visit to Wicksteed Park; a pretty little girl called Gill – in my brother's class – befriended me with a lovely smile and an aniseed ball, and a photographer arrived to take the school photos. It was to be some years before the young girl spurned my adolescent advances, and many more before the school photo enabled me to pick her out of a Nurses reunion photo in the Cambridge Evening News!

The years ground on. Thurleigh School was never a pleasant place for me, for besides being bullied at every opportunity, I was often caned – ours was one of the furthest routes to school, so my most regular caning was for lateness. However caning was common throughout the school anyway: on one occasion every boy was caned because no one would own up to smashing a bottle of waste oil that was used to oil the gardening tools – some of the lads then ganged up on me, because I was the one who had volunteered to provide it in the first place. Later that day a member of the Home Guard called in, and apologised for 'Breaking a bottle of oil last night.' But we received no apology. I believe I was a good example of the futility of caning, for all it did was harden me and make me hold the teachers in disdain – there were occasions when I arrived midmorning because rabbiting and botanising along the way had taken my mind off the time. On one memorable occasion I arrived as the classes turned out to go home! Even so, during the next three years I still managed to stay in the top three in my class, and a bright light occasionally lit up my day with a smile and a proffered sweet.

The war was to affect me in varying ways. We had already been host to two London evacuees in the council house at Colmworth, and after we moved to Bolnhurst, I often played with the two children of a White Russian family whose father had been shot. After our first visit, when their mother poured well stewed tea from a watering can into jam jars for us, mother toured her friends, begging household articles for them. Father had already joined the Local Defence Volunteers, later named the Home Guard, and at first paraded in civilian clothes with only an arm band for identification and for some time was the only one with a rifle – his own 'rook' rifle. I can remember mother crying with laughter when he put on his new uniform: being about 5 feet 9 with very muscular biceps and 48 inch chest, his jacket was a tight fit with the sleeves reaching some 4 inches beyond his fingers, the crotch of his trousers was about level with his knees, with the bottoms laying on the floor some 10 inches beyond his toes, whilst his 'greatcoat' was a great coat – the hem swept the floor! She spent days making alterations.

Polish 'displaced persons' were already working on the farm, when one afternoon the Russian lady ran screaming across the field, 'BEEL, BEEL, Fwance as fallen, the Bosch vill be comin ere.' Even an eight year old caught the gloom. A day or two later father set the Poles ditch digging beside a large wood, and as he returned to the farm buildings, yells rang out – they were running after him waving their arms, pointing behind and shouting, 'VIPS, Bill, VIPS.' Heart in mouth, he turned and ran like blazes to get his rifle from the barn, and three women just arriving to do some hoeing, snatched up pitch forks and joined the race – the wretched parachutists hiding in the wood were not going to have it all their own way! There was much hilarity and great relief, when it was discovered that one of the men had dug into a wasps nest.

Planes, Bombs and Souvenirs

At Thurleigh I was much nearer the action! Our farm was close to the small Twin-woods airfield, flying mainly Bostons and Blenheims, with some of the approach lights on our fields: Thurleigh airfield was just over two miles north of us, flying mostly B17 'Flying Fortresses', and Staughton, some six miles north-easterly, flew Lancasters. Engine noise, either overhead or warming up on the runways, was with us day and night. The Fortresses often arrived back in the late afternoon and it was not unusual to see one trailing smoke as it limped home – to add to the drama we often got the news directly from those men billeted among us, or their village girlfriends.

Every playtime there would be a group of boys haggling over a spent 303 Home Guard cartridge, or the lead bullets dug out of their practice bank. I was never into 'swopsys' to build up a collection, with me it had to be, 'my find', but I didn't mind exchanging duplicates to the highest bidder, for how else could I build up a marble collection or get a good whipping top? This meant my keeping a good look out in the countryside around – a spent cannon shell or a Very light cartridge from the American planes could occasionally be found. One special prize was a hatch that fell off when a gunner baled out, but I am afraid I cannot remember how on earth I managed to get the piece of new tank track home – it had fallen off the rack on the side of a tank, and must have weighed some 30 kilos. It was used as a barn door stop for years.

The best finds came from keeping my ears open, and it was surprising how much – a now ten year old – could pick up by listening in to his Home Guard father's description of the happenings of the previous night. A Fortress had crashed on takeoff, at Mr Hope's farm, so naturally I managed to cross that field on my way to school, even though it was a couple of miles out of my way. The friendly American guards let me wander over the site to pick up bits of the smashed 'Plexiglas' windows, a much prized plastic that older boys used to make into brooches and rings; little did the guards know, my pockets were also laden with live cannon shells and Very light cartridges – worth quite a bit to a syndicate of older boys who made fireworks out of them.

A Boston from Twin-woods crash-landed on one of our fields and provided me with hundreds of live cannon shells, some still in sections of belt. Alas the firework syndicate – and my best source of wealth – broke up soon after, when a boy was injured in an explosion. My first piece of a reputed thousand pound bomb, was gleaned from the soldiers about to bulldoze the crater – a very uninteresting torn piece of metal, that I thought could have come from anything. Another piece, decidedly larger, came from a 'Doodle Bug' which dislodged part of the roof of the next farmhouse to ours; what I really aspired to was a piece of bomb that really looked like a bomb, and better still, have a few German hieroglyphics on it. One theory was that all bombs had a hard point to enable them to penetrate, so all I had to do was measure the centre of the crater, dig down, and the point would be mine. My chance came when my father came in one morning during the summer holidays, to announce that the bombs during the night had straddled Twin-woods, and made a crater in 36 Acre.

My breakfast was the quickest ever and despite my father's warning to keep away, some twenty minutes later, accompanied by my eight year old brother Bob, I was measuring across the crater, and soon digging down with the largest digging implement that I had been able to hide inside my jacket. After only a few thrusts I heard a metallic clink, and soon uncovered a disc, some six inches (150 mm) across. I then dug down the side, with no sign of it receding to a point. 'It is longer than I thought,' I informed my brother, and asked him to search for a stone, whilst I dug down. When he returned with a decent one, I proceeded to whack the 'point' a few times to loosen it, with no result, and decided to dig even deeper into our tenacious Bedfordshire clay. It was when I came to the second projection around the side that the light dawned. 'It's a fin,' I announced to my brother, and even I quickly decided that a live, upside-down bomb, was not all that desirable. But at least I now knew that not all bombs had a pointed end!

We had only just arrived home when a policeman called to ask for directions to the site. And it was well into the afternoon, before a yell from my father informed me that, both a policeman and an army sergeant were wanting a word! My emotions were rather split, for both the policeman and my father's faces forewarned of trouble, but the sergeant I had met before, and he stood there with a splendid whole – now empty – bomb. It ensued that the policeman had quickly judged the situation, the only point in my favour being that the crater would probably have been filled in, with the bomb remaining down there, if it had not been for my uncovering it – although that fact was not told to me until long afterwards – I was then severely lectured on the danger to myself and Bob. 'My bomb' had not gone off because another incendiary in the pack had melted a small globule of the aluminium case, which had stuck the detonator – a glass vial of acid in a tube – so that it could not slide and break, and because it was now up-side-down, the dents, showing where I had been hitting with the stone, happened to be above where it was situated!

That particular bomb – even steamed out – was denied to me as mother said it gave her the shivers. I do think I redeemed myself later though, when I found a

'German booby trap bomb' in a hedge, and informed the police. It's only since reading about wartime boffins, that I now know that I had in fact found an RAF bomb. There had been a trial run over Bedfordshire, with hilarious consequences. A plane was to fly across the path of the incoming German bombers, dropping small bombs – the shape of two soup plates welded face to face – on the end of wires attached to parachutes. When a plane flew into a wire, the parachute would drag the bomb back up to the wing, and the detonator – all round the edge – would set off the bomb on contact. For various reasons, no bombs contacted enemy aircraft, just draped themselves over the Bedfordshire countryside. The following day, perplexed folk were carrying them in from all over, and depositing them at army posts and police stations. One policeman had cycled some distance with a half a dozen clanking on his handlebars!

When Sparrows were Vermin

I was also heavily occupied in the 'war effort' and as well as collecting salvage of all kinds, in season, there were horse-chestnuts for explosives, rose hips for syrup and blackberries for jam – I was paid on a per pound basis for the last two. I also did pea picking and potato picking, and this took my interest to another level, for my mother invested this money in National Savings for me: much of it was advertised for specific purposes – so every time the radio spoke of Spitfires destroying German bombers, I hoped that the one I had helped pay for, was one of them. And I was particularly upset when the Bedfordshire Times headlined, that the submarine HMS Thorne, that I had helped pay for, had been lost.

Vermin control was high on the 'war effort' agenda – and for us lads it could also be fun! Our father taught us all the ways to catch and kill, quickly and efficiently, and how to pluck, skin, and quarter just about anything. Skins and feathers still fetched a ready penny – but only if they were prepared properly. Our large 'weather board' barn was always decorated with stretched skins, varying in size from moles, average 6d, (two and a half p) to fox, best quality £1/10s, (£1.50) – you have not lived until you have skinned a smelly dog fox by the light of an almost equally smelly carbide lamp – and wings from jays, magpies, and carrion crows – don't ever tell me crows are dull black creatures! At that time my father earned about £3 per week as a farm foreman, working all hours.

I remember Bob and I attending a chicken farmer's threshing-day. We checked all his permanent wire netting on one side of the stack and used the rolls all threshing sets had to carry with them, to seal off the rest once the tackle was in place. There were three good mousing cats, a small dog, and around a hundred hens also in our enclosure. Mice started running whilst the thatch was coming off the rick! By the end of the day – and the stack – the cats and dog just lay, looking like balloons, watching mice run past their noses; only an occasional hen still ran forward to snatch them up as my brother and I flailed left and right. For us though, the icing on the cake was the number of dead rats – well over a hundred – for which we got a penny per tail from our local policeman, but only after I had given them to a friend in another village who took them to the School Master where he was kept at arm's length, and made to count them out and then take them away for burial. Upon his return, we shared the loot, and then cycled to our policeman, who despite our offer to dispose of them, always declined.

Another money earner was sparrows. We joined the national 'Sparrow Campaign', and along the way earned a halfpenny a head from the farmer, and often – if our mother was fed up with the repetition – another penny or two per dozen, from local housewives for the ingredients for sparrow pie. We also joined with other lads to roam the hedgerows on winter nights – it needed to be windy and moonless – then with either clapper net, or simply a sturdy stick with the twigs left on to form a fanlike shape, one lad would walk on the windy side and tap the hedge, and at least a couple of lads on the lea side with carbide cycle lamps, would hold the net over the top as birds flew out, or simply strike them down with the branch. I liked the net best, because we could let out any pretty birds, although I was sometimes howled down if it was a lean night, and a particular lad's mother was expecting enough for dinner. I got quite expert at identifying a particular bird even before it left shelter, so I could often shout, 'Leave that one,' even with the striking method. One problem that made us keep our wits about us was the blackout, for although we had permission to go 'sparrowing', the local Bobby would have been onto us like a ton of bricks, if he had seen our flashing lamps, and there were occasions when we doused them in fear, as German bombers droned overhead.

There were always a lot of sparrows around the farm buildings in those days, many lived out their whole lives in the vicinity, nesting under tiles, in thatch, ivy clad walls and trees, and any nearby overgrown hedge. They were the mice of the air where the farmer was concerned. For most of the summer they spread out over the adjoining fields, getting their food from anywhere they could, but during some of that time in Bedfordshire they worked for the farmers and gardeners; for much land was planted up with the brassica family, which were quickly found by the egg laying cabbage white butterflies, and as this coincided with the sparrows need for protein for their young, they meticulously worked their way along the rows, searching for the caterpillars – even chasing the butterflies.

But for the rest of the season, once the wheat started to fill out, they changed from carnivores to vegetarians. I have seen 50 metre wide strips of standing-corn alongside the hedgerows, which should have yielded some tonnes, without a single grain in the ears. With the harvest gathered in, they foraged the fallen grain from the fields, finally moving into the stack-yards, burrowing under the thin thatch and letting in the rain, even tugging out straws from the sheaves in the walls. Once the stacks were thrashed, there was the luxury of picking out all the light grain and weed-seeds, blown out with chaff and cavings. Also at this time, all the cattle were in the yards, and the birds descended into the troughs even whilst the animals were feeding, but still getting good pickings after they were finished, by searching every nook and cranny that meal and grain had fallen into. And if any door or window was left open in the granary or food preparation areas, a swarm of sparrows would descend in moments!

In the hard weather, and especially when the land was covered in snow, all this activity caught the eyes of birds who usually never came near the farm buildings. I have seen flocks that numbered thousands, containing not only birds from the woodlands and hedges around, but birds from abroad. The orchard would be scavenged for every last rotting apple by a noisy throng of starlings, blackbirds, thrushes, redwings and fieldfares. The sparrows on the waste heaps in the stack-yard would be joined by yellow hammers, chaffinches, bull finches, etc. Every scrap would be scratched through and through; here and there, a patch of feathers would show where a sparrow hawk had made a quick dash in for a meal too. The carts used to carry hay and straw into the yards, and especially any horse droppings, would be searched over, and every time a person walked through, this noisy cloud would take off and sit silently on roofs and trees until it was safe to return.

If the frost and snow persisted, as the outer bounty vanished, hunger became acute, and even the shyest birds lost their distrust of humans, and all would move into the warm yards, pecking among the animals feet. There were days when you could be forgiven for thinking that you were in a foreign zoo, the colours so vivid against the dung of the floor or the white snow on the roofs. This was for my brother Bob – with one or two of his friends – a time of great activity, putting any amount of time and effort into bird catching. Officially they were supposed to be after sparrows – and starlings of which only the breasts were edible – but any of the larger birds were thought to be fair game. They always had a few brick traps set around, which generally only caught one bird at a time; these were made of four bricks, three set on edge in a U shape, and the fourth fitting exactly in the U, one end on the ground, and the other just resting on the top edge of the front brick, so leaving a triangular cavity inside. In operation, a flat topped twig was stuck in the ground, another, similar but shorter, was stood on the end of it and tucked up into the 'frog' of the brick, thus holding the brick up to leave a gap, then another small forked twig, trimmed flat for a few mm, was placed between the two twigs, the weight of the brick keeping it all in place, until a bird alighted on the fork to peck the bait inside. The brick fell into place, trapping the bird in the space below. A sparrow was killed and such as robins released – some robins got used to this handling, and made a nuisance of themselves!

Bob scaled this up to a framework covered in wire netting held up by a stick, with a long string attached, and placed on a levelled chaff heap. Hiding nearby, when enough birds were pecking beneath, he tugged the string and ran over to gather in his booty. The Land Girls going about their business, kept a sharp eye on these activities, for even though these town bred girls had by now overcome their distrust of some of the ingredients of my mother's delicious stews and pies – possibly much to do with hard work causing acute hunger pangs – they still drew the line at eating song-thrushes or yellow hammers.

Despite the fact that laws existed to protect wild birds and nests, many country people ignored them. Egg collecting was not yet outlawed – boys in every village vied as to who had the best collection, as well as adults – often the local vicar. Probably mostly due to my early nature lessons and rambles with the enthusiastic Miss Arter, I was never interested in owning a collection, although I still enjoyed helping others in the hunt. However I often caused dissension, for I did insist on a code – I am not sure from whence it came, Miss Arter or my mother – probably a bit of both, but I stuck to it – only taking one egg, but there had to be at least two, and none at all if the bird was sitting.

The taking of wild birds to put in cages was against the law. My Uncle Cecil still did this – although to give him his due, it was only occasionally to avoid too much inbreeding in his aviary! He was quite crafty about it – he obviously knew the implications. Searching for the nest of, say a goldfinch, he would bring the eggs home to be brooded by one of his own, or if he had no sitting bird, he would ring the young the moment they were hatched, and leave them to be brought home just prior to flight. It would not surprise me, if unscrupulous breeders still do this today.

The taking and taming of fledgling jackdaws, magpies and carrion crows, in that order of popularity, still happened; these were single birds to be household pets – the ultimate was to get one to talk. I was often introduced to a 'talker', but on only one occasion was I ever able to understand a single human sound – and that from a magpie. It was understood, that for a talker, the bird had to be taken from the nest as early as possible, and Bob was a past-master at hand-feeding these tiny birds. He would dash in from school, mix up a bowl of food, and then run round his cages, from whence a cacophony of sound would emerge, as they saw 'mother' coming. Some he would keep – much to my mother's annoyance – but most were for his friends. The occasional public house in the area had one of his jackdaws in the bar.

Two birds in particular I remember – I must have been about thirteen. One was a wood-pigeon that was tamed for me, to be a decoy for when I was pigeon shooting with my 4.10 shot gun. A special string harness was made to my uncle's instructions, so that it could walk around and fly up onto a perch unhindered – I expect it was illegal then, but highly successful. It all came to an end, when a friend of my employer's – an army Major and a rifle champion – asked if he could borrow a twelve-bore shot gun, and go pigeon shooting with me. Despite at least a dozen shots, he missed every one, then with his last at a low incoming bird, missed that too, but killed my precious decoy.

The other bird was a jackdaw my brother kept. Anything misplaced, and you went to Jack's cage. Anything heard crashing to the ground, and Jack would be seen hurriedly hopping away. It did more hopping than flying, adored my brother, and would fly to meet him from school, but was the bane of my mother – she would insist that it stayed in the cage when my brother was not around. It especially upset my father! First when it started pulling thatch out of our roof, and again when a neighbour came to complain that it was attacking hers. The end of his limited patience came, when he was planting Brussels sprouts, and upon finishing the row, straightened up and looked back, only to see Jack close at his heels pulling up the last plant. Luckily for Jack, the dibber missed him. But the ultimatum was: 'He goes to a new home, or I wring his neck.' Yet another public house got a feathered bar-room character.

A Boys Work on the Farm

The main reason why I missed joining in with most of Bob's deeds was the fact that I always seemed to have a job to do. Looking back, much of it was my own fault, for I often volunteered my services, and if I was asked to help, usually dropped whatever I was doing, whereas Bob would make a song and dance. From about nine years onwards, I regularly helped after school and weekends, such as taking the cows half a mile to the fields after milking for our neighbouring farmer, Mr Tew – although this could be quite eventful and even dangerous at times. Our little road was the main thoroughfare for the American Airmen travelling to Bedford, and their jeeps and lorries travelled through at breakneck speed. The wretched cows seemed to resent this, and despite most of the time walking sedately in single file on the wide grass verge; upon hearing the sound of an engine, would resist all my attempts to keep them there and at least half of them would walk into the road. On one occasion, an open lorry, full of airmen standing in the back, careered round a bend: as the road was perfectly clear, the driver took no notice of my frantic signals for him to slow down, until half a dozen cows simultaneously walked into the road. The driver slammed on his brakes, and the lorry slewed across the opposite – fortunately empty verge – sliding sideways into the ditch. Not one of the cursing airmen fell out; having all locked arms together, they were just pressed rather tightly against the lorry's cab.

Other regular, but uninteresting jobs, entailed collecting sticks to light Mother's following week's fires and boil the Monday wash in the copper, collecting the farm eggs, and churning the butter. I have already mentioned pea and potato picking; of the two, I liked pea picking best, for not only did you have a seat – usually a wooden beer crate – whilst pulling the bines out of the ground to pluck off the pods, but you were given a ticket for every full bag weighed, to be paid at the end of each day. Potato picking was backbreaking work, with heavy buckets to empty into sacks, you were grumbled at if you held up the machine on the next run, and the pay was weekly. Blackberry picking was a favourite money earner and I knew all the best bushes – still do! A jam factory used to send a lorry to collect them, and the whole family spent all their spare time picking. I still have the brass 'stilliards' my mother used to weigh mine with, to make sure she knew my total, before she tipped them into the large barrel the lorry had left with us. I am still quite a whiz at it, and disdain going to pick less than a small pail-full, often staying until I have a couple.

Looking back now, it seems there were an inordinate number of tasks that required the use of the ubiquitous galvanised pail. Not only were there different sizes and shapes, but many were often for one purpose only: I acquired a now rare – almost new – 'lavatory' bucket a few years ago, and it made a splendid log bucket. Painted matt black, it stood beside our log burning fire of the same colour. I was amazed at the number of visitors – some quite young – who would give the bucket sidelong glances, then whisper, 'Is that bucket what I think it is?' One task needing a lot of buckets was calf feeding – another of my chores – and these were kept scrupulously clean, and often, if a clean bucket was needed, one would be 'borrowed'.

Early one morning when I was about nine, I was told to clean out and scrub the brick floor of a small empty shed, and have two of the calf-feeding pails ready, as the butcher was coming to kill a pig. Meanwhile, the large copper just outside – usually used to cook potatoes and peelings for the pigs and hens – had also been cleaned out, filled with water and lit, and I had further instructions to keep feeding the fire from the pile of wood beside it. At about 10.00 am, an old man arrived on a motorbike and sidecar, and with a flurry of activity, father, labourer Maurice and Betty the Land Girl, chivvied the chosen pig from the sties into the clean shed.

Once inside, the girl hastily shut the half-door on us and retired. I was now told to be ready with a bucket to catch the blood. Father grasped one ear of the now squealing animal, and Maurice the other, heaving it into a sitting position, and above the noise, the old butcher shouted instructions to me, where to stand and how to hold the bucket, then before I knew what was happening, he plunged his large knife into the throat of the pig, and a fountain of blood shot out! What with the dying lunges of the animal, and my own shock, it was a wonder that I caught any of it. The men quickly tied a rope round the back trotters, and throwing it over a beam, hauled the animal up, with me continually trying not to miss too much of the precious liquid.

The pig was soon lowered and dragged outside to be placed onto two sheets of corrugated iron, whilst I carried the two buckets up to the farmhouse kitchen, where two ladies waited to turn the contents into 'black pudding'. On my return, the butcher gave father and I a four inch (100 mm) piece of blunt scythe blade each, and then father dipped a bucket of the now boiling water from the copper, poured it over the pig, and the three of us got down to scraping off the bristles. It must have been close to a couple of hours before the old man was satisfied, and we then dragged the animal back into the shed and strung it back up, this time with a special piece of wood holding the rear legs apart. A final bucket or two of cold water, was sloshed over it to wash it down, and sluice the floor clean – at least I now knew why this little shed had such a strong cross beam, and a brick floor sloping to a central drain – then two galvanised baths were brought in and the butcher did the disembowelling; dropping the gut and intestines in one, and the offal in the other, for the only part that would be thrown away was the pigs last meal and the bristles – or as the butcher said as he scraped the bristles off even the ears and tail, 'The only part we waste of a pig is it's squeal.'

A time was agreed for the next day, when the old chap would return to carve the carcass into joints, and he bid us good-bye. The rest of the afternoon – prior to milking – we spent washing out the contents of the stomach and the metres of intestines, for all of these would be shared among the farm staff, who would all be enjoying 'chitterlings' for tea or supper the following day, and the resulting dripping, would be spread on bread – with a sprinkle of salt – as a treat, for a few suppers after that. I helped at a number of pig killings, and possibly one of the last of the really fat pigs to be killed in Britain – the average weight of pigs being killed in 1946 was around nine score (100 kilos). A nearby 'smallholder' asked my father if he could spare someone to help at his pig killing; now just over fourteen, I was considered an old hand at the job and told to attend by 7.00 am on the day, in order to fill their copper and get it lit in good time. The couple must have been in their eighties, and seemed overjoyed at having a keen young lad helping, and treated me royally. After I had tied a pulley to the branch of a large walnut tree, and whilst the water in the copper was heating, I was invited inside the pretty thatched cottage, to partake of an enormous breakfast. This consisted of a 12 mm thick, by 250 mm long and 125 mm wide, fatty rasher of salt bacon, potatoes and two thick slices of home-made bread, all fried in the lashings of fat oozing out of the meat!

I had already noticed a huge pig eyeing me over the wall of the sty, but thought that was the mother sow, expecting we would be driving a youngster out of one of the surrounding sheds. I found out the truth, when the butcher arrived on his motor cycle – he was now really getting on a bit – and looked over the sty wall, saying, 'I reckon she must weigh all of 26 score (260 kilos) we shall never hold her,' and calling over the old lady, instructing her to entice the animal beneath the tree with a bowl of meal; then as it waddled under, he plunged in his long knife to the hilt. There was hardly a squeal as the animal fell to one side – thank goodness they were not interested in collecting the blood – and we soon set about scalding it where it lay on the grass, and removing the acres of bristles. I don't remember much about the tussle involved in rolling it over, or even the harder task of hauling it up the tree, but I do remember it's nose still lay along the ground.

When I told father about the day, he said that I had been privileged to see the area's last travelling 'pig sticker' kill a pig on the run, and asked me to take special note of the heart when I helped with the butchery the next day. Sure enough, when the heart was removed, I could thrust a finger into the cut the knife blade had made the previous day!

One of my hardest tasks was pumping up from their well the gallons of water needed to wash out the huge mass of intestines. They had a similar brick shed to ours, but with elm, lead lined troughs on legs around three sides. Into these we proceeded to lay the joints – taking both me and the old man to carry one side of bacon – whilst his wife busied herself smashing blocks of salt, and rubbing it into the meat – this would keep her busy for many mornings to come, as she turned and rubbed in salt, until all was cured. My last task was to lug two buckets the half mile home, my payment for the two days: a huge joint in one and chitterlings – or chitlins – in the other.

22

Another reason why I was expected to do my bit so early in life, was that manpower was in such short supply, also father's employer had run off with our first 'live in' Land Girl and he had been promoted to farm manager, so come harvest time – and the school holidays – I was really needed, and worked a full day, helping at milking time, and leading those large horses back and forth twixt field and stack-yard, and stook to stook. By the time I was twelve, I was loading the carts as fast as the two 'pitchers' tossed up the sheaves – and woe betide me if the load had to be roped on – unless it was travelling along very uneven tracks. With our two-wheeled carts, care had to be taken as the load was built, not to either bear down on the horse, or even lift the poor creature off the ground. So, as work progressed the pitchers would keep an eye on the shape of the load, and might put a shoulder to the shafts, and call out, 'Yer angin,' or, 'Yer bearin,' if things were not as they should be. I can only recall one of my loads falling off. As it was midday, I stayed on top whilst a Land Girl led it in to the stack-yard, and as she pulled into place, the load slid onto the elevator – me included. I was told to stay and clear the lot off in time for work to start afterwards, happily both Land Girls stayed to help, and I was able to rush my own dinner before returning to the field.

Although it is common to see mainly 'round' corn stacks in old pictures – both photographers and artists loved these – the expert stacker looked down on them, both figuratively and literally, for generally they were small and easy to build. On larger fields and holdings, oblong stacks with rounded ends and the roof tapering in all round, were more common. But what every 'stacker' worth his salt aspired too, was being able to build oblong stacks with corners and the roof flush to the end, rather like a brick building,. However a consequence of these large, higher stacks, was much more settlement causing instability. Hence small round stacks were easier to build – and keep upright.

An important part of the scene was of course the gentle giants, the horses. But they were not always so. They all had their personalities, we all had our favourites. There were one or two I positively hated leading – I still have a couple of deformed toes as proof that a ton of horse stepped on them, and I most certainly wasn't the first in the life of that particular animal, for some wit had aptly named her Clommocks. And Polly, a lively Percheron, who could shy at a white butterfly, lifted me off the ground on many occasions. One favourite was Captain, a Clydesdale – his nose was scarred, it was said, from a previous owner's beatings. The whole farm went into mourning when he suddenly died of tetanus. Bonnie, his mother, was the matriarch, rather an old dear, and at twenty nine years plus, knew her way around every field and task, and she quickly learned that the new Land Girls were a bit of a soft touch.

It was muck-carting time. Bonnie groaned and grunted as she pulled her load out of the yard, so the message went back, 'Not so much on poor old Bonnie's cart.' Bonnie pulled ever lighter loads. Then my father arrived. 'Why is that cart travelling nearly empty?' Back it had to turn, and to the girls anguish, he loaded the cart to the brim, then instructing me to take her out, called, 'Giddup Bonnie, and no more silliness.' Bonnie sailed out of the yard without a grunt. Prince was also a Clydesdale – recently bought at a sale, young, very headstrong, always pulled the heaviest load with the utmost ease. But any fright, such as a partridge whirring up, and fully loaded or not, Prince was off! His last, and worst occasion, was in the harvest field. The load was almost finished, he had no one at his head, nobody saw the trigger, but by the time the battered Prince was back in the stable, one man had concussion, another a broken finger, three carts in the way were unusable, another horse injured, and Prince's own cart smashed to smithereens. That brought the horse era to an end for me.

A Love of Tractors

A trailer was bought to be towed by our one rubber-tyred tractor, and a similar outfit hired from the 'War Ag' depot. Because the trailers carried more than four cart-loads between them, the work force could now all go to the field together, and return to stack together, halving the labour needed at a stroke! Although it meant an exhilarating ride out to the field it also meant that someone had to be on the tractor towing the trailer to be loaded all the time. How I remember that droning tractor, the hot days, my eye-lids growing heavy, often missing the call, 'Hold tight,' which was not only the signal to the man on the load that the tractor was about to move, but for me to let in the clutch – so a pitchfork would clatter down on the mudguard to wake me. The poor man on top must have been grateful that he at least had heard the call as I let in the clutch with a start! Yet now that everyone returned to the stack yard together, I was able to learn the craft of stack building.

I loved tractor driving and using any of the machinery involved with them. I can still remember dad taking me to see my first little Fordson tractor ploughing – I was no more than five – and it seemed to have huge balls of clay for rear wheels, which squidged off in large lumps across the field. I was to learn later that the farmer had been worried about the weight pressing down on his Bedfordshire clay, and during the first months of ownership, he and his two sons had taken it in turns to hacksaw out the wheel centre between the strakes! The Ford Model N that I drove most in the beginning came second-hand from a factory in Leeds where it had been used for towing. Father's employer, Mr Topham had been ousted as a 'stay away' tenant by his brother-in-law, an Air Vice Marshall in charge of airfield engineers, who was able to pull strings to get this urgently needed tractor, but what a disappointment when it arrived! It had almost smooth 'road' tyres, a very worn clutch, and needed to be kept running fairly hot or the plugs oiled up in minutes.

However, our new employer took leave, and taught me the beginnings of engine overhaul – fitting nothing more than new piston rings and using a file on the little and big end bearing cups. However, the moment we dropped a cultivator in the ground it stood still, so over that summer it was only used for light work. The Bedford factory that rebuilt clutches – they had no replacement clutches – were able to do the job, and during Mr Martindale's next leave, he decided to drive it there, but on coming to the first hill it refused to budge any further, and he abandoned it on the verge, and walked home. They all laughed, when I came home from school and said that he should have turned it round and driven up in reverse; but sure enough, when he and my father drove out to it the following day, they turned it around, and up it went. The old girl – on cast iron wheels – weighed over 1.7 tons, and come April each day after school, I was driving it to harrow and roll the fields of corn.

Betty, the Land Girl was keen to get tractor driving experience, and grumbled, 'If young Billy can be left to do such work, surely I can too?' The following morning she happily drove over the fields to hook onto the roll. It was cold, she wore the regulation overcoat, and it is believed that it got between her foot and the clutch pedal. The outcome resulted in her being thrown off as the tractor hit the rolls. These tractors were started on the severely rationed petrol and switched over to paraffin whilst still hardly hot enough to vaporise it, so they easily stalled. Dad heard her screams from the buildings, and raced to the scene, to find her under the rear wheel, blood oozing from eyes, nose and ears. She moaned, 'Lift it, Bill, lift it. Oh please lift it.' He grabbed the axle stub and lifted. 'Oh that's better,' said Betty, 'lift, lift.' Finally he had it off her body and placed his knees under the tyre to take the weight. Unfortunately she was so badly injured, she was unable to move: it was now father's turn to shout. Three men eventually arrived and pulled Betty out, but unable to lift the tractor, one ran to inform the employer, and fetch a jack, whilst the others propped the tractor with wood. Father

26

believed he stood for about twenty minutes, before the jack lifted it off him. My guess is the tractor – which was fully fuelled – would have weighed some 1,344 lbs to 1,568 lbs at the rear wheel (609.6 to 680.3 kilos). My 1971 Guinness Book of records lists one professional achieving 1,200 lbs in a 'squat lift' and another managing 820 lbs in a two handed 'dead lift'!

Father suffered of course. He refused to visit the hospital or even receive doctor's treatment, but he got mother to regularly rub him all over with goose grease – something that we always had plenty of. I remember seeing him walking about like a zombie from a film set, every muscle picked out in ever changing lurid colours, starting with orange and red and going through bruise blue to inky black, from his ankles to the base of his skull. Unable to bend, he ate, milked cows and drove the tractor in a standing position for many days, and during that time didn't go to bed, just walked about the farm, and dozed for short periods on a door that he placed on one of the horse mangers

My father was the most honest man you could wish to meet, and I believe he would have ripped the hide off me, if he had had cause to think that I was dishonest, however, in his efforts to look after family or farm, he would not hesitate to overstep the law. He often kept me from school whenever important jobs needed doing, despite letters from my teacher, who lived close by and knew what was happening. On one occasion we were drilling wheat in a roadside field, and to my dismay I saw Mr Woodbine-Haylock the schools attendance officer, waiting by his bicycle at the roadside as we approached. On our side of the low hedge lay a sack of wheat. Father, especially when he was busy, usually had a grim face, and today he was busy. Standing on the platform behind the drill, he threw the mechanism out of gear as we crossed the headland mark, flipped open the lid, and jumped off to run straight ahead to pick up the sack, whilst I turned in a wide arc to pull up alongside him, now standing with the sack on his shoulders to tip the wheat into the drill. To this day, recalling the speed with which Mr Woodbine-Haylock jumped on his cycle and sped up the road, I believe he thought he was going to be thumped!

Another time I was sent to Sharnbrook railway station with the tractor and trailer. A heifer had died in the night, blood oozing from her nose, and the vet had confirmed father's fears – she had died of anthrax, and must be burnt as quickly as possible. Father and two others spent the morning digging a large hole beside the body, and collecting wood to put in it, whilst I drove the ten mile round trip, with an 'emergency licence' for one ton of coal – signed by the vet. Soon loaded up, I was back on the road, but as I approached Sharnbrook police house, a sergeant ran out and waved me to a stop. 'Are you from Red Gates Farm?' he asked. With quivering voice and knocking knees, I admitted I was. 'Oh good, I hoped you were, you can give my constable and I a lift. Just wait a moment until I fetch him and our cycles.' I can still see my father's face, as I drove into view with two policemen riding 'shot gun' on my twenty sacks of coal! The constable had to stay and supervise the rest of the day's proceedings, and so it wasn't until evening that dad was at last able to ask, 'What on earth were you thinking of, giving those two policemen a lift?'

Looking back now, I am at least pleased that I was kept from school to mow the hay, for it is still indelible in my memory just what the average meadow contained in the way of wild flowers – even back then I would lift the cutter bar over the occasional orchid – and the innumerable moths and butterflies of every species lifting out of the falling swarth as I passed, would outdo the best of today's Nature Reserves. We mostly used a hay sweep, and built the stack in the field. This machine was akin to a huge fork with wooden tines, and two wheels at the rear. In practice the tractor pushed it down the windrows of hay, and once it was full, over to the stack – where two people forked the hay into the elevator. It was similar to reversing a two wheeled trailer – with poorer manoeuvrability – no one liked using it, but I took to it like a duck to water, tearing all over the field in top gear. This probably didn't please the folk stacking – they used to rest while waiting for the next load – but delighted father, and was yet another excuse to keep me from school.

Little did I know that I was about to be at the forefront of a coming revolution and years of controversy! I cannot remember the year, but remember Mr Martindale volunteered to finish the job, so that I should not be kept from school. I was spreading a brown powder – Gramoxsone? – it arrived in newfangled paper sacks, and for a still 'weedy' lad, contained a back breaking 50 kilos, and as I slit the tops open, and spread the contents along the trough of the fertiliser spreader – converted from horse drawn – I got covered in the light chocolate-coloured dust! The fields were a sea of young charlock, so thick that you wouldn't know what crop was really there, and I remember I was most disappointed that not a single one seemed to be drooping by the time I finished on Sunday evening. I didn't get to see the fields until the following weekend. What a transformation! Not only was the charlock browning over, even the creeping thistles, our other most persistent weeds, had their heads hung low. All the farm workers were ecstatic. No more back breaking charlock-pulling in the potato fields. No more hand-hoeing the corn fields. No more thistle filled arms and hands whilst stooking the corn at harvest time. Collectively, we all thought it was a wicked shame that it could only be used on corn crops and the potatoes before they emerged. However, my father cast his eye around other problems – thistles, nettles and buttercups aplenty in the grass fields: "Let's try it on the worst patches before the cattle move in." I remember being quite pleased that those weeds had thinned quite drastically, but didn't notice if the orchids and the cowslips had suffered too!

Ploughing was one farm activity that gave me much enjoyment, not only for the expertise that was necessary, for you not only had to set the trailing plough up to make a good job, you had to measure out the field into accurate 'lands' or 'stetches', then set up gun-barrel straight ridges, that came together in gun-barrel straight finishing furrows as you ran up and down the field. It didn't matter what shape or how hilly the field, any deviation, however small was noticed and commented on by one and all. Even so I enjoyed the challenge, and once all the measurements and ridges were done, it was relatively simple to keep the rest in shape without too much attention, leaving plenty of scope to look at what was going on around me.

And because of the very nature of the job, the most interesting happenings were usually the bird life. In those days it was often a thousand or more rooks and a hundred or two jackdaws, getting as near as they dare, to snatch the worms and grubs. I would often be able to pick out a certain individual acting more bravely than the others – No wonder it was bigger and stronger, when it was getting the best, and most. One pure white rook certainly stood out, but only for one autumn – it probably still survives in a glass case somewhere – there was also a white jackdaw and a couple of blackbirds, but mostly it was just white patches or single white feathers. Migrating birds dropped in as I prepared land, and drilled winter wheat – I especially looked out for golden plovers; and during the spring cultivating and harrowing, I would see wheat-ears, ring ousels and yellow wagtails passing through.

During the later harrowing and rolling of the growing corn, I became proficient at seeing plover scrapes – they are among the best camouflaged eggs of any bird – less than four eggs in the nest were taken home, but four were probably incubated, and I would stop and pick them up, then with the birds wheeling and calling overhead, carefully watch the spot as I moved over it, stopping again to renew the scrape with my hand, and replace the eggs. It gave me great pleasure to see the hen return and snuggle down when I was far enough distant.

I only ever saw one hooded crow, but all carrion crows in those days were very wary, they needed to be hungry to follow the plough, and would land at the far end of the field, then keeping an eye on the tractor, would fly in a wide ark to always be at the opposite end. One winter, a pair got exceptionally bold, and ended up following me quite close. Father, who hated them with a passion, was very annoyed that I hadn't informed him of this when he came to see how I was progressing, immediately returning home for his gun. He arrived back with it concealed in a raincoat, and sat on the mudguard of my tractor, with the gun still hidden. The two crows meanwhile, perched in an oak tree about ten gunshot lengths distant and preened themselves. At last, father's patience ran out, and he shouted in my ear, 'The crafty old devils know something is up with two of us on board. I'll leave the gun under this coat: slide it out carefully, and you should get the chance to shoot one,' and off he jumped. The crows floated out of their tree and cruised in my direction before he had left the field, and followed me closely. I leaned down and slid the gun from under the coat, turning in my seat to see the pair already a couple of gunshot lengths away. They never followed me again!

Adventures with Bulls

The first time I was needed to help with a farm animal, was during a difficult calving. The cow was lying down, and every time dad got the calf's feet out, and put his hand in to turn the head, the calf slipped back in. My job, after he had tied a cord on the feet, was to keep pulling whilst he manipulated the calf. It was 10.00 pm when the calf finally slid to the floor, and I saw, what I only realised later, was state of the art resuscitation. He held open the comatose calf's mouth, and pressing his own into it blew hard, alternately squeezing its ribs. After what seemed an age the calf gurgled and started breathing, and not until it was up and suckling did we go home, mother angry that I had been kept out till after midnight. I still believe that was the most incredible late night I have ever had!

31

The recalcitrant bull, was a different story and for me at the time quite traumatic. It was potato harvesting time, and as usual I had been kept from school to help. A gang of some 20 soldiers were picking them up, but on this particular day the weather had turned to drizzle, and they had been told they could have an early lunch, and to take it into the farmyard. The buildings – probably mid-19th century – consisted of a cow shed, dairy, six loose boxes, three open-fronted sheds, stable for eight horses, chaff house – with granary above – and a large weather-boarded threshing barn, once thatched, but now with a corrugated iron roof, all set round a square forming four cattle yards. The farmhouse was placed well back from the side that had a section of wall, with a five barred gate set in it – the main thoroughfare for cattle entry to yards, stables and cowshed. My father, his brother Cecil, a Land Girl, another permanent man, and myself had stayed behind to put the last sacks of potatoes on the trailer and haul them off the field, and as I drove the load into the dingy thrashing barn with my father clinging behind, a small door was flung open on the far side, and my uncle dashed in yelling, 'Bill! Bill! The b***** bull's out.' I stopped the tractor, but before following on, cast around for a suitable stick, and spying a broken pitchfork handle on a ledge, snatched it up, and rushed through, to be confronted with a scene to be forever burnt into my memory.

In the open – and empty – sheds there was over a metre thickness of dry dung – so most of the soldiers had been sitting in the mangers on the bit of straw still in them, with their feet up, as if in easy chairs! Unfortunately, this meant they were at a very good 'skittling' height for a rampaging bull, so most of them were now clinging to every available rafter, with kit bags, gas masks and greatcoats scattered all around. In the centre was one very angry bull, with the door frame of his loose-box around his shoulders, kept in place by his near two metre – tip to tip – horns: my uncle and the other labourer were as terrified as the soldiers, and were begging my father to go and get his gun.

I was immediately called over to where the bull stood glowering at my father. I rushed forward waving my stick. 'Use your voice boy. Use your voice,' he barked, and as the animal turned to face me when I shouted, he grabbed the bottom of the door frame, and twisted it sideways and off, whence the bull immediately turned its attention back to him. He yelled, 'Throw me the stick,' then, 'Fetch the bull pole,' and giving the most horrendous bawl at the bull, drove it back towards the loose boxes. In moments I had the stout ash shaft with a latched hook on the end, which always hung on the wall in the dairy, and dashed back. The bull was now showing his anger by pushing up huge heaps of dung. My uncle meanwhile from the safety of the wall, informed father that he had walked into the yard, just as the bull burst out at a couple of soldiers teasing him over the half door.

The serious part now had to commence. Father knew that the only way he would ever be able to lead him in and out to serve cows again, was to totally dominate him right then. After swopping pole for stick, I was instructed to approach the bull from the front, not to take my eyes off it for a single moment, then stand and yell and lift my stick, but jump to one side if he charged – and under no circumstances to turn and run! I lifted my stick: the bull glared. I yelled fit to burst: he lifted his head out of his latest muck castle, and in a flash the pole was hooked into his nose ring. Painful for his nose or not, he was throwing father all over the place, who, between superhuman efforts to keep the bull's head up – a bull can only do damage with his head down – was shouting instructions to me, 'Keep close by his flanks. Hit him as hard as you can behind the horns. NOW.' I knew it was useless, for he lunged around more violently than ever. 'I SAID HIT HIM HARD FOR GOD'S SAKE, NOT JUST PART HIS B***** HAIR.' Clenching the stick with both hands, I gave a second wallop: the bull rolled his eyes, turned his head and quietly walked into the box next to his own damaged one. If I did feel any jubilation, it was soon dispelled by another shout, 'COME

IN HERE QUICKLY. Inside he was holding the bull's head in the corner, over the manger. 'Put the chain round his neck.' One end of a Y shaped chain, used to tether a cow was bolted through the wall; the rest of it lay in the manger! All I had to do, was bend under the bull's massive neck, and retrieve the chain, stand up between it and the wall, pass one end over its neck, then bend back under, and latch the two ends together. To father's frustration, I took at least three tries. I can't remember him giving me a single word of praise afterwards; it was just something that had to be done.

Sadly, the bull was often a problem from then on, and one Saturday a lorry arrived to take it to Bedford market to be sold for slaughter. The poor lorry driver's face fell when my father led the cavorting animal out, and even with his own pole latched in on the opposite side, they had quite a struggle to get him up into the lorry. My last dealings with the bull, was to pass a couple of chains around his neck, attached to the corner post at the front of the lorry, whilst my uncle and the other hand, once again stood safely behind the wall. The lorry driver commented, as he closed up the lorry, 'That's a brave young lad you have there, a right chip off the old block.' I heard the Land Girl mutter, 'The poor little devil is probably more afraid of his dad than he is of the bull.'

The next bull was a roan coloured Shorthorn, chosen chiefly as a mate for Bertha and her daughter. She was not only the largest and best looking cow we had, she was also the heaviest milker. However, she had been bought very cheaply as a first calved heifer at Bedford market, with 'calf at foot'. She had obviously not been milked – even the rough cowhands at the market had been unable to tie her up. There had already been some hilarity as farmers hopped into her pen for a closer look, and jumped out again at speed as she charged. No one bid for her, and father negotiated less than the reserve price. Needless to say, he had her tied up and being milked within minutes of her arrival at the farm. A year later, just after her second calf, Dad – still the only one who milked her – caught a bad case of flu, and I was instructed to milk her. With the aid of a bowl of cattle cake, I chained her up in moments, but I didn't dare sit on the stool. I jammed the bucket down into the straw and milked with one hand, the other holding the bucket in readiness to jump out of the way of her vicious kicks. On the first occasion, the old devil held her milk back for some ten minutes before she let it down, but I went into the dairy triumphant with a full bucket, for I had taken two buckets with me, and kept tipping one into the other, which I had placed at a safe distance. So proficient did I get, that I dispensed with that bother, and only my very last bucketful – as recuperating dad came to look over the door – went flying. Bertha obviously thought she should keep up her reputation.

The new bull was quite docile – and his horns seemed minuscule compared to his predecessor – so he was allowed to roam with the cows: even my uncle occasionally fed him in the loose box, though he always carried a hefty stick when crossing any field the bull happened to be in. He obviously heeded my father's advice, 'Never trust a bull or a stallion, or turn your back on them, however tame they may appear.' However one morning, during harvest, Mr Tew sped into the stack yard on his bicycle shouting, 'Mr Clark! Mr Clark!' and we scrambled off the corn stack and cart as he puffed out, 'Your bull is killing my bull.' We in turn, all ran for our own cycles, and raced the mile or so to his field, to find a broken gate, and all his cows milling around our large bull – who was bellowing with rage and scraping clumps of turf high over his back with his front-hooves. Facing him, doing a poor imitation, was Mr Tew's half sized young Shorthorn. In his favour, he was light on his feet, and as we arrived, skipped to one side giving our lumbering beast a sharp sideways poke in the rump as he passed. This only served to enrage our bull even more, and he swung around with a terrible bellow: nothing short of murder would now suffice!

Our group took up station behind a stout fence, and looked towards father, who was already striding into the melee. He rushed at the little bull and drove it off. Oh goody, ours must have thought, I've got some help, and started forward. Too late, he found out his mistake as the stick thudded on his crown – but he was too enraged to let that stop him, and still surged forward. Dad now had a bull, back and front, bellowing their heads off. He called for someone to come and drive Mr Tew's bull away. No one moved. 'Billy,' he shouted, 'Bring a stick here.' I raced over. 'I want you to keep off Mr Tew's bull. I'll hit him, then you stand in front of him – and don't take your eyes off him, and if he moves forward, USE YOUR VOICE AND HIT HIM HARD.' We rushed together, our bull keeping us close company. Father yelled and whacked the small bull, then leaving me to manage, turned to face ours. I could hear loud shouts, hefty thwacks, and the most bloodcurdling bellows from our bull, but there was no way that I was going to take my eyes off Mr Tew's bull. It stood glaring menacingly at me and pawing the ground, thankfully not fancying another thump on the head. I suddenly realised the hullabaloo had quietened and to my relief, Mr Tew and his farmhand appeared at my side, and we drove their bull into the nearby yard. Later during the midday meal, the Land Girl regaled us with the end of the saga. She had followed dad, pushing both their bikes, and said the bull appeared to be scared out of his wits and just wanted to get back with his herd. Luckily the road was empty at the time, and were it veered in the wrong direction for the bull, he simply crashed through the hedge, and leaving dad behind, lifted his tail and raced across the intervening field, giving a joyful bellow to his ladies as he smashed through the final hedge.

I quite enjoyed going with Dad to the Bedford cattle market, when he would often finish up at the associated auction yard. (He always cycled the six miles, as he suffered from travel sickness – in later life, he has had to jump out of my Land Rover before we had crossed the first field!) You could find just about anything in 'Peacock's Auction': dead game, live chickens, geese and ducks, plants and shrubs – bare root only in season – small farm implements, and various household articles, often complete house clearances. Once there, father would walk along the lines of goods, keeping an eye open for anything that took his fancy – mostly some hand tool, but sometimes it would be a gift for mum. Once it was a tuneless harmonium that he purchased for half a crown – 12.5p – and made into a sideboard. Any exceptional bargain was often sold on; one was a full sized snooker table for £1.50, which he sold for £10 – his foreman's wage at that time being about £3.50. He once spotted a gold hunter watch among some items worth about a half crown, but another bidder ran him up to £2, at which point the Auctioneer stopped the bidding, and asked the porter to look through the box. As a result the watch was sold separately for £10.

A memorable buy, was a magnificent 15 metre 'thatching ladder' made from a single ash sapling, and furnished with round oak stiles, weighed over two hundredweight – 100 + kilos. As there was no suitable hire vehicle at the sale, father at the front and his brother Cecil at the rear, cycled the six miles home with it on their shoulders. I not being tall enough to reach the middle anyway, was instructed to cycle ahead to stop the traffic at junctions, and not move from the middle of the road until they had passed over – a major problem being, that once they stopped, it was a struggle to get moving again. Folk turned to gape in amazement from the busy pavements, and wag after wag made ringing bell noises, and shouted, 'Fire, fire,' as we passed along. Was I glad when we finally left the city streets behind.

My first foray alone was because father was engaged with cattle at the same time as a special cycle sale. Although this bicycle would be my first adult model – paid for with my own money – strict instructions were given as to what to look for, and when to stop bidding, and under no circumstances to buy a 'racing' bike – his older brother had recently been killed whilst riding one. A good quality new cycle could be bought for £8, and a second hand model for around £2. To my delight prices seemed extra low that day, and three or four presentable ones were let slip by, because my eye was on an 'as new' model. I could hardly contain my excitement when the only other bidder faltered, before bidding £2/2/6d, but as my hand lifted for £2/5/0d, father's voice called from nearby: 'Why has that bike got black tape round the crossbar?' A voice in the crowd answered, 'It's obviously to stop it getting scratched where the foot goes over.' The Auctioneer, pencil poised to knock it down to me, said to the porter, 'Take the tape off please.' A broken crossbar was revealed! The only good bike left, was a sports model with low handlebars, and I despondently turned away – only to see that father was bidding, and it was knocked down to him for £1.50p. My great joy was tempered rather, when he made me wheel it round to a repair shop, and for another ten shillings they swopped the handlebars for ones that didn't allow me to ride with my head down. After that baptism, I often visited alone, sending my Flemish Giant rabbits by the local – horse drawn – carrier, and occasionally buying a new buck, which the carrier would deliver for me on his return.

Post-war Tractors

The war ended and the secondary school system started again, enabling me to spend a final – happy – year at Keysoe School. This was helped greatly by the Wednesday afternoon woodwork classes, using excellent tools, and being put in charge of the large school garden that provided many of the vegetables for the school's kitchen – although I did blot my copybook on one occasion, when the headmaster caught me eating the tomatoes. All must have been forgiven, for on the day of my leaving, only weeks later, he said. 'Well young man, I have not known you for very long, but with your enterprise and enthusiasm, I expect you to come back and visit me one day in a Rolls Royce!' But my apex of transport at that time – my bicycle – was all that I needed to get me back to the farm within a couple of hours of his encouraging words, and on 'my' Fordson Major, Model E27N, bought some months earlier.

It was, according to our supplier, the first one in the area especially fitted for row crop work. However, to my disappointment the implements to fit on it were in very short supply – even the hydraulics arrived later for us to fit ourselves. I was none too happy having to tow a borrowed Oliver plough, which proceeded to fall to pieces, aided by the fact that I gleefully used the wheel brakes at every opportunity to turn in a tight circle: another problem also accrued from this predilection! I later felt the tractor swaying, and to my horror found that all but two spokes on one, and three on the other, of the smart red 'Skeleton' wheels were broken at the welds. Aching to use the hydraulics, to my joy the cultivator finally arrived – in pieces in a crate – but no ridging bodies for me to get the potato ground ready for planting. Yet again I had to use old trailed equipment, and copped it from everyone when I found it impossible to make straight furrows.

One big problem I had – still do – was being so immersed in my work, I lost all sense of time! Even mother's idea of waving a cloth when I was in view, didn't work, for I only looked when I remembered. My father thought I was silly buying a wrist watch: 'Mark my words, if you don't break it with the hard manual work we do, it will fail from being smothered in sweat, and being out in all weathers.' Sure enough, Swiss it may have been – the best I could afford was a mere five jewels – but the only correct time it showed was at 6.00 am, when I set it by our American wall-clock before we left for work. 'Get a good Ingersoll pocket watch,' I was told.

Eventually I saved enough, and proudly put it in a special leather pouch in my pocket. If it didn't stop altogether, it gained anything up to two hours each working day. I surmised that it was me. Father said that was ridiculous; it happened to be a poor watch, and he would personally take it back and get it changed next market day. The following day I was ploughing 'Oak Close', whilst father cultivated 'Burnt Ground', and as he took out his watch to see if it was time to get the cows in, the gun that he carried on the tractor, fired! The watch took most of the pellets, a few entered his fingers, and some ricochets ended in his face. Never having possessed a gun licence, he deemed it unwise to visit the doctor, and picked out what pellets he could himself.

Come Saturday he changed my watch and bought himself one, handing me mine that evening, with both watches showing the correct time to the minute. Once in my pocket, mine played up like its predecessor. Despite swapping the watches around over some days, they would both behave perfectly in my father's care, and be outrageously inaccurate with me. One of the workmen agreed to buy mine, and I decided to save up to buy a quality watch. Meantime I would do some research – and cause some hilarity by carrying around a large   alarm clock, and carefully set it down near my work. One difficulty was in getting people to lend me their watches, once it got around that being in my possession made a watch so unreliable it could even run backwards!

Only days after the potato planting ended, the cultivator tines, hoe blades and discs – all the parts to turn the cultivator into a steerage hoe – arrived, but not neatly in a crate, just left in a heap in the barn. Now the race was on to get ready for the first hoeing of the mangolds: Mr Martindale was on weekend leave, and the pair of us set to work at first light on Saturday, constantly referring to the sheets of instructions – which got ever blacker and more crumpled. It took us all day, with father adding to the pressure, by popping in from time to time fretting because he was sure rain was on the way and likely to stay. Next morning the radio confirmed his fears, and as soon as milking was finished, we drove to the field. After a few stops and starts for adjustments, with father anxiously looking at the sky, we were off! And as he got his 'eye' and 'hand' in, he kept calling out for more speed, until I was in second gear and at full throttle. We reached the end of the long field. Simultaneously, my right hand twisted the hydraulic lever to lift the hoe, my left swung the steering wheel and my right foot slapped down on the right wheel brake and the outfit immediately stood in the next row, facing the way we had come. I dropped the hoe, glancing round to see if father was ready to start back. Consternation! He wasn't on the seat way out at the back of the hoe. Then I heard very angry swearing and bawling from the middle of the bramble hedge. Henceforth I had to stop at each end for him to dismount before turning.

The October potato harvest arrived – the wartime scheme to let schoolchildren have two weeks' potato picking leave was still in operation, and dad had applied as usual. And oh my joy, when among the group that cycled in on the first Monday morning, was one young lady, still able to dispatch that vivacious smile, which now made me go weak at the knees. Oh what a fortnight! The joy of driving the tractor and trailer to the field, loaded with passengers, but always with carefully chosen Gill and her friend sitting on the mud-guards of the tractor. At eight or nine miles an hour, hit the ruts at the right angle, and the girls had to fling their arms round my shoulders to stop from falling off. By the end of the fortnight one arm stayed put for most of the trip. I should have recognised though, that her attentions were more due to her friendly nature. One clue I missed, was when we spent a wet day sorting potatoes in the barn – Gill's girl friend playfully pinched her leg under the sorting table, and I got the slapped face – though with profuse apologies when the mistake was pointed out.

With his part in the war over, the Air Commodore fancied being a full time farmer, and his and father's opinions clashed ever more frequently: it was time to move on. And in the autumn of 1947 dad found a position at Keysoe, where the elderly farmer had decided to engage a working foreman, and with two of his men about to retire, was also pleased to take on my brother Bob, who had just left school, and me, now considered to be a proficient tractor driver. Knowing the area, and coupled with the fact that I should still be driving a nearly new Fordson major, I happily agreed to give a week's notice, and then cycle over for the duration of father's one month's notice, to get on with their autumn ploughing.

Bees and Rabbiting

Unfortunately this was to put a stop to me starting beekeeping! I had recently spun the honey out for a local beekeeper, whilst he and his wife took the combs off the hives. They had kept bees through the war years, and he boasted at how much a jar he had made selling honey on the 'black market.' Although many bees clung onto the combs they brought into the extracting house, and I got stung several times, it had only made me more determined than ever. Then when an old carpenter engaged on repairs to the damaged carts, mentioned, as he said his farewell, that he was also a beekeeper, I immediately bombarded him with questions. 'How many hives did he have?' 'How much honey did he get?' etc. Father, who hated bees, knowing immediately which way the conversation was heading, pushed me off. But I ran to the road and waylaid the man, asking if he ever sold hives and could I visit him sometime?

Having received positive answers to both questions, I badgered father until he gave permission to keep a hive – it had got to be as far from the house and people at work as possible! I prepared by fixing a second parcel carrier to my bicycle in readiness for the 9 mile ride, and upon hearing what I was up to, Betty, our Land Girl, asked if she could accompany me. It was a pleasant afternoon, and we arrived at the man's workshops about an hour later. Looking back, I now realise he was not the world's best beekeeper. In fact he was I suppose typical of the old saw: 'A cobblers children are the worst shod.' He had a row of a dozen or so hives, standing at all angles, with roofs covered in bits of roofing felt and pieces of rusty corrugated iron, all held in place with bricks and stones – although to give him his due, they were the modern Nationals. After walking along his hives I broached the subject of cost, and was horrified to find that the three pounds burning a hole in my pocket, needed to be multiplied by four to buy one of his hives filled with bees! After a bit of searching around his workshop, he managed to find the parts to make up a whole hive – in some semblance of good order – and said I could have the lot for one pound ten shillings – £1.50. Also come next spring, he would bring a swarm with enough combs to hive it on, but it would cost another three pounds. With some difficulty, we strapped the hive parts on my bicycle, and made the return journey, with Betty commenting, 'You have been done.'

Now only weeks later, with the furniture lorry packed to capacity, it took little thought from father to decide what would be left behind! A bonus for the family was the new barn conversion cottage: for the first time we had the luxury of a flushing toilet – even the new Council house had not had that, only an inside cold-water tap – a bathroom with hot water on tap, and electricity. Not that dad held any of this in high esteem, his byword was always: 'What was good enough for my parents is good enough for me,' a consequence being that he refused to buy an electric cooker. I offered to buy it, and mother and I travelled to Bedford, where, for the first time, she took out a 'never-never' policy, for she refused to let me buy the cooker outright: I could pay the deposit and first instalment but she would deal with the rest. It was a joy to see her face when it arrived the following day. Father just grumpily commented that I had more money than sense.

Being so busy, only rare chances came my way to socialise at the Thurleigh Village Hall Dances, but always Gill was in the company of her older sister and a cousin, which rather cramped my shy style, but I did manage to pass over one box of chocolates – still needing the saving of sweet ration coupons, it should surely be enough to turn any young lady's head!

The fact that my present employer was a strict churchman did mean that at least I always had Sundays free, so I was able to cycle over to Thurleigh to keep up with my fishing and rabbiting pals. One morning I arrived at my friend Peter Holowell's house, only to find he and his brother Fred were just leaving to cycle in my direction – rabbits were being a big problem on the farm where their father worked and they had been asked to ferret them. They also had a good rabbiting dog, and he padded the couple of miles alongside us until we arrived at some large fields of sprouts, the headlands of which were just about devoid of any sign of greenery. Peter lost no time in telling his dog to enter the hedgerow, whilst we strode along, one either side, sticks in hand, with Fred trudging behind carrying the ferret box and a few 'bolt nets'. We walked for some time without the least sign of a rabbit, or even interest from the dog, then arrived at a good sized warren; the dog showed no interest in the holes, although he needed cajoling to stop him sniffing around the adjacent bare ground. We walked on further, then I heard Peter swear. He called me, and I struggled through the hedge, to find the brothers surveying freshly dug ground just out in the field. 'No wonder we haven't seen anything,' raged Peter, 'Some b***** has been here in the night and ferreted them all, they dug their ferret out just here.' He was now feeling very embarrassed, for he had spent most of the journey surmising how we would manage to carry all the rabbits home on our three cycles. Despite my protesting that it didn't matter, Peter was smarting.

A discussion followed as to the most likely place that the poachers would have missed. I pointed out that the nearby combined wheat field – a rarity then – with the rows of straw, should have a rabbit or two under it for the dog to flush: Peter agreed, and with Fred still lugging the ferret box, we proceeded across the rows. There was no sign of a rabbit until we approached the far side, when four or five dashed through the hedge into a large mass of brambles. We crawled inside, to find a large warren – Peter was ecstatic – and we quietly set about netting the holes. Fred had no sooner put the ferret in, than I heard Peter swear again. 'Now we are for it, look over there.' I peered under the curtain of blackberry tendrils; a man with a gun beneath his arm was striding towards us. Quick on the uptake, I asked if the man owned the field we had just crossed? At Peter's nod of the head, I realised it was no good us saying, 'We are looking for an injured rabbit.' We were about to crawl out and throw ourselves on his mercy, when I noticed a Jack Russell terrier darting about in the long stubble: I hissed 'Stay put, he's rabbiting.' We all shrunk down. 'Watch his gun, if he aims our way, stick your head down a hole.'

The next moment his dog was in among us. Peter had his arm tight round his own dog, with one hand round its muzzle – even so the growls seemed frighteningly loud. I put my hand out to the Jack Russell, and murmured, 'Good dog, go home.' The farmer's boots came so near I could have touched them with my stick, and if he had bent down he would have seen us all. However, he called to the dog, 'Come on out stupid, you'll only get stuck down a hole.' I quietly shushed the dog again, and to our relief, he meekly ran after his master – who was still only a few steps away when a rabbit hit the net under my face. Terrified that it would squeal, I thrust in my hand, and pushed it back down the hole. This worked perfectly, and only muffled sounds could be heard as it busied itself sinking its teeth into my fingers. I watched desperately for the farmer to get a safe distance away, and still worried that any rabbit his dog put up would certainly run in our direction. I then heard noises below ground as more rabbits bolted! I glanced round. Peter was still hanging onto his complaining dog, and Fred was laying head thrust down a hole, with the box in front for added protection. By my legs another rabbit shot into a net. I swiftly threw one leg over – squeezing the rabbit between my thighs, and looked back towards the farmer who was now thankfully moving away. At last I was able to pull out the rabbit still clamped onto my fingers, and dispatch it, not

45

at all pleased that all the blood was mine! Peter, still with one hand on his dog, turned to deal with the rabbit between my legs but was unable to do anything for laughing. I turned and sat up, only to see Fred also joining in the hilarity. There lay a dead rabbit, and nestled between that and my private parts and blood covered trousers, was the ferret, gorging on its throat.

This was to be my last 'pleasure' foray into the Bedfordshire countryside, for my life was about to undergo a big change. Father was hunted down by his first employer at Thurleigh. Now married to his Land Girl and running a Civil Engineering contracting business he had recently bought a farm near Buckingham to use for a machinery store and workshop, and having only recently heard that father had been unhappy, had arrived 'hot foot'. Dad was overjoyed at the prospect of working for Mr Topham again and in early 1948, just after my 16th birthday, I left the last vestiges of childhood behind, to start a new life in Buckingham.

Little did we realise, that the only 'improvement' father had ever made to my schooling, was about to become mostly redundant. Watching me doing some homework one evening, he had enquired as to why I was labouring right handed? When I said that the teacher insisted I changed, he went incandescent. Turning to mum, he stormed, 'Why haven't you said something to the b***** woman. Doesn't she realise how handy it is to have a left handed man in a work team!' And with that, he leapt on his cycle and raced to her house. I was never again told to alter my hand. Now the combine harvester was about to ensure that I would not need to stand on the right side of a corn stook, whilst dad stood on the left, to pitch sheaves. The tractor loader and 'muck spreader' would mean we no longer positioned to fork the dung onto carts, and driving a tractor-mounted hedge cutter, would no longer see me on one side of the hedge, and him on the other, striding in the same direction with our hedge slashers swinging almost in unison. Though I would still be handy come Christmas time: standing on the opposite side of a hanging duck or goose, so making the plucking of the left-hand wings easier. But all that was still to come.

3. To Buckinghamshire and Contracting, then Dairying and Cattle

From Contracting to Hospital

Much of my time was spent in the agricultural contracting side of the business. My weekly wage had risen to £3, but by working overtime often doubled it. However, as I was mostly working up to a seven miles radius from home, I needed transport, and despite father still prophesying doom, bought a Dawes racing bike. This gave me my first serious brush with the law: a motorcycling policeman pulled me over as I hurried through Buckingham, and lectured me for exceeding the speed limit, which I am afraid rather pleased me – but I should have thanked my lucky stars that he wasn't around a few weeks later.

Having finished a farmer's ploughing by Saturday lunchtime, I rode to tell Mrs Topham and collect my wages, she remarked that my father was urgently needing a field ploughed, and asked me to wait whilst she phoned the transport manager. Howbeit she turned from the phone with a smile, and said, 'At least you can have the rest of today off, they can't get your tractor back before tomorrow.' Next morning I arrived at the workshop as Mr Topham drove up in his Jaguar, and we walked in together, only to see a mechanic lying beneath the engine of the lorry, and the manager peering in from above. He turned, with a frown, saying, 'This will be out of commission until at least

Wednesday, and I've been unable to locate a hire lorry for today, the ploughing will have to wait.' 'Nonsense,' said Mr T, 'That old Allis Chalmers has fairly worn pads, Billy can drive it back; I've driven it on the road many times and there will be little traffic this morning,' and turning to me, 'Away you go then, it will only take just over an hour: try to keep on the verge as much as you can.'

I had quite a difficult time keeping to the grass verge because of the many telegraph poles, having to skew well out into the road to avoid many of them – regardless of approaching blind corners. Now and again the first share of the six furrow plough would turn a large sod onto the road as the wheel dropped into a rain gutter, so I had to stop and drag it back into place. I arrived at the outskirts of Buckingham soon after 10.00 am – grass verges now absent, it was full blown clatter on the street. So whether to go at ploughing speed, and only make enough noise to bring out the nearest residents, taking half an hour to go through, or go like the proverbial 'bat out of hell,' and take about half that?

I went for it! As I passed the wide cattle market stretch, the racket dissipated a little, but as I came up towards the Old Gaol, the noise bounced back at me, and I was pretty well deafened. I shot past at about nine miles per hour – which felt like a teeth rattling fifty. As I skewed across the centre of the square, I noticed the Salvation Army Band standing in open mouthed silence – I don't know when they were able to start up again, for I lost them to view as I turned into the narrow confines of Cannon Street. Anyone in residence along my route through those narrow streets, will surely remember that awful rumble, growing steadily louder as their house shook in unison: then as they ran to doors and windows, instead of at least 'Armageddon,' all that trundled past was a rusty track layer and six furrow plough, with a young lad at the controls. Luck was on my side, no policeman appeared, but had they wanted to pursue reports, they could have tracked my progress in much of the road surface, for many months afterwards.

Some time later, driving a little grey Ferguson on rubber tyres I was stopped by a constable, who said I didn't look 16: had I got a licence? With a flourish, I took out my 'Pass Certificate' for agricultural tractors – and road rollers – signed only the previous day. With this tractor I was again at the forefront of the farming revolution, but only the fact that it was brand new kept me in a good humour – having had to leave my man-sized crawler. The little tractor sped up and down the field, effortlessly turning two 12 inch wide furrows with the mounted 'deep digger' plough, ending the day ploughing a similar acreage to the lumbering crawler. I was smitten, but what was more, on short journeys I could drive it home.

Some six months after leaving Thurleigh, my friend George Johnson wrote to tell of a forthcoming 'Social' with the invitation to stay over Saturday night. Despite being busy, Thurleigh was never far from my thoughts – absence certainly worked for me, and I ached to see Gill again. I pedalled the thirty miles, but my old friends must have thought I was a bit of a 'damp squib,' for the evening was spoilt by Gill's absence, and I could hardly wait to jump on my bike for the return journey the following morning.

Much of the firm's civil engineering fleet was akin to the crawler – far from new, and with ex-army equipment now becoming available, even our 'new' stock, generally came from that source. I was often put as 'driver's mate' when heavy equipment needed transport. The main driver was an Irishman, who did whatever was asked, but once we got under way would be shouting complaints across the mid-mounted engine – 'Most of our machinery should be scrapped!' Usually followed by such as – 'These brakes are useless, we shall have to keep off busy roads,' or, 'The engine is clapped out, we had better miss such and such hill.' Often finishing with a list of all the problems we had if the police should stop us. On one occasion – on a country road a mile from our destination – we came to a steep hill, 'If I call, 'Bale Out' make sure you jump far enough to miss the bulldozer's blade,' he shouted. Arriving at the bottom we swept round a bend, only to be confronted with an even narrower road, and an avenue of small willow trees. Sadly six of them gave up their lives that our bulldozer blade might pull us up safely. The rest of the day was spent unloading the bulldozer and angling the blade: so that we could drive between the others for the few hundred yards to the farm and commence our hedge removal and pond filling – after tidying up the roadside!

Then another invitation from George sparked my ardour back into life. It took hours in torrential rain and a lashing gale to get to Thurleigh, hardly giving me time to say hello to George's mother before leaving for the evening's entertainment. Again no sight of the one person I wanted to see. Sunday dawned fine and clear. It was now or never. I cycled towards her house and was just in time to see a motor cycle drive out of the gate towards me – it was Gill. I waved but she gave no glance of recognition, and swept past in a cloud of exhaust smoke. Not even a backward glance! My trips to Thurleigh had come to an ignominious end – It was to be 1992 before she briefly touched my life again – I was replacing our tired interpretation signs at Wandlebury, which involved trips to the Bedford firm producing them. On my final journey to pick them up I decided to return through Thurleigh, and call at Scald End Farm where I had been friendly with the boys during my schooldays – we neither recognised the other – but spent a happy couple of hours catching up. I was delighted to find that they ran their farm on conservation lines – barn owls still hunting the field edges – then the younger brother mentioned that he had just taken delivery of a Thurleigh Parish history. He opened the wrapper, and we flicked through, and there on page 27, was the 1940's school photo. We were able to pick me out – fourth from the right in the centre row. A photo I had not seen – along with many other childhood photos – since my mother had her voluminous handbag stolen. Gill, the girl pupil who had been so kind to me, also fourth from the right, was in the front row. They allowed me to purchase the book, and at home, I noticed an even earlier photo of Gill (about 4 years old) standing by a well-known stile, and a 1990s photo of her standing on the same spot. It was this photo that allowed me to see that she was the same Gill among a group of nurses, pictured in the Cambridge Evening News in 2003 – celebrating the 50th anniversary of their starting nursing at Addenbrookes Hospital. We had spent part of our working lives within spitting distance. Perhaps my meeting Gill was preordained to set me on life's road in a proper frame of mind to find the right girl. It's just a pity she couldn't have made herself a fortune with her discovery of an administration of carbon monoxide as a cure for love sickness!

By now I was shuttling between the agricultural and civil engineering on a regular basis. The 'Agricultural' part of the business was quite new, and belonged to Mrs Topham, who believed in purchasing the best, so I was getting a good grounding in driving all the latest combine harvesters, pick-up-balers, manure spreaders, hedge cutters, etc. If a machine came onto the market that could do the work better or faster, it was soon with us, whereas on Mr Topham's 'Civil' side, a machine was only replaced if it no longer worked. One such was an ex-army shovel loader, brought over on 'Lease-Lend'. A powerful track-layer that used hydraulics to lift and lower the shovel, but to tip it, you yanked on a lever that unlatched it, allowing the contents to tip out, and to clip it back, it was lowered to the ground whilst reversing. I was loading lorries from a huge heap of brick rubble, and trundled up to a wooden bodied tipper with a heaped shovel, lugged the lever, and with an almighty thud the load crashed through the floor to sit on the chassis in a mass of wooden splinters.

Unfortunately I had a chest weakness, and I was soon suffering badly in the dust and fumes from those cabless machines. I endured six months of various doctors performing tests, minor but unpleasant surgery and suggesting a plethora of remedies, culminating in a 'chest specialist' diagnosing that I needed urgent major surgery. I had lost all faith in Oxford's Radcliffe hospital by then and walked out – though I did have to visit them later regarding minor accidents. The first was after a stampeding bullock and I collided. My twisted nose still bears witness to the fact that their ENT specialist was wrong in his diagnosis that my nose was not broken, and would later spring back into shape. To add insult to the injury, I was also given an incorrect injection, and had to lie still for two hours with a pretty nurse holding my wrist – so it was not all bad. Another time was as a result of being struck on the head at work, and I was told that I should stay the night for observation; at about 7.00 pm a nurse dashed in and gave me an injection, and soon after, she and a porter arrived and pushed my bed into the corridor: I woozily asked what was happening, to be told that I was being rushed off to have my burst appendix operated on, thank goodness I was still conscious!

What the Milkman Saw

In between hospital appointments, I had been helping with weekend deliveries at a local dairy: being a town round, mine was large in number, but short in length, so was still worked with a horse – a van would meet me halfway to load more milk and take away the empties. It usually took me from 7.00 am to midday. As with most dairies we used bottles with cardboard disc closures – the customer pushing a finger into a centrally scribed spot to lift the disc out of the rim inside the neck. In practice it often wasn't scribed deep enough, and the whole disc shot in squirting milk everywhere! Even the one third of a pint bottles for school delivery, where the centre was only used to poke in the drinking straw, treated the young customers similarly – also because the disc was recessed some milk often lay on top to gather dust and germs. One Saturday, a 'working' lady complained that upon arriving home she had found her bottle tops had been 'chewed' during the previous week. I

54

did the lady no favours suggesting 'rats or mice'; however, as I walked back I disturbed a Great Tit pecking at a bottle on the cart and dashed back to inform her, and she remarked on what a clever bird it was. This bird – and a cousin, the Blue Tit, often live in close proximity to houses and gardens, pecking up seeds and berries, scavenging for insects under window ledges and inside porches, etc. It was obvious what had happened. The odd bottle had a drop of milk on top, in plain view of the foraging bird. It would not take long for it to decide there must be more below, and joy oh joy, it had now settled into solid cream!

I had already decided it would be sensible to get out of dust and fumes, and when the dairy owner offered me the job of helping in the dairy, I jumped at the chance. Once again I was in the forefront of change! Britain had at last caught up with America, and here was I in 1949, helping to position the last of the machinery to change the dairy into a modern pasteurising facility. Even the bottles and closures had been changed, a disk of aluminium foil was now crimped over the top, so no more puddles of milk on top to pick up germs, or for a sharp eyed bird to see. The damp atmosphere was ideal, and I was not only soon fit, but put in full charge. Then during the winter – due to a rounds-woman's illness – I had to take on a round for some weeks whilst my employer managed the dairy. The first Sunday was especially mild and sunny – the horse clip-clopped to a halt, and I stepped quickly down a path and round a corner to a covered patio. A tall, slim, blonde woman, in nothing but the briefest of undies, was standing with her back to me, one foot on a stool as she smoothed on a nylon stocking. 'Thank you Esme,' she called, 'Could you put it on the table?' and next, 'OH MY GOD,' as I plonked the milk down and fled! Then two weeks of hard frost ensued, freezing the milk even as I travelled, and little columns of cream lifted 'above the parapet' as the ice expanded, forcing off the caps. Here and there, small birds noticed.

A horse-pulled milk cart was not the fastest transport, but it was one of the easiest to drive: the horse mostly stopped – without being asked – at regular customers' houses, moved along at my command from a distance, and often caught me up with no command at all. I had plenty of time to observe my surroundings. During the following weeks as the mild weather returned, those sharp eyed birds that had enjoyed their frozen cream, must have been quite disappointed to find tightly fitting caps again, and one or two tried pecking through them. All birds are quick at noting each other's movements – even listening out for other breeds excited calls, and I was soon seeing more and more strips of bottle top foil. Thinking back, I can remember regional differences, and individual milkmen had an input too. On the start of early rounds, it was dark, the folk were still home, and probably all the milk was taken indoors. The milk left on the doorsteps by the later starting roundsmen and at the end of long rounds, would stay until the scattering of working mothers who had already left, arrived home – giving plenty of time to freeze, and longer opportunity for 'copy-catting'. One suburb of large gardens, filled with trees and shrubs and lots of resident birds, became a 'no go zone' unless I threw a sheet over the crates. In this area of large houses, the ladies got out of bed much later, but no longer had live-in servants to take in the milk. Their birds soon got onto milk rations: however, on a new housing estate – mostly young mothers at home – and not much in the way of tree cover, only an occasional bottle would be attacked, and I cannot recollect a single bird chasing the cart.

The milkmen soon started leaving instructions for customers to leave out the required number of cups to be placed over the bottles, and later still provided special plastic beakers; they next had complaints of light ones being thrown off, so more sophisticated lidded crates arrived, some with inbuilt number indicators, and finally, insulation too. The writing was on the wall for those thieving birds. It is probable that if the bottles were left uncovered today, they would not be touched by the present generation, the learning sequence would have to be gone through all over again.

The Allure of Cattle

However, the pull of farming was too much! And I applied for the job of 'second-cowman' on a farm that had just been bought by an industrialist. Money was being spent in large quantities, resurfaced drives, oak fencing, new buildings, the latest machinery. Even the farm house was in the process of being modernised and enlarged – for the factory owner's future home. I spent my first week desperately trying to memorise all 60 cows. This was my first time with a pedigree herd, and I could not be starting with a worse breed, for until you really got to know them, Red Polls were like peas in a pod, there wasn't even the occasional crumpled horn to make one stand out. Also a first for me, was the ultra-modern milking parlour, with milk recording linked to weighing each cows food – it would take all day for one milking if I had to shine a torch in every cows ear to read her tattoo. To add to the pressure, the head-cowman had already made it known that come hell or high water he was having the next weekend off.

On Saturday morning I arrived early to be sure of a good start, and was immediately puzzled by the fact that everyone else was early too – including the head-cowman standing talking to the farm manager. I busied myself readying the milking equipment and record cards and filling the main food hopper, etc. Then opening the gate to the holding yard I walked out for the cows; noticing that everyone was still standing around. Next, as I approached the herd, I realised that the large bull, Honest Lynx, who all week had resided in his brand new pen, was in the centre. Damn, I thought, I hope he is not going to play up, I haven't got a stick. My answer came immediately! And as he snorted and came towards me, an old memory snapped into place! I shouted and threw up an arm – but he just kept coming, and as I dodged behind a cow, he swung round, expertly flinging a few clods over his back. I decided bare fists would not stop this lad, and bending low, dodged through the herd to the nearest hedge, leaving him wheeling about in frustration.

I had noticed an ash stump with some fine, three year growth: I wrenched one off, and a nice knob of stump came with it. A quick trim with my pocket knife, and I had the most perfect 'shillallee' that anyone in my circumstances could desire. I now noticed an audience in the distance – and realised I had been set up. I strode back, and the bull, catching sight of me, trotted over. He came with a final rush: I yelled – he didn't hesitate. I raised my stick and bawled again – he never flinched – then at the last second, with a Matadorian side-step, I brought my stick down on the back of his head. He slid to a stop on his knees, eyes rolling. I turned and pushed the cows on, but as I approached the yard, I heard the thunder of hooves. I turned and shouted – he faltered – I raised my stick and yelled even louder as he started forward again, and he stopped and threw more clods over his back. These niceties over, he evidently thought, 'Right that usually frightens the hell out of them, now, let's get on with it.' He snorted, and surged forward. I could hear my father's voice, 'HIT HIM HARD, NOT JUST PART HIS B****Y HAIR.' This time he went down and rolled onto his side. I closed the holding yard gate, and let the first six cows into the parlour: over the half door I could see the other men casting glances in the direction of poor Honest Lynx, as they went about their duties.

Unbeknown to us, our employer had decided to camp in the house the previous night, and as I was attending the second cow, he burst in. 'I say young man, that bull out there cost me 600 guineas, and you have b***** nearly killed him, the poor devil is only just getting to his feet.' 'I am very sorry sir,' I replied, 'But I believe I am worth even more.' At that he slammed out. I suppose, with hindsight, I should be grateful that it was so early in the morning, for at most other times, he had a film camera in his hand, making a full record of life on the farm. The head-cowman and farm-manager kept well out of my way for the rest of that weekend. I learnt afterwards, that neither of them would ever go into the bull's pen, it was designed so that he could be moved around by pushing slides and gates – rather in the way of a lions enclosure! For added safety, there were narrow gaps in strategic places, so that a man could slip out. Three months later the head cowman quit, and I was offered the job, which I accepted, taking the opportunity to offer brother Bob my previous position. From then on, I happily walked the bull most days on the pole, and often allowed him out with the herd – which he enjoyed even more.

Simultaneously with starting at Castlefields Farm in 1950, I met Wendy Spurgeon and her mother at a local dance. Mother had originally brought Wendy and older sister Stella to rural Buckinghamshire to avoid the Colchester wartime bombs. Whilst Wendy attended – the also evacuated – St Boniface school at nearby Gawcott; both girls kept up with their dancing, and had become quite popular in the area. Wendy – soon to be the true love of my life – had just returned from a professional dancing tour, so perhaps I should not have been too surprised when my mother later confided in my sister, 'Is she the right girl for him: will she cook him a proper meal?' After I was made Head Cowman I invited Wendy in to look round, and met her at the drive entrance. The cows were grazing on the other side of the new oak fence, and I pointed out Honest Lynx; she was very impressed by his size, and begged me to take his photo with her little camera. I jumped the fence, and camera to eye, took a photo when he filled the frame, then crouching, advanced closer – ignoring Wendy's warnings – clicking the shutter again when his head filled the frame: lowering the camera I found we were almost eye ball to eye ball. He just carried on contentedly grazing. It is the only photo I have of any of, 'my bulls.'

It was the middle of the 50s Foot and Mouth epidemic, and every day I paid special attention to noses and feet as the cows entered the parlour, and wandered among the other stock after milking, to examine them too. Then one morning I noticed redness and blisters around a cow's mouth, replicated by the same around her hooves. With heavy heart I rang the vet – his shock matched mine, as I described what I had seen. 'I believe you are correct, I shall inform the Ministry Vet immediately.' The vet arrived in the afternoon, gave one look at the animal, shook his head, and said, 'Oh dear, I wonder how it got here!' We toured the rest of the farm, but not another sign did we see. He seemed satisfied with all my precautions but advised that he could not make an order until it was confirmed in the laboratory, but recommended the builders should be sent off site – after their boots and vehicles had been disinfected – and that the farm entrance gates should be locked. I decided to quarantine myself too, and spent two anxious days expecting to find more cattle with symptoms at every tour. With the cow now dribbling, I even selected the site to dig the pit for the funeral pyre. Then the Ministry Vet returned, 'They have not been able to confirm, and want another sample.' We walked into the cow's box. 'There is no doubt in my mind, looking at her now,' he commented. So two more nights of sleeping in the manger! But meanwhile the cow was looking better: then mid-morning on the fourth day, my own vet arrived. 'Good news Mr Clark, you do not have Foot and Mouth,' then he burst out laughing, 'Although, looking at you, I could believe you have.' He then went on to explain that the cow was suffering from a rare virus, with all the look of Foot and Mouth, and fortunately, because I had quickly separated her from the herd, we had avoided an epidemic, the worst outcome of which would have been a big drop in the milk yield.

The scare over, my busy time was about to start. It was early October, and during the next few weeks, all sixty five cows were due to calve – the farm policy was to get the highest milk yield during winter and spring. I had already spent enough time with cattle to know that around three quarters of them would calve during the night, and like my father, no animal in my charge was going to get into difficulties without me being there to help. And so any evening that a cow looked as if she wouldn't make it through the night – and sometimes it was two or three – I bedded down in the manger, with an alarm clock to wake me, in case I did happen to fall into a deep sleep. This time in my life coincided with the start of the winter dance calendar.

Wendy and I had been dating only a short time, yet I now regularly, either stood her up, or rushed her home early from some enjoyable venue. I ought to have thought myself exceptionally fortunate that she still met me with a smile – well mostly – and expressed concern as to the latest birth. In fact, come to think of it, a large part of our courting was spent around the farm, or in the milking parlour – I even proposed to her in there: at least I did go in for a bit more romance, by sitting her on a tree stump out in the meadow before slipping an engagement ring on her finger.

Whilst working at the Dairy, I had put in for my driving test: unfortunately the driver ferrying me had forgotten to fill the van with petrol, so on arrival at the Test Centre emptied in the spare can. As the last of the petrol poured in we noticed the colour change to a rusty red, at which moment the examiner hurried over – we got as far as the first traffic lights. I said 'It's water in the carburettor, won't take a minute.' It took two or three, before we proceeded to the next traffic lights. They were of course on red! And again the engine died as I took my foot off the accelerator. 'I'm sorry,' said the examiner, 'I'm cancelling the test, I will walk back.' Now, six months later, I arrive at the Centre in the farm's new Land Rover. The same examiner climbed in, and to my surprise remembered our last encounter. 'I hope you filled up with better fuel this time.' All went well until we arrived back at the Centre, but as we alighted he gave an exclamation. 'We haven't done the emergency stop!' We climbed back in and I manoeuvred out into the traffic as he said. 'The next street is quiet, turn in, and when I tap the screen with my papers, stop as if a child has just run in front of us.' I was just below 30 mph, when his papers hit the screen – followed by his head! For what seemed like minutes he just sat head in hands. Finally, he sat up, 'I shall most certainly remember my first ride in a Land Rover.' – I must be one of very few drivers to pass their test despite returning the examiner with a large bruise on his forehead!

All my care and attention in that first season's calving certainly paid off – I didn't lose a single calf, or once call on the vet for help – though there was an upset at the beginning! I had been up all night, but was well pleased that the first three calves of the season were all heifers. The news travelled fast, and everyone, from my employer down, wanted to see them – including the recently engaged carpenter, who brought his wife and two lads before they left for school. At last I was able to help Bob with the milking, but as I opened the milking parlour door, the carpenter's four year old daughter ran up in tears, 'I wanted to see the calves too,' she shouted. Taking her by the hand I led her to the calving yard. The three calves were now lying down in the straw. 'I can't see them', she howled. Bramble, the last to calve was nearest, so I stood the child on the bottom rail of the fence and slid through to lift up Bramble's calf. As I reached it, Bramble let out a bellow; and I turned just in time to hurl myself at the child running behind me. As I gathered her in my arms, the enraged cow knocked me flat, sideswiping the child; I hugged her close as I got to my knees, and was hit again from behind – this time I was able to use the momentum to throw her under the fence, where she slid to a lifeless heap. I rolled to one side, only to find myself pinned down by the cow's knees, her angry face curving down into mine. Bob having heard the racket, arrived with a welcome stick, and I threw myself over the fence, gathered up the prostrate child and ran like blazes to her house. By the time the doctor arrived she had regained consciousness; he could not find the slightest bruise, and thankfully she had no memory of the incident. In fact I was the one with the handsome bruises.

It was only in my final season, that a calving tested me to the limit – Red Poll calves have larger heads than most, so it was often a struggle before a calf was clear. This large heifer started about 2.00 am, with twins, each a doubled up breech presentation, and only when Bob arrived at 7.00 am, were we finally able to get the first one clear. And not until 10.00 am – with veterinary help – was it brought to a successful conclusion! During those last two years, my employer, who had not the slightest knowledge of farming, took more and more interest in the cattle project, and interfered in every way possible. Because I disagreed that his breeding plan could raise milk yields quickly, he started looking at all the different feeds and the relative costs. He had a fantastic brain for figures, and in seconds could run his finger up the day's columns of milk and rations given, and whilst walking through the short length of the parlour subtract the costs from the Milk Board's expected cheque. Following it with a favourite phrase, 'I would sack my factory manager if he gave me such a poor return.'

He must have been the salesman's delight, and would not accept that you could not change an animal's diet at the drop of a hat. The crunch came, when a large tank was delivered, and a lorry later arrived to fill it with a yellow porridge-like substance – waste from a glucose factory. It smelt sour, but the, 'expert' who arrived soon after, assured me that it had all the qualities to give a high milk yield, and the cows would soon get used to it, and proceeded to give instructions as to amounts to feed per gallon A week later, only three cows were eating the regulation amount, the milk yield was plummeting as the rest either refused to put a nose near, or at best, gave an exploratory lick before bawling in disgust, and as like as not, kick off the milking machine! They, like me, were getting very edgy. Out in the release yard, they butted one another about, and on this Friday afternoon, just as I was about to dash to Buckingham before the barber closed – I was due at Wendy's sister's wedding the following day – one fell against the water trough and broke the inlet pipe. Running a hose from another tap, I turned it on gently, left the cows still queuing and dashed into town. On my return at 6.00 pm, I was surprised to find the hose turned off and cows jostling at an empty tank: I turned it back on and busied myself until they all drank their fill, and left the tank full again.

The following morning as I walked the bull out, the builders were being spoken to by Mr Jarman before they left off work for the weekend. But upon seeing me, he rushed over and demanded, 'Why the hell did you go home at exactly five o'clock yesterday? I pay you an inflated salary, for the very reason that I do not expect you to watch the clock. And you left a pipe running in the cattle yard. Do you realise how many gallons would have run to waste overnight?' Not only could I not get a word in, but my companion on the pole, was, to say the least, getting agitated. I cannot remember all I said in the heat of the moment, but do know that it ended with me storming off, helped immensely by Honest Lynx. The grinning building gang obviously enjoyed the altercation, and with some of them about to do their weekend round of public houses, much of Buckingham knew all about, 'the row at Castlefields Farm,' even before I had the opportunity to tell Wendy that, a month before our own wedding, I was looking for work!

4. A New Job – and a New Life with Wendy

Very late that evening – his second try – a rather dapper little chap with a strong Irish accent, called to say that he had been drinking in the White Hart, and heard that I was looking for a job. He was Farm Manager for Michael Richardson, and could I go to see him in the morning, as they were needing a head cowman. By ten o'clock Sunday morning I had rushed through my chores, and by twelve o'clock I had been offered the position of Head Cowman to the Efril Herd of pedigree Jerseys, to start in two weeks' time, at nearly a third more salary. I accepted, on condition that two weeks later, I could take the week off for my honeymoon – my first ever holiday!

I started on the 20th of March 1953. The head cowman/farm manager before me having left to start his own farm, the farm labourer/tractor driver had been promoted to farm manager, and two seventeen year old lads helped where they were needed, whilst a man near retirement age looked after the piggery attached to the Richardson Paint-factory. By the middle of the week I was aware that all was not well with the new manager, and on the Friday morning – also my 21st birthday, he informed me, 'I have had a row with the boss, and given him notice.' This was rather upsetting, as I had been relying on him to look after the herd whilst I was on honeymoon: luckily I was able to talk him round to changing his one week's notice to two! On the following Friday before the wedding, a note pinned to the cowshed door, requested that I call on Mr Richardson at his paint factory office – which I passed by daily on route to deliver the milk to the dairy. His secretary ushered me in, and said he would be with me shortly: after a few minutes he bustled in, puffing on a large cigar, and asked if I was happy with the work. I remarked that recent events were a bit unsettling, but personally I was OK. After another puff or two, he said, 'I think you are just the chap that we need. How would you like to manage the lot? Cows, pigs, and the arable land, starting when you come back from honeymoon.' Upon my answering, 'Yes,' he stepped forward and slapped me on the shoulder, 'Good man, do a good job, and you shall share in the profits,' and with that he called to his secretary, 'See Mr Clark out,' and I reeled out in a daze.

The following morning I progressed through getting myself ready for the midday ceremony, whilst the rest of the family went mildly haywire around me. At least I didn't have my sister Betty chivvying me, for as one of the two bridesmaids she was with my bride to-be. Our homes were quite near to one another, and in view of Buckingham church, so once the ceremony was over, it seemed no time at all before our two families had finished the wedding breakfast, and were escorting us the few steps to the station. With much hilarity we were helped aboard the steam train, and with some borrowed chalk from the stationmaster, the legend, 'Just Married' was lightly scrawled across the door as the train moved out. We both slumped gratefully back into the seats for the first stage of the journey to Brighton. Where the weather was kind, and we enjoyed idyllic long seaside walks and evening theatre visits, made special by being devoid of work problems. Although, like many other young couples we quickly realised we still had a lot to learn about one another. Wendy as soon as Wednesday, found out about my short-term memory, when upon complaining about an awful smell in the vicinity of the wardrobe, I dashed to retrieve a large crab that I had hidden for a Sunday night feast! And on Friday I learnt that Wendy positively hates public surprises, when our host brought in a birthday cake, and all the other guests sang 'Happy Birthday' in honour of her 21st!

I don't remember much about our welcome home on the Saturday, other than it did not go on too late, as I would need to be at the farm the next day to take up my managerial post.

Jersey Cattle and Spanish Dresses

I had changed to twelve hourly milking: 7.00 am and 7.00 pm, for I had long thought it was not kind to expect heavy milkers to have to carry their load seven or eight hours longer during the night. But now I would have to slot in the supervision of the rest of the two small farms, especially keeping up with the food needs at the piggery, and sale-ready porkers. It all went smoothly, except that I had to forego my afternoon free time. From now on, Sunday would be exceptional only as the day I worked less than 14 hours! The Jersey herd was collectively very handsome, but Tolande, the first import – a darkly blotched blonde with eyelashes that any girl would die for, was outstanding. She was due to calve soon after we returned, and by Wednesday I could see she was close; I looked over the half-door of her loose box, before leaving at 8.30 pm, and could see that she would not need me before midnight – I could either walk the two miles over the fields, or cycle three by road with a long hill both ways – I returned at 12.15 am, to be greeted by the sight of two glistening hooves, and within the hour I was back home, pleased with how easy the calving had been, and that it was a splendid heifer the image of its mother. I decided it would be registered as 'Efrill Tolande the 2nd.'

The following morning, with milking and bottling finished and delivered, I returned to milk her, and was gratified to see such rich colostrum, – not just for the calf's sake, it was also one of my favourite milk puddings, known as 'beastings' and various other names around the country.

It was tradition to offer enough for a pudding to the 'house' and the farmhands. Fortunately for me, it was not to everyone's taste, most probably because few folk baked it to the consistency of an egg custard – it was either solid and dry, or still liquid. I became a reasonable expert on it, and believe even today, some fifty years since I last saw any, I could still judge the percentage of water needed, if any, to make a perfect pudding. That evening I glanced over at Tolande as I passed, she stood placidly with her head at the corner hay rack. In the dairy I readied all the equipment, then fetched the cows, again glancing over the door at Tolande, now laying beside the calf. As I milked, my mind kept returning to Tolande. Still feeling uneasy, I looked in on her each time I carried a bucket of milk into the dairy, she still lay there completely relaxed. At last with the shed washed, and utensils sterilised ready for the morning, I only needed to relieve Tolande of enough milk to leave her comfortable for the night, and I could return home for supper and bed. As I opened her door, like a bolt from the blue, the reason for my unease hit me – she had not been chewing her cud! I rushed over, and felt her flesh. She was boiling hot, and swayed when I made her stand. 'Milk fever,' I groaned.

Except for once seeing my father tackle a Shorthorn with it, this was my first time. Knowing that Jerseys were more susceptible than most, due to the heavy demand from a rich, heavy milk yield on their calcium supply and small frame, I had ready all that was needed for such an eventuality. Having done all I could, I settled beside her, for she was lying down again. I talked to her continuously, her now bulbous eyes, seemingly unseeing, and as her head sunk to the floor I lifted it up onto my lap, but slowly and surely she relapsed further. In desperation, before she went totally unconscious, I poured another 'drench' down her reluctant throat, then sat back down, and laid her head back across my knees. Very slowly her breathing seemed to be returning to normal, and the tremors in her hind legs subsided. I thought she might be turning the corner, and leaned back against the wall exhausted, but with hope in my heart. Goodness knows how I had managed to fall asleep, but the next thing I knew, was a breathy nuzzle in my face, and I opened my eyes, to what at that moment was the most beautiful picture in the world. Tolande standing on her own four feet, and about to slurp what must be the roughest of animal tongues across my face. I arrived home as day broke, to find Wendy slumped fast asleep in an arm chair: two of us had had an uncomfortable night!

The Jersey bull, Woodfield Antares, was not very impressive. Even though he was furnished with a decent pair of horns, Honest Lynx could have flattened him with a puff, and in fact the Large White boar at the piggery commanded more respect. However I remembered my father's edict – the smaller the bull, the lighter he is on his feet – and this one could certainly move. Being Jersey Island bred, he was used to being pegged out with a chain, and the previous cowman had followed on with the tradition. A chain was attached to a halter, and ran between his horns, down his forehead and through his nose ring, to be hooked to twelve metres of chain fixed to a stake driven well into the gravelly ground, allowing him to graze a 24 metre circle. This needed moving at least once each day, or he might be unhooked and walked to the buildings if a cow needed his services. It was not the easiest situation, needing all your attention to hit the stake, and be aware of his occasional cussedness and speed – especially when bending down to pull the stake out! So I devised a swivelling anchor out of a scrap car's front wheel hub, welding on three 200 mm spikes to the underside and a metre long 'T' handle and a snap-hook on the axle stub. I could now attach his chain, give a couple of jumps on the wheel to bed it down, and to move him, lift the handle to prise the stakes out of the ground, turn it on edge, and push the tyreless wheel to the next spot before turning it back onto the spiked side again. This worked perfectly, except for one night!

The pigs and the twelve hourly milking was enough to fill my day – even with Wendy helping me by bottling the milk in the mornings, washing out the cowshed and returning the cows to the field – but now impending harvest promised to make my seven day week even more hectic. This was when George, the friend of my teens, tracked me down. He was an aircraft electrician, living in a town house, whilst we had just moved into the farm cottage in the tiny village of Radclive. He spent an ecstatic Sunday trailing me around the farm, amazed at the beauty of the meadows, the mill stream and the Great Ouse winding all through the farm, but utterly mortified that I no longer spent time angling. 'I know what I'll do,' he said, as we ushered him off, preparatory to starting the 7.00 pm milking, 'Next Sunday I will arrive at about 4.30 am – don't worry about breakfast or a flask, I'll bring it all with me, and we'll fish until you have to go and start the morning milking.' 'Don't you dare;' said Wendy and I together – though I told him he was welcome to fish if he wanted. The following Sunday at 4.45 am, there was a loud hammering on the front door. I dashed and opened the window, 'I am not coming out, buzz off,' I shouted – and from under the porch stepped my employer's wife! 'Oh Bill,' she called, 'I am so sorry, but the bull is loose, he just now put his head in the open window and snorted at me.' I found him at the bottom of her garden feasting on cabbages, but despite my best efforts, I was unable to get him into the yard, and he fled up the road to a neighbour's field. No need for me to dwell on our efforts – I gave my father and brother Bob an early call – to catch him and put a new ring in his nose. Suffice it to say that we woke up the rest of the hamlet in the process. My employer's wife, who had been packing to follow her husband and children to Cornwall, had left before I could explain and apologise; however another problem the next day, probably put me back in her good books.

I had been asked to keep an eye on the mill house, but meanwhile the au pair – who couldn't speak a word of English, had been left behind to do some last chores. I noticed her tripping backwards and forwards to the washing line with a large washing basket – she was quite a pretty, well-tanned, slightly plump girl and looked every inch as I imagined a Spanish girl should look – even dressed the part, in a white cotton blouse, slightly off the shoulder, bright red, fully flounced calf length skirt, and sporting large dangly ear rings! I gave her a cheery wave, and a 'Good Morning' on the first sighting and she responded with a smile. Later, as I unloaded the clean bottles and churns from the van, I noticed that the pint of milk I had put on her doorstep was still there and in full sun, so I walked down to remind her to put it in the fridge. As I approached I could hear sobbing and broke into a run: realising it emanated from the washroom, I dashed in, and the sobs changed to squeals. With both palms towards me, she was obviously imploring me to go away. The situation was clear! She had been lifting clothes out of the large, old fashioned washing machine and feeding them into the electric mangle fixed to one side, and turning quickly, her skirt had been gripped by the rollers and she had only managed to reach the switch as her bottom came against the rollers. She was now naked up to the waist, except for a scrap of knickers – enough in place to save some modesty. She was so tightly tied, I doubted if I dare use a knife. I threw her a towel and said, 'Don't cry, I can help,' and dashed off for my tool box. She looked even more worried when I returned, for I expect she thought I had gone to call some authority or other. However, in a few minutes I had dismantled the cover and taken off the drive chain – luckily at the far side from her, and spun the skirt back out. With a last sob – and I know not whether it was a curse or a thank you, she rushed past me into the main part of the house.

By 1954 the farm my father managed was a model of what he thought a modern mixed arable and grazing farm should be: neat machine-cut hedges – an ungainly machine, mounted on an old standard Ford tractor, which I was among the first to use – and larger fields, although he did only bulldoze a couple of hedges and ponds! By now most of the unsightly patches of nettles and thistles had disappeared from his grazing land, and the corn poured at

71

such a rate from the new 'Tanker' combine harvester, that drying and storage facilities had to be built. I of course, was not only keen to emulate him, albeit with a smaller unit, but aimed to be more modern still.

Following my change to 12 hourly milking, I had started electric fenced strip grazing, and ploughing and reseeding the rush infested grazing land. Mr Richardson was pleased that despite his previous losses, my first year turned in a profit, and no doubt if the phrase had been coined then, I would have said, 'You ain't seen nothin yet.' Even so, when I found wild flowers entirely new to me growing in the improved pastures, it did not stop me from admiring them – although I had already learnt not to pick a bunch to take home to Wendy, for she preferred to see her flowers in their natural habitat: but she did say, after I had taken her to see these unknown blooms, that I should make enquiries. Through the kindness of an elderly Buckingham botanist, we found that one, a Yellow Star Thistle was very rare. She thought that no more than three other plants had been noted in the Buckingham area in the previous fifty years, and religiously entered my name as the finder for 1954 in her copy of the record. Sadly, the plants only appeared that one season. Nonetheless, unbeknown to me, another seed had been sown – to lay at the back of my mind.

There was one modern innovation that I had inherited, which I was certainly not going along with. In an upstairs converted granary stood a four year old battery system, containing 200 hens. I was horrified, both to see them, and smell them, and within days I had dismantled the cages, strawed the shed down to let them have the free run, and next brought some abandoned 'arks' back into use, putting a dozen hens in each, and moving them about the fields, so thinning the number in the loft down to a hundred – I still find it hard to believe that at the time of writing, the majority of this country's eggs still come from battery hens!

Teazel and Beth

I must tell of 'Teazel', Wendy's little Cairn Terrier – getting old, but still full of life, and like many ladies' pets, used to getting his own way, liked good food, and was a tad overweight: and still had much to learn! That of course was my opinion. Teazel thought he knew all he wanted to know in his role of being a ladies pet. He would attack an Alsatian and swing on it's tail if he wanted to, in fact do most things, as and when he wanted to. He would not sit, or come to heel at the first time of asking for anybody – and most certainly not for the new member of his family. Having always lived with dogs, I thought I should take Teazel in hand! Wendy agreed, and so whenever possible, Teazel accompanied me on my walks to inspect the crops and animals, especially my trips back and forth with the milkers. Keeping him to heel proved to be a doddle – he quickly learnt that close to the heels of his trainer avoided hulking great cows sniffing at him. Sitting by the gate outside the field was much more preferable to wandering among skittish heifers. He was soon sitting patiently waiting without being tied. And of course all the walking got him lean and fit.

Eventually the cows gave not a second glance when we walked between them – until one morning! We walked through those waiting at the gate. Further off, the rears of three cows protruded from an angle in the hedge, and as they took no heed when I called, I guessed they were sniffing at something interesting – my thought was a fox kill. I walked over; and simultaneous with rounding the corner and seeing a fourth cow and calf, the three turned, saw Teazel, bellowed, and charged! I vividly pictured the trouble I would be in as I carried home Teazel's lifeless body. The first cows – sedately walking up the lane – now turned and came rushing back. Even if I could have picked him up, the enraged cows would have knocked me down too. I just yelled, 'HOME TEAZEL. GO HOME.' He needed no more telling. Unfortunately, home was the route we walked – no short cuts through hedges for him. In desperation he dodged between flailing legs and threatening horns and with only slight relief I saw him breast the first rise ahead of the galloping cows, distended udders swinging and spurts of milk going in all directions. Shutting the gate on the cow standing guard over her calf, I dashed up the lane to the road – not an animal in sight, but at least there was not a trampled shape either! I trotted on, fearful of the carnage I would find in our vegetable garden, with the rows of glass cloches, runner bean tripods and rows of peas climbing up their sticks. But as I drew near I could see there was not a single cow there, just a bemused Wendy leaning out of the bedroom window – it was still not 7.00 am. The thundering hooves and bellowing had certainly given her a good wake-up call! 'Have you seen Teazel?' I gasped. At the sound of my voice, a grinning little face, with tongue hanging nearly to the ground, peered round the corner of the cottage. I had no time to stand and explain, for at the brow of the hill beyond the farm buildings – just short of the main road into Buckingham – was the local 'Road-man', frantically shouting and waving. Having turned the front runners around, the tired herd was now ambling back as if nothing had happened. The only written record, until now, was the sudden drop in milk yield – some five gallons – for one milking only. Teazel happily soldiered on until age – not cows – overtook him.

It was soon after this that Wendy decided to buy me a Welsh Border Collie pup. The farmer in Wales took it to his station at 5.00 am, and she was to be put off the train at Buckingham Station at 4.00 pm. I walked through our fields and the half mile of streets, to collect her. The pup, having been cooped up for so many hours, would surely appreciate a walk instead of another ride. At the station-master's office I was shown a flimsy little chicken-wire cage and I bent down to open it up; the tiny mite – hardly 8 inches (200 mm) high and not much more from head to tail, looked up from her straw bed without the least sign of concern. The kindly Station Master arrived with a saucer of water as I lifted her out, and we both laughed when I offered up my new collar and lead as she drank – a piece of string would have to suffice.

From that day forward Beth seldom left my side; no matter if I was driving tractor, van or lorry, building a bale stack or loading a trailer, Beth would be there. Ladders, heat or noise held no terrors for her, and it seemed no time at all before fully trained – mainly to whistles – she was trotting along the roadside to the railway bridge, then down the lane beside the railway to fetch the cows, whilst I busied myself getting the milking equipment ready. I would then cycle along to open the gate to let the cows onto the road. One cottager told me he set his clock by her: I in return, said I wondered why she always crossed to the opposite side of the road to pass his house? He chuckled. 'I'm afraid my tabby once jumped down from the fence onto her back, I was terrified he was going to blind her, as he raked his claws down her face, but your dog knew what to do. She turned and crashed straight through the hedge, leaving my cat tangled in the brambles behind her.'

She was my pride and joy, and many were the compliments I received, both on her healthy looks, and behaviour. I knew I could put my trust in her, whatever I asked her to do. Even when she took to having a little wander each morning whilst I milked, I was unconcerned – she was most probably only relieving herself. Then one afternoon I stopped to pass the time of day with the railway crossing keeper working on his vegetable patch piling seeding cabbages and sprout stalks into a wheelbarrow. Finally, grasping the handles he remarked, 'The sooner I throw these into my hen-run the better, perhaps a bit of green-stuff will start the lazy beggars laying, I have never had so few eggs!' I opened the gate for Beth, then cycled back to the farm, knowing the cows would soon be with me. The following morning the cows trooped into the yard as usual, Beth trotted to her bed, curled up, and went to sleep. At 8.00 am, as I bent to wash a cow's udder, a mere shadow slunk past and out the door: I watched, as she crossed the yard, crawled under the gate, over the road and into the field, where she broke into a lope. I put the milking machine on the waiting cow, then jumped on my cycle, peddled furiously to the chicken run and creeping the last few yards, I saw a well-worn track under some brambles and then the wire-netting. A few moments later Beth's head appeared in the 'pop hole' of the hen house, egg yolk round her muzzle, and a whole egg in her jaws. I waited until she squeezed out, before I said, 'BETH, what are you doing?' She dropped the egg, ran to the wire, yelping as she shot through, quite sure that she was going to get her first ever smack. She was laying on her bed shaking from head to tail by the time I arrived back. I said, 'Never do that again,' confident that she never would. At least I now knew why she had such a glossy coat – I thought it best not to ask the crossing keeper if he had ever given her a cracked egg or dropped any along the roadside.

Despite my working day and night, and turning in profits for each of the three years I was in the post, Mr Richardson reneged on his promise to give me a share – though after my first reminder, he did make us a present of his old black and white, nine inch TV set with magnifier – and I decided to cut my losses.

5. Oxfordshire – Farm Maintenance and Poaching The Duke's Pheasants – Return to Buckingham and More Contracting

In December 1955, I took on the post of, 'Machine and Building Maintenance' for three farms covering seven hundred acres – part of the Marlborough Estate in Oxfordshire, farmed by tenant Mr Walter Green. I was also to be relief milker, relief crawler driver, and driver of one of their two combine harvesters. This may sound a lot of work, but except for the combine driving and the occasional weekend milking, no overtime work was carried out, so I hoped that Wendy and I would be able to spend a bit more leisure time together. We moved into a quaint little stone cottage at East End, Coombe, rented by the farm from the Duke – a pass enabled us to use the Palace road to get to Woodstock and walk and cycle around parts of the Estate that the public seldom got to see.

Mr Green resided at the 'Home Farm', where the buildings maintenance workshop was situated; he was supposed to be retired, indeed the reason for my appointment, was to take over the work that he had personally been attending to for some years. I soon learned to replace every tool in its allotted place immediately after any use – for if he walked in, and it wasn't in my hand, he would ask, 'Where is that half inch wood chisel?' The estate upkeep was in such good order, that less than six months per annum on my part would probably keep it that way, so hence my other tasks and the machinery maintenance – which was either in the field, or at Geoffrey Green's – GG –

workshop, which was in complete contrast to his father's. It was easier to take my own box of tools there, than spend ages trying to find the right tool in all the muddle. However, he was a most excellent farm manager.

Unfortunately Beth was now out of a job. Even when I worked with the herd of Friesians – as they were unused to a dog, she was not welcome. With hindsight, I should have let her go to another owner, but with Wendy now without a dog, we thought Beth would happily fit in at home. She reluctantly watched me cycle off in the mornings and raced to see me in the evenings, but apart from Wendy taking her for walks, mooched around the garden for the rest of the time. Then along came Alan; there was only one thing that the Radcliffe Hospital had managed to get correct where I was concerned, and that was to inform me that my childhood mumps had been at a most inappropriate time. Now, after years of vetting, we had been entrusted with this delightful five month old child. Beth looked a little askance at this newcomer taking up so much of her mistress's time, but she was so well trained I was confident she would soon take to him. We realised that all was not well when she growled at a passing milkman, and later chased the postman, breaking a couple of spokes in his cycle wheel. We took extra care once Alan was on his feet, but one Sunday I was repairing a toy in my shed, Beth happily dozing at my feet, when Alan toddled in to see if I had finished. Beth leapt as I shouted, 'NO BETH.' I cried tears of remorse for my stupidity, as we rushed a profusely bleeding infant to the nearest doctor. However, all was not as bad as we feared; my yell had stopped Beth in mid-bite, but Alan still bears the puncture marks. And I had another tearful session the following evening, as I carried Beth's body over to Blenheim Park wall, and buried her beneath a beech tree.

Mr Green brooked no interference as to what he thought needed my attention! I often found myself being suddenly spirited away in the Austin 7 he used as his farm runabout – to unblock a sink, or replace one tile on a roof –

no matter that I was under a tractor and covered in oil, or thick with dust in the heart of a broken down combine! He also regarded the pedigree Friesian herd, and the Landrace pigs his domain. The milking herd was grazed at the Home farm and the cowsheds were situated a few hundred metres from his house – the wintering yards in full view from his upstairs windows meant that any discrepancy was noticed. If I happened to be in the workshop, there would be a cry of, 'William, can you go along and ask Rodney to straw down the second yard, it's looking messy, if he is too busy, ask Young Tom' – he was a young labourer who did any menial task, but could be miles away – so it was often easier and quicker to jump on the nearest tractor, and do the job myself. I only realised toes where being trodden on, when the wife of one of the five tractor drivers remarked, 'I saw you using Young Tom's tractor today, you need to watch out; Harry is just waiting for you to touch his, before he blows his top!'

I next gained the attention of one of the Duke's nine gamekeepers – an ex-army man. During quiet times on the farms, both Mrs Greens 'borrowed' an older labourer to work in their gardens, and having noticed the speed with which I was getting my own garden into shape, elderly Mrs Green inquired if I would be willing to give her a hand for a few Saturdays. The first thing I noticed was that the pigeons were clobbering her sprouts and cabbages – they were using a large elm tree out in the meadow as a settling point and I volunteered to shoot them. I owned a .22 rifle with a silencer, I liked it especially for rabbit shooting, for when two or three were in range, I often shot two, and occasionally three, as all they heard was a noise like a cracking twig, followed by one of their number falling over. With such a powerful weapon I took great care to ensure ricochets would be going away from any road or habitation, and if I saw any activity in the line, I wouldn't shoot. During my second Saturday in the garden I was running back with a pigeon in my hand, when GG and a man in green tweeds, came striding down the path towards me. 'What on earth are you doing William – running them down?' said GG, with a broad grin. The man in the tweeds brusquely snatched the bird from my hands and examined it. He seemed quite disappointed when I said that Mr and Mrs Green had given me permission, and as I started digging again, he said, 'You can't be getting much gardening done if you are watching for pigeons.' For answer, I plunged my fork into the ground, picked up the rifle leaning against the fruit cage, took aim at the tree, pulled the trigger, and as a pigeon dropped like a stone, picked up my fork, commenting, 'I shan't run for that one, its dead, I only go if they're injured.' I knew I had made a mistake when I saw the pallor of his face as he returned with the pigeon. 'Through the head! I don't know if His Grace will allow this Mr Green,' and off he stalked – taking the pigeon. 'Don't worry William, you're doing a grand job, I'll tell Father and he'll have a word with the Head Gamekeeper, but I should think he will want to see you.' Both the Greens were well aware of the importance of keeping on the right side of the gamekeepers, in fact, one of the terms of my employment stated that any employee found taking game on Mr Green's farms, or guilty of poaching elsewhere, would be instantly dismissed.

A few days later, a tall, quietly spoken, elderly man in green tweeds accosted me as I repaired a dry-stone wall. 'Good afternoon young man, I must say you are making as good a fist of that wall as I have seen for many a day, the Duke will be well pleased when he next passes: but then a fellow that can shoot a pigeon through the eye at two hundred and twenty paces, should probably make a good job of most things, hey?' He then introduced himself as the Head Keeper, continuing, 'If you ever want to come and beat for us on a Saturday shoot, you will be most welcome, and I'll see that you get a couple of pheasants too. He then pointed to a corner in the Park – where stone had been quarried. 'There's a large rabbit warren down there, making it safe for rifle shooting, feel free to get one whenever you want.' And after shaking my hand, he walked on.

'Our' gamekeeper must have been mortified with this outcome, for a day or two later, the wife who warned me of upsetting the other men, passed on our keepers conversation with her husband: 'If he so much as looks at a pheasant, I'll have his guts for garters!' Sure enough, whenever a hare ran past, or pigeons clattered off, I would know that he was lurking. Sometimes, when I was shooting, I would give a cheery wave and a 'Hullo,' in that direction and he would slink out with a sickly smile. The harvest finally arrived, and I found myself very busy. Besides driving one combine harvester for every hour possible, I repaired and maintained both, and even the third retired one on the occasions it was needed, when GG also drove.

If I thought my being tied to the combines would relieve our gamekeeper, I was mistaken. He would be stealthily moving through the trees if we were near woodland, but out in the field if we were too distant, no matter what time we worked to – if the weather was 'catchy' it could be midnight. We were allowed to catch any rabbits of course, and all the men had a stout stick at the ready on the tractors and combines, and on the occasions when GG took over from me – whilst I dealt with some problem – he would take his gun on board. One time he dumped some twenty rabbits in the trough behind the cutter bar before driving to the next field, then swung in, pushed the gear lever down to start thrashing, and too late, remembered the rabbits – and I spent an interesting couple of hours clearing bits of rabbits and their guts out of every nook and cranny.

Another time, after fixing a problem at the drying plant, I hitched a ride back on the grain trailer, first walking behind my combine to examine the straw and chaff to check the threshing – it still upsets me to see the amount of grain lost from many machines, due to poor adjustment, or being driven too hard – when moments after GG put the emptying auger into gear, I could hear a strange rattling. I jumped on board to look in the grain tank, and to my horror I was looking down the barrels of his gun jiggling around: I have never ducked, or pulled a gear lever so fast, ever! It took some time to extricate, for the butt was well splintered and stuck in the start of the auger – whilst I was trying my hardest not to be in the way, if it did 'go off.' Not the best place to keep your gun safe – especially if you have a poor memory!

In some fields the young pheasants trotted along in front of the combines like chickens going to be fed. It was nothing to see a score run out at the corner, just in front of the machine; some would carry on running towards the woods, whilst others would hide under the first row of straw or run back into the standing corn to trot along to the next corner. As darkness fell and we put on the headlights, those birds left would often only move when the reel was actually knocking the straw above their heads. Thankfully the combine of those days was very slow, but occasionally one would go inside with a whump, so I carried a heap of small stones on the platform – not for nothing was the next village called Stonesfield – and towards evening, toss them among the pheasants to flush them out. One evening the inevitable happened, and one lay quivering as I droned towards it: it would be a sin to waste a good dinner, and our man was on the far side! With my foot I pushed the bag that my food had been in, to the front of the platform – no cabs in those days – slipped the gears to dead slow as the bird disappeared under the cutter-bar, dropped to the ground in time to pick it up, slipped it in the bag, and was back in my seat again in seconds: I had been so intent – one false move and I could be under the wheel – that I had not noticed the trailer coming up to unload. As I pulled the lever to start the auger, the driver gave me a big grin and a thumbs up. Once his load was full, he stopped and climbed aboard. 'Well done Bill, I have often wondered how I could get away with one, without that old s** over there knowing. Can you get me one too?' Before the evening was over, I had provided him, the other trailer driver, and my colleague on the other combine with one apiece.

A large acreage of potatoes was also grown – consequently needing a number of pickers: all female, these

82

were brought in from Coombe by Young Tom on a tractor and trailer, from Stonesfield by GG in his Land Rover, and from Long Handborough by Mr Green in his car. One day GG detailed me to pick up from Stonesfield as he would be away all day. The women waited in a group, and there was some hilarity and ribald comments, as one or two larger women needed help from me to struggle on board. For the rest of the day I was doing some repair or other, but at my arrival in the afternoon, the same jocularity ensued as in the morning, then suddenly all went quiet, and following the concerned nods, I espied Mr Green walking over. 'It looks as if you are having problems William,' and he stepped forward to help us lift a large pram into the centre of the melee inside the Rover. 'No, no, we can manage,' spluttered the two red faced women. However he took the handles and heaved, the plywood bottom – no doubt weakened by years of leaking nappies – burst, and a heap of potatoes fell at our feet. With a smile at me, he said, 'Oh dear, William! Quickly, fetch a sack, we mustn't keep these ladies waiting.'

The potato crop was stored in a large stone barn. As Elder Tom was in hospital, it fell to me to take his place when the time for sorting came around. The work was not too onerous – Elder William shovelled the potatoes into the ground level hopper of the sorter, from which they were elevated into a revolving cylinder. Mostly dirt and dust trickled through the first small round holes punched through metal plate, while marble sized 'chats' fell through the second, square holed section of woven wire into a two handled tub. And in the last section, the 'seed' or 'feed' potatoes fell through further woven panels onto a side elevator to be bagged up – these panels could be changed to concur with the Potato Board's latest minimum 'ware' sizes. Balancing this elevator – on the opposite side – sat a single cylinder engine, put-putting away, with a little cloud of steam rising from the water jacket. The ware potatoes spilled out of the end of the cylinder and jiggled along a short roller elevator – presenting all sides to the eagle eyes of three ladies – who tossed damaged ones into buckets for immediate farm pig feed. (We were all allowed to take any of these potatoes for our own use too, so no embarrassment this time for one certain young lady!). Green and rotting ones were thrown onto a heap. As the ware potatoes filled the hundredweight (50 kilo) hessian sacks, I – when in the company of Elder William, answering to 'Young William' – weighed, tied, and stacked them in one-ton piles – attending to the bags of seed too, which didn't have to be weighed and were stacked separately.

Young Tom was only in attendance first thing each morning with his tractor and trailer, when Elder William and I shovelled up the dirt for him to dump in the fields, and the rotten and green potatoes, to be tipped into a quarry – he would then drive off to collect the ladies for their 9.00 am start. Each day soon after 4.00 pm, a lorry arrived to pick up the load of ware potatoes. On one occasion the order was for extra, so we three men started sorting first thing. Once the ladies arrived we got up to speed, but as the morning progressed and we pushed the machine forward, the previous day's soil heaps got in the way, so I just levelled them out, and we all just stood a little higher. The tallest lady – who was rather aloof from the other two – commented that we ought to leave this dry soil all the time as it was warmer than the concrete floor, and the shortest young lady said she was finding it easier to reach across. Then, soon after lunch – as I heaved a sack onto the pile – there was a yell, 'Stop the engine!' I swung round to see the tall lady struggling with the seed potato elevator. I leapt to the little engine, and snatched off the drive belt with my hands, then rushed round to the sobbing woman expecting to see blood, only to find the youngest woman grinning from ear to ear, saying, 'For goodness sake, stop making such a fuss, I am sure Young William has seen as much – and more – before now.'

The distressed woman was begging us men to leave the barn; and no wonder, for the two cogs at the top of the little elevator – normally out of the way – had caught hold of her frock as she leaned over, and she was now standing hard against the cogs with breasts bared, and her frock pulled up, showing bright blue knickers. We waited outside, until finally a voice called, 'We can't budge her Young William, you'll have to come.' I at last managed to remove the cogs and tease the tangle from the spindles to set her free. Then, whilst both women helped to sort out her clothes and mend her bra with string, I rushed the machine back together. It seemed quite surreal, as for the rest of the afternoon, in the glare of the single light bulb hanging above the sorting table – the proud looking tear stained lady, in her torn, crumpled and oil streaked frock, carried on working in front of me!

During the following two years I found myself being ever more useful! Most small items I repaired on site or made new in the excellent workshop. Large items, such as five barred oak gates, posts and rails, window frames and such, were ordered from the Duke's saw-mill and workshops. Unfortunately, no matter how careful, I still stepped on toes whenever I helped with the farm work! I had to drive the crawler for potato planting as Old Tom was still in hospital. It needed all my concentration to make decent ridges in the exceptionally long undulating field. I later cringed as we gathered to collect our wage packets, when Mr Green remarked loudly: 'Young William, those potato ridges across Eighty Acres, are the straightest I have ever seen.' And whenever I relief milked, the yield was always 'up', when it is a well-known fact that cows hate change, and it is mostly lower at such times. My usual confidant said the cowman reckoned I was over-feeding the expensive concentrates. Armed with this information, on the evening he left for his two weeks' holiday, I counted all the sacks of 'dairy concentrate', and weighed the opened one. The milk yield rose steadily, until by my last day I was filling an extra ten gallon churn. Upon his return, the angry cowman, made the allegation directly to Mr Green. When I was asked why I hadn't kept to the milk yield to cake ratio charts, I merely passed over my list of quantities in the store on the Friday night before I started, and the amount still there on the Sunday evening when I finished. GG later congratulated me, saying, 'Father and I have been through the figures twice, and we both reckon that you should have used much more concentrate to get that yield.'

But my time there was coming to an end – Mr Topham had made me an offer that I couldn't refuse! On my last day, the Head Gamekeeper came to where I was loading manure spreaders. 'I hear we are losing you.' He then took and shook my hand, leaving a ten shilling note in it, 'Have a drink on the Duke, we shall miss you: there hasn't been another combine driver on all our farms that drives the pheasants out of the way like you do.' My guilt was not wiped away entirely until a few years later, when a name I recognised was headlined in a daily newspaper, my old adversary was in trouble. Now a head gamekeeper himself, he had been caught selling dozens of his master's pheasant chicks!

I was still hankering after my own farm, and with the promise that my salary would be doubled – and probably quadrupled with bonuses – I thought this would surely enable us to get there at last. And so in June 1958 we moved to a pleasant little hamlet on the edge of Hillsden, near Buckingham. The downside being, I was now at home less than ever, and missing a lot of Alan's growing up. Despite our scare with Beth attacking him, we both still felt bereft with no dog in the family, and when a shooting friend of my brother visited in some distress, imploring us to take in his beautiful Golden Retriever for a while, we jumped at the chance. He and his wife were out to work all day, and despite his wife returning to walk the dog at midday, it still barked and disturbed their neighbour/landlady. The ultimatum was, the dog or they, had to go! Julie was the most delightful dog, some ten months old, well into her obedience and retrieve training, and made herself at home immediately. Best of all, she looked on toddler Alan as her best mate. We daily got more apprehensive as to how he would cope when her owner returned for her. When he did call though, it was to tearfully tell us that they had decided that it was unkind of them to expect Julie to be alone all day, and would we like to keep her?

We were all overjoyed. I still did occasional shooting for the pot, and thought it would be nice to carry on with her retrieve training. Julie was soon perfect with all the commands, stuffed rabbit skin finding, picking up, and carrying; and after she showed no fear of the gun, I decided it was time for the real thing. I walked the farm that my father managed from end to end – not a rabbit ran out of the stubble, nary a pigeon came within range, then, as we walked the last field, a hare leapt up! Julie quivered and looked to me. I said, 'Stay', aimed and fired. The hare rolled head over heels. 'Good Girl', I said, 'Go, fetch'. Julie ran like the wind, and as she bent to pick it up, the hare lifted its head and blared, as only an injured hare can! Julie bolted back to me, staying close behind my legs whilst I dispatched it. That settled Julie's role in life. She refused to have anything further to do with shooting – playing ball with young Alan was all she wanted from now on!

My work was to be mostly with civil engineering machinery this time, much of it subcontracting to build Britain's first motorway, the M1. I wasn't the only one excited by the chance of big money: businesses, both large and small, were sinking large sums into new machinery and fleets of lorries in readiness for this bonanza. Mr T had bought a stone quarry near Lower Heyford – it had not been in use for many years but still had planning permission – and he was pleased at the low price he had paid. Once the large stone crusher arrived from the 'Parker' factory, I could make a start on getting a few hundred tons stock-piled in readiness. In the meantime, the very latest model 'Drott Skid Shovel' – designated the 'Four in One' – had been delivered, so I was contracted out to a demolition firm at Bicester Army Camp. This job proved 'memorable' right from the moment I arrived. First I was held up whilst the sentries removed the smashed crossing gate which an army steam train had just run through, then, on finding heaps of new ventilator cowls, from 100 mm to 300 mm in the first building I was to demolish, I walked over to investigate the neighbouring – large dormitory with shower block – and found three workmen inside painting. It transpired that they had signed a contract with the army to redecorate all but the first building, prior to Ministry officials deciding to demolish them instead – the army was not in the habit of giving money away, so a sergeant regularly inspected their work, making sure it was up to standard!

Once I had established the cowls were legitimate demolition – we sold them for £100 to the contractor who was going to build on our cleared site – I found that any attempt to lift more than half a shovel-full with the 'Four in One,' tipped it on end and I had to use it gingerly for some days, which was probably just as well, for even then, we were so close to the painters at times, that paint came off on the two labourers gloves as they removed doors, windows, cupboards, etc. The inspecting sergeant visited ever more frequently, until, at the penultimate building, he informed the painters that they could call it a day – which was just as well, for we were ready to knock the walls down as they waved goodbye! I worked late into the evening removing every last vestige of foundations and drainage, for Mr T had informed me that the stone crusher would be arriving in two days' time – since the disbelieving reps had viewed me at work, mechanics had fitted a large weight on the back end, and the Drott now heaved and lifted whatever I put it to.

At the Guard Hut the following morning I was scrutinised, and hurried over the level crossing: simultaneously with thinking, 'I never looked for trains,' I heard a loud crash, and my rear view mirror filled with engine and bits of the new gate clattered past! Still shaking, I parked my van by the Drott, and prepared it for the day's work. That done, I glanced at my site map, and drove it the few hundred yards – past some new looking houses – to find nothing but a grassy clearing among trees! It took a little time – our sergeant was on leave – to find out that the building had never been built but had remained on the Ministry books. This was the second time that painters had

88

been paid to paint it, and now we were being paid more than £200 to demolish it! As the officer said, 'Cheap at twice the price to get it removed from the books.'

My quarry work proved to be nearly as farcical, although not so profitable. The first blasting of the rock face demolished the new hut, then the huge machine wouldn't crush the stuff – the firm's expert opined the rock was too 'soft': which brought the comment from Mr T, that the only soft thing was the expert's head. Howbeit, after changing the jaws, it at last crushed stone – but slowly – with only a dozen loads in the stockpile when the first stone was required. Only for it to be rejected as 'too soft!' Despite Mr T's best efforts, it stayed banned from the M1 – at least he found a buyer for the crusher, but he couldn't off-load his quarry and during the next three years I worked wherever I was needed. Some of it I am afraid to say, was removing farm hedgerows and a hundred acres or so of woodland, besides filling in a few ponds.

I did get to work on some M1 verges, but most of my work was in association: such as pushing surplus soil from cuttings into land-fill, and opening up a new gravel pit. Once it was seen just what I could do with the Drott, I was more involved with groundwork for new factories, and housing estates, including some of the first for the new town of Milton Keynes. In all those environments I saw sloppy work being done – I was present at the fiasco, when fabricated beams, meant to carry the M1, fell to the ground as they were being lowered into place: the buttresses had been built too far apart! Wherever I was working, corners were cut and poor materials used – and as to the waste! Usually being the person to landscape the finished site, I was often instructed to bury all the left-overs. I would not want to buy the last house built on many estates, knowing what lies a few feet below the surface of the garden! There have been occasions since, when mention on the TV news of some problem with a housing estate or road, such as a need to demolish or up-grade, or there has been subsidence – when my memory clicks in, and I remark, 'Has it really lasted that long?' – Anyway, I had now had enough of 'civil' engineering; it was time to get back to farming.

1. *Thurleigh School photo 1940. I am fourth from the right, middle row. Courtesy Thurleigh Through the Years.*

2. *Harvesting in the 1970s. Me with Stooks.*

3. Honest Lynx allowing me to take his photo.

4. My cows were very approachable. Me with Lantigen and a slightly jealous Beth

5. One of Topham's two Vickers crawlers at the new Aylesbury sewerage site. The chief engineer celebrated the opening with tea made from the 'out fall'.

6. Tracking back on the Drott after using the new Rock Scoop to load the Parker Crusher. The Matbro was used to load lorries with crushed stone.

7. *Young Alan and I cutting cucumbers. Stewart gave Alan pocket money for picking tomatoes. It came in a proper wages envelope. "You will note I haven't taken any tax off, like I have your father's," he said. "I would rather not join that if you don't mind," answered Alan.*

8. *Building a corn stack. My father's adage: keep the middle full! After a photo in the Cambridge Collection.*

6. Move to Essex – Market Gardening – Mixed Farming and the Interest in Nature Begins to take over

The changes that were taking place in the way farming was done, was being noticed and having an effect even outside farming circles. I realised that much of what I had thought was 'cutting edge' on only a few modern farms, was now being multiplied over the whole of Britain. I began to examine whether I did, after all, want to be an ultra-modern farmer? Smallholding looked more appealing – and not just because it increasingly seemed it would be the only size I could aspire to. We moved to Essex in mid-1960, bought a large caravan and rented 30 acres of land and buildings in Tendring, and I took on garden work to earn our daily crust, but come the winter the work dried up.

A temporary job in the Palgrave Brown wood yard at the Colchester docks saw me through. Two incidents whilst I was there, confirmed two of my mother's oft repeated mantras – never believe all you read in the newspapers – and your sins will surely find you out! Whilst having a tea break, I watched lorries bringing in scrap iron next door. One driver leapt out and papers in hand rushed into the dock-side office, meanwhile his loaded lorry ran backwards and over the edge. The next day, a local newspaper carried a splendid photo of the driver who had risked life and limb to try and stop his runaway vehicle! The second incident involved a work colleague – he had made a mistake in his conversion from metric to imperial, and finished up with ten off-cuts of expensive hardwood – 300 mm x 300 mm x 900 mm. It was dusk, the tide was racing out, so over the side with them. For five days the pieces passed back and forth – with a large red eagle and source number emblazoned on one end of each piece!

Market Gardening

In the spring – keen to learn more about market gardening – I joined a large tomato growing concern near Clacton, and besides helping put up a two acre, 'Dutch-light' greenhouse, worked in both lettuce and tomato houses throughout the summer. They were pleased with my work and wanted me to stay, but I had other plans. Our farm stock was coming along – we already had Saddle-Back pigs, hens and New Zealand White rabbits in our farm buildings – which Wendy looked after during the day – but I had held off from tilling any of the land, as the elusive owner had still not signed our agreement. Right next door to us was an eight acre holding with three one-acre greenhouses, and earlier I had struck a deal with the owner to repair his unused one during the evenings – he had a stack of years old greenhouse parts, and hundreds of sheets of glass – and expand his next winter's crop of Freesias, which would provide extra income for the following spring's heating. I gave him time sheets, with the condition that he could pay me whenever possible.

I had been shocked to find what a hand to mouth existence, middle-aged Stewart was living. Besides a third of his glass area being unusable – he couldn't afford the repairs – he could only manage to heat what remained to grow the lucrative early tomatoes anyway. His outdoor land was uncultivated, and neither would he be able to plant a later tomato crop in the repaired house, because he could only manage to employ two part-time workers. I was now going to take on any part time work in the vicinity, to earn my daily bread, and till his land ready to plant Brussels sprouts and runner-beans. By February 1961, the repaired greenhouse was in full production of Freesias and the other two houses were stocked with tomatoes – then about 30 cm high – in a heat of never less than 70°F. The sixth of an acre propagating house staging was covered in three inch pots containing tomato seedlings. These would later take the place of the freesias as we cleared them. We also had plans to plant the un-staged side of the propagating house with a cucumber crop on straw bales – a new procedure that I had seen in the Clacton nursery.

On a particularly frosty evening, after spending the day working at a nearby farm, I were sitting reading, when there was a barrage of fists on the door: I flung it open to see Stewart standing in the lamplight, with tears streaming down his face. 'Oh Bill, Bill,' he cried, 'I am finished, after tonight I will be bankrupt. And after all our hard work. But there is nothing I can do, I am so sorry.' Mystified, I threw on my coat and rushed after him as he stumbled home. He had been watching the TV news, and it had been announced, that the rota of threatened power cuts would start that very evening. East Anglia would be off power until at least 6.00 am the next day!

I rushed over to the two automatic coal fired boilers, which provided the heat through 150 mm cast iron water pipes, and could just manage to keep 70°F in the two acres of glass during the coldest time. Each one was in a pit under an open fronted shelter, with a hopper of coal – lumps no bigger than sugar cubes – providing some twelve hours of fuel on full heat. I switched on the first light and climbed down, eyeing up the small, half HP electric motor, which was driving a gearbox via a 'v' belt. From the gearbox, one shaft slowly turned a screw below the hopper, and delivered coal into the furnace, and a second shaft spun a fan that forced air up through the grate to make a roaring fire: the water circulated under the momentum of heated water rising up into the houses, and cooled water returning. 'It's going to be OK,' I called, and with no further explanation ran to his workshop/store. It took some minutes to fill and light one of the two paraffin 'Tilley' lamps hanging there, then I

started taking the engine off a little 'Merry Tiller' cultivator –
I was just placing it in a wheel barrow when the electric
light went out. By the light of the Tilley, I sawed off a metre
and a half length of scaffold plank, selected suitable bolts,
necessary tools, finally completing my load with a couple of
concrete blocks along the way.

I managed to get a doleful Stewart to remove the
fuses and unbolt the electric motor, whilst I measured up
and fitted the petrol engine to the piece of scaffold board –
freezing fingers and deep shadows slowed things up. But at
last, I placed my foot behind the concrete blocks holding the
motor in line and the drive belt at the correct tension, pulled
the starter cord, and the few embers in the boiler sprang into
flame. This was still not enough to lift Stewart's spirits. He
had seen the small propagating house was almost down to
the minimum air temperature the seedling tomatoes
required, and dashed into No 2 house. 'This thermometer is
even lower,' he called, 'It'll take half an hour for the water to
get up to heat, we have still lost, you might as well shut off
the engine!' But I was already running. 'The engine on your
lawn mower is the same model. Light the other Tilley and
take the motor off the other boiler.' This time things were
easier, which was fortunate, for Stewart had given up, and
just stood inside No 1 house wringing his hands, and calling
out the latest temperature drop, before – thank heavens – his
wife dragged him off to bed. I stayed all night cosseting the
engines, topping up the tiny petrol tanks, and stopping them
from time to time, to check and replenish the oil. As soon as
the electricity was restored in the morning, I switched back
to the electric motors – not a plant was lost, and fortunately
there were no more power cuts.

Nature on an Essex Farm

The owner of the land I was renting was still resisting signing
our agreement, and I now had a suspicion that he was only
waiting for me to get the land into good order, before he put

100

it up for sale. My Solicitor agreed, and said we should give him an ultimatum, sign by this week end or else . . . Two days later I received notice to quit! That, together with the frost episode led me to decide that smallholding was too precarious after all, and despite some misgivings, I started to look round with a view to either farm, or dairy herd management again. Perhaps in Essex I would have more luck in my choice of employer. Despite being offered three different dairy and farm managerial posts, none appealed, then the local newspaper carried an advert wanting a 'good all-round man' on a farm near Wivenhoe and we decided to take a look. The elderly Mr Dutton, had turned over the management to his farm-college trained son. A modern house, that had been the home of a foreman, was ready to move into. The son – Jim – and I, 'got on' immediately, and two weeks later I was working all hours to get the autumn ploughing done. I had plenty to keep me interested, for not only was I now working fields of light sand, the Ford tractor had evolved – in fact there were now three sizes – with 'mine,' being the mid-sized '4000,' also the plough now turned over, so that the furrows could be turned to left or right. No longer was valuable time spent measuring out and setting up ridges, you just dropped the plough in the ground at one side of the field, and roared backwards and forwards until you finished the field. On the rare occasions the 400 mm furrows blocked, it could be hydraulically lifted high in the air, and even shaken, which was just as well, for there was no way you could you get off – leaving the tractor toiling forward – and push a blockage through with your feet, as I had done with the old 225 mm plough. This one was travelling along as fast as a gently trotting horse.

This higher speed meant that the birds that followed had changed their habits too – they had to be more adventuresome to get the first peck at the worms. Wivenhoe was within easy reach of the coast, so the raucous seagulls crowded in, giving the land-birds little chance. The weather out at sea had a bearing too: the rougher the weather the more followers, and if few others folk were ploughing, the flock could be so dense, that it was difficult to pick out individuals, as they swirled around the tractor like huge snowflakes, always coming in against the wind to drop as close as possible to the turning furrows. If the wind was across my direction of travel, they landed as the soil was thrown at them, but on my return, they would be dropping steeply over – and occasionally between the upturned plough shares, to be thrown with the furrow, still frantically grabbing at worms. Occasionally, a half buried bird would need to be pulled out on the next run! The squawking and screeching could be heard above the tractor engine, and things could get even more interesting if I was travelling into the wind – for then the bird that only just missed my head, was guaranteed to hit the furrow as it turned, to madly grab at least three worms. The others, landing three or four together, meant that one certainly went hungry. One black-headed gull got very adept at this low altitude approach, now and again brushing my hair with a wing-tip, or making me smile as it got too close to the exhaust, and was flipped off course. On one occasion, I playfully plucked it out of the air by its feet, only to have a couple of hundred worms regurgitated all over me – well, I had been wondering, just how many worms a gull was capable of swallowing!

You always knew when a mouse – mostly field mice – had been turned up, for there would be a sudden upward swirl, leaving a noticeable patch devoid of gulls, some landing around the edge to watch whilst two or three of the bravest – usually herring gulls – would be circling overhead and snatching at the mouse as it ran towards the nearest hedge. Once a bird had it in its beak, all the others would give chase; seldom did the first – or even the third – get to swallow it. Early one morning, a great black-backed gull landed some way off, and I reckoned it was shy of the tractor. A couple of hours later, as I neared the hedge, up went a swirl of birds, as a field mouse dashed out. I turned the tractor round and started back. The mouse was now running across the unploughed land with two gulls fluttering over it. Then headlong over the tractor swooped the great black-backed gull, beak latching onto the mouse as it landed, and with a swift arching back of the head the mouse was gone! The big bird then proceeded to show me its expertise – not for him the hurly burly of snatching up worms. On my return run, I saw it was stamping around part of the mouse's nest lying on the surface – and another mouse broke out to run for cover – it didn't stand a chance. Next, the wily bird, still giving the odd stomp about, pulled every vestige of nest out of the ground, exposing the pink bodies of baby mice as I roared past. It joined me every autumn for the next three years, always standing on a slightly elevated knob of soil, flying over to pick up fleeing mice, or give any bunch of straw the 'great black-backed dance treatment!'

After years of carting an alarm clock around, I was given a pocket-watch that kept – for me – remarkably good time, never gaining more than ten minutes or so each day. Sadly it only lasted a year, before refusing to tick again, so it was back to the alarm clock. Then an electric wristwatch in a Colchester shop window positively beckoned – and after persuasive negotiations on both sides, the jeweller let me have it on a week's trial. I thought if it is my electricity that has been affecting watches, perhaps this is the one I have been waiting for. It was basically a 21 jewel, Swiss movement, wrist watch, with an ugly bulge on the side that contained a battery, providing impulses to regulate the balance wheel. At last I always knew the time to the minute – indeed, if other folk wanted to set their timepieces accurately, from thence forward, I was the one they asked!

A Child's View

Despite the long working hours, I did pursue a hobby or two: A little shooting for the pot, some wine making and gardening. The last two getting me involved with the village show, when I twice won the cup for the best homemade wine! I had been a keen wine maker since assisting my mother in the 1940s, and usually had one or two bottles and gallon demijohns in the cupboard, but I had to punish myself to get the gardening done – often doing the digging by moonlight – but between us we grew most of our needs and lived well, much to the disgust of eight year old Alan, who's gustatory highlight was a certain brand of, 'cardboard pastry' pie.   He once asked Wendy, as she put roast pheasant with all the trimmings on the table, 'Why do we eat peasant food?' He did take an early interest in the joys of the countryside, as many of the entries in his school books show, but he leaned ever more towards motor bikes, sport and pop music. When year old Caroline came into our lives, he was gentle and protective of her, but perhaps a little more enthusiastic towards encouraging her to play football than Wendy liked! With his aptitude for anything mechanical, I pushed him into trying the small local shipyard: and after only a few weeks they offered him an apprenticeship, but on condition he attended college – at their expense. Alan was adamant that he did not want to return to school life, and I put much pressure on him to accept their generous offer. The crux of my argument was that ship building would be a job for life. That shipyard – and many others – have long gone, howbeit, he finally found himself a job on a garage forecourt.

Caroline was interested in every flower before she could toddle, and by the time she was four, wanted to know everything about anything! She had also reawakened Julie's enthusiasm for retrieving again. If any soft toys were lost around the garden, she only had to rummage under Julie in her bed, to triumphantly find her treasure: the pair were almost inseparable. They would run to meet me as I walked back over the fields for meals, Caroline pointing to some, 'new' flower and I would name it, and answer her questions on various matters. Little did I guess that it would be my life that would be most changed by, and gain the most benefit out of, her early years. I soon discovered that a small child's capacity to assimilate knowledge should never be underestimated, and that I had to be careful with my delivery – One mistake was when I was loading manure from a heap in the corner of a nearby field, then driving back and forth, with the spreader flinging it in a wide ark behind me. Caroline met me at midday and asked, 'Why?' I explained how all of the countryside relied on the death and decay of what had gone before – nothing was wasted: we baled up all the straw to use for winter bedding for the animals, we fed the animals, and when they went to the toilet, this soaked into the straw too, and by the end of the winter we had a deep solid layer. This we cleared out, and put in a heap with any other stuff we had available – the septic tanks that collected the waste from our houses got pumped there, wood shavings mixed with droppings from the turkey houses, even any dead pigs or turkeys got buried there. And I finished with, 'And now it has all rotted, it makes good food for all the crops that we plant,' pointing out the difference between some fat-hen plants we were walking past and two or three extremely large ones, growing on the heap. She was very impressed.

Then one Sunday morning a week or two later, I was preparing our greenhouse to plant tomatoes – a task made all the more pleasant by the help of a small person with her own tools. I had already sterilised the soil, by cooking it, the weekend before – which had involved quite a bit of discussion – and was barrowing it into place. Next I cut open a bale of peat-moss – something that I would never use today – that had been soaking, and with Caroline enthusiastically joining in, started mixing it into the soil. 'What is this Daddy?' 'Peat, Caroline.' She leapt up with a scream, and burst into tears. I quickly examined her hands expecting to see blood as Wendy rushed out of the house, 'What on earth has happened?' Caroline pointed down to the heap, 'It's P P P Pete,' she sobbed, 'I didn't know he was dead!' – Peter the pugnacious pig-man, was quite overcome at her concern, when I told him. Another mistake did not produce quite such dramatic results, but it was further proof that I needed to hone my teaching skills. We saw a big, red tailed, queen bumble bee, burrowing into a dandelion

105

flower. 'What's that bee doing Daddy?' I explained how it was in the process of building a nest, somewhere nearby; and its need for both nectar and pollen, ending with how it was also fertilising the flowers, so producing, seed and fruit. A couple of days later I was broadcasting Nitro-chalk on the wheat next to our house. At lunchtime, I was asked what I was doing. 'Fertilising the wheat,' I replied. Caroline's eyes opened wide, 'Oh Daddy, you are clever, what a lot of work you have saved the bees.' I have kept to, 'bee pollination' ever since.

Poisoned Banks and an Osprey's Visit

All this questioning was getting me ever more interested in what was going on in the countryside around us, and I decided to join the Essex Naturalists Trust. Later, whilst looking for frog-spawn in a pond – we couldn't find any – I noticed an effluent outflow from a farm, running into a ditch that fed it: I approached the farmer and he sorted it out. We had fun looking for sticklebacks in, 'our' nearby brook – we didn't find these either – but saw minnows and great numbers of caddis fly larvae. I was now increasingly looking over hedges, not at other farmers' crops, but at what they were doing to their streams, hedges, and meadows. I got into much trouble at a winter conference, arranged by a national chemical manufacturer. I was appalled that there was not one mention of taking care of wind direction, wind speed, or spray drift onto hedgerows, ditches or nearby woodlands – only onto nearby susceptible crops, and especially no mention of timing in regard to flowering periods when using insecticides. Despite making it plain that I had used sprays for many years, the speakers bristled at my questions and suggestions. And after I mentioned that on our farm at least, often half the recommended dose of weed killer was adequate, our hosts really showed their annoyance. For the rest of the day, they made snide asides to my earlier questions; encouraging the farmer/spray

106

operator audience to regard them as nothing but nuisance interruptions, jokes, and even a danger to good farming practice. By the end of the day, I was ostracised by everyone.

In July 1971, the Essex River Authority workmen came weed spraying the banks along the brook. I drove my tractor close to their parked Land Rover to note the chemical being used. Identical drums in our store, included instructions to avoid spraying over ditches and ponds, with particular emphasis on not discarding empty spray containers into such areas, for fear of poisoning the river life. Six year old Caroline was not to know it, but our next visit to the brook had a serious purpose. To her disappointment, the banks were covered in withered plants, and the pretty yellow irises and water forget-me-nots, in and on the edge of the water, were all brown. I explained what had happened, and that the River Board seemed not to know that plant roots held banks together, and that I was expecting that the minnows were lost. We were unable to find any, but were pleased to see plenty of caddis larvae – until closer inspection proved that most of them were dead in their cases. It was time for, 'public' conservation action! I passed on my information and anxieties to the Essex Naturalists Trust Chairman, and due to his involvement, and a subsequent visit from the local press, the River Board eventually agreed, that weed spraying the banks of streams and rivers, was probably not such a good idea.

It was becoming apparent that I had much in common with the mindset of the Trust folk, and I next signed up for a field trip arranged by the Colchester Natural History Society. Wendy, sometimes being a bad traveller, I just took Caroline who enjoyed it immensely, her non-stop questions taxing my knowledge to the limit as we trailed at the rear of the group. Our dual observance skills missed little, and it wasn't long before we had our own separate group discussing what we were observing. Then in September I was to see another side of people's enthusiasm for wildlife. I was ploughing a field by a large gravel pit lake, using our latest Select-O-Matic Ford tractor with a built on cab – although it was the envy of the other men on the farm, I disliked the cab, for I would much rather have the wind in my hair and an unobscured vision. At about 11.00 am, I was swinging over the one way plough as I reversed round at the cliff edge of the lake, some six metres above the water, when into the view of my open rear screen, a large bird swooped down over the lake. As I turned, it remained in the centre as if framed, dropping its feet, to effortlessly lift a two or three kilo carp out of the water. By the time I had pulled back into the furrow to return across the field, it was visible through my front screen, coasting across, to perch on a dead branch at the top of an oak tree behind our house.

Wendy could hardly contain her excitement when I arrived for my midday meal. I was lucky to see any food! She had my binoculars in her hand as I opened the door, and a bird identification book on the table. 'There's an Osprey sitting in the tree at the bottom of the garden,' she gasped, 'and looking through these binoculars from the lounge, you feel you could almost touch it.' And indeed there was certainly no need for any visual aid – as we sat watching it from just inside our open door whilst we ate – except by using the binoculars, I was able to identify it as a young bird. I hurried dinner and crept down the hedgerow as near as I could with my camera, I had all the equipment to take close-ups of flowers and insects, but this huge bird, only some thirty metres away, was still only a sparrow in my view finder. I returned to my ploughing, vowing that if the bird used this same route from Scotland next year, I would be ready with a telescopic lens. The following afternoon it caught another fish, although this time I was too far off to see, but Wendy and Caroline – just home from school – had all the fun of watching it feeding. That evening various folk came to ask if it really was an Osprey that had been sitting on the tree below our garden. I had already told my employers what had happened, and I had said that my friends in the Colchester Natural History Society would be very hurt if I did not inform them, but suggested that I should hold off as long as possible, because once it became common knowledge, we would be overrun, and the poor bird would not be able to perch anywhere to eat in peace.

The following morning, the gravel pit manager called to see me – I had been instrumental in suggesting a scheme to save their Sand Martin colony, and, how better to reinstate some land for ground nesting birds, which had already encouraged Little Ringed Plovers to breed: 'Bill, some fishing club members have told me that a large bird is fishing the lake, they think it's an Osprey.' I confirmed that it was. He thanked me, and said he was going to phone the local 'News', and did I mind if he gave them my name? During the afternoon, reporters from two newspapers came to speak to me, so that evening I phoned the Secretary of the Colchester Natural History Society with the news. I then carted straw-bales off the nearby field, using some of them to build a wall out from the hedge at the end of our garden, and with the remainder, constructed a roofed hide, large enough to squeeze in a dozen people. There were openings facing the oak tree, allowing four or five folk to look at a time. I then blocked three nearby field gateways, and hung roofing slates on the bales, with 'This way to see the Osprey,' chalked on them, adding arrows to avoid any confusion. On my garden gate hung, 'Please enter and keep close to the hedge,' nearer the hide, 'Quiet please,' with the last on the open-backed hide, 'Please stay inside.' At only some 10 metres from the tree, if the bird did return, it would give folk wonderful views – even first time bird watchers could not mistake how they should behave, and Wendy would not have her day constantly disrupted.

We had only just started breakfast the next morning, when I saw a man – obviously having climbed over the first blocked gateway – standing in the middle of the field, shielding his eyes against the rising sun as he scanned the horizon. When I returned at midday, there were many people pacing up and down the road, and others milling around the straw hide. Wendy said it had been continuous, and there had been no sign of the Osprey. I went out, and told them all – in no uncertain terms – that no bird would come near with all their activity. It would be better, to either stay in their cars or the hide. I was then informed that many of them had been furiously motoring back and forth to other lakes, a round trip of some 30 miles. That evening, as I walked home, I became aware of magpie chatter among the remaining bale heaps. Creeping from heap to heap, I finally saw the reason for the fuss. The Osprey was on top of the last heap, feeding on a carp more than half a metre long. I watched from behind a bale at almost 'spitting' distance, until the brave magpies drove it off.

It stayed around all week, eating most of its fish in 'our' tree, perching there for an hour or two, usually only flying off, when some stupid person moved out of the hide, to try and get closer. One evening a man had just left, after knocking on our door to thank us profusely, 'You provided me with the view of a lifetime!' And as I returned to our living room, I espied another man with a camera on a tripod with a lens about as long as his arm, striding straight across the field towards the tree: I nipped into the lounge, in time to see the Osprey take off, and the erstwhile photographer stamp his foot in frustration, before turning back. When I caught up, and berated him for spoiling the evening for the other bird watchers, he said he didn't care a jot about them! 'I have spent a whole b***** week trying to get a photo for my editor; have you any idea where it's heading now?' 'Africa I expect,' I sharply replied. As it happened, I was probably correct, for that was our last sighting.

Jake the Cocker Spaniel

On Christmas day, our gamekeeper came knocking on the door. 'Happy Christmas Bill,' he said, and handed me the lead of his liver and white Cocker Spaniel, Jake. Confused, I said, 'Well, yes, I am sure we can look after him, where are you going?' He laughed, and said, 'I'm not going anywhere, he's yours; Wendy has bought him for you.' I was a member of Jim's small 'shoot', and knew of young Jake, the biggest and bravest of the keeper's four dogs, and the occasional misbehaviour when working – which I believed to be due to the way his master handled him. Wendy had obviously thought I could soon put Jake to rights, and this would go some way, to make up for my loss of Julie as a gun dog! Jake and I exchanged enthusiastic greetings, and every spare moment from then on, was taken up in training. The following autumn I was invited to beat for a prestigious shoot, and specifically asked by the head gamekeeper, to take Jake. The first 'drive' was heavy going, but Jake obeyed every whistle, and the pheasants flew forward at an increasing rate to the finish. The second drive was through mature woodland and open ground, but I was asked to take Jake into some very dense bramble patches. None of this made any difference to Jake, he crashed through like a, 'hot knife through butter', as the head keeper, so nicely put it. Then suddenly, silence; and in answer to my shouted queries, no one else could see him either. My heart sank! This was the behaviour that had made his previous owner angry. I traipsed around in the wood when the drive was over, whistling and calling, but no sign of him. I reluctantly joined in the drive through the next wood, still giving my 'Come to heel' whistle from time to time, much to the amusement of the beaters who had been in the know as to, 'Jake's wonderful improvement.'

Despite a sudden flurry of shots up ahead, I gloomily kept in line, whistling ever louder and more frequently, with the odd call from nearby grinning beaters. 'Sounds as if Jake is pulling out all the stops,' or, 'Don't look so worried Bill, he is making up for lost time.' As we neared the end I could hear frustrated and angry voices, 'Who's damned dog is that, get it out of there.' 'That blasted dog, has just retrieved my bird.' And as I burst through the hedge at the end, one called out, 'If you can't catch the b***** thing, shoot it!' I gave a desperate shout, 'HEEL JAKE,' as he flashed between two dogs to pick up a bird; thankfully he suddenly remembered his training, and head down, slunk to my side.

111

Unlike his previous owner, I knew it was not a bit of good cursing him now. That would only make him more reluctant to come to heel next time. He knew he had done wrong I could only apologise profusely to all concerned, and in my turn, slink off, and quietly put him in the car. That would be punishment enough, as he listened to all the shots and calls for the rest of the day. I was invited to the next shoot, but the Head keeper thought it advisable to add, 'You won't bring Jake will you?' Jake was still welcome at Jim's shoots – he put all the other dogs to shame when flushing game from dense cover, or finding wounded birds, yet just once in a while he would disappear for an hour or two; I decided there was some quirk in his nature that excitement brought to the fore

The Ford Select-O-Matic tractor, I remember now, for the attempted cover-up of its failures! We took delivery of this, Ford's first semi-automatic gear box tractor, in late spring 1970 and soon realised what a boon it was. One task it excelled in was the lifting of early potatoes. It was quite a problem to lift this crop without damage and ensure that the women pickers on piece-work, clean picked them. After the exact depth of the share of the 'Hoover' lifter had been selected, it was imperative to travel at the correct forward speed in the varying soil conditions, so keeping the soil to potato ratio right, thus preventing bruising or reburying them. This tractor was the 'bee's knees' for this work, and also with just about every other machine we affixed to it. Usually, the tractor I used was changed when the 12 month guarantee ran out, but due to the high cost of this one, Jim had decided to keep it for two years: until a neighbour made a good offer for it. The second one was kept though, but only days after the guarantee ran out, there was a loud clunk from the gear box and I used a 'courtesy' tractor for a couple of weeks.

Jim thought that with the event so close to the twelve month cut off, he should have some dispensation, and when he was given the enormous estimate for repairs, made such a fuss, that Colchester Tractors said they would meet him halfway – 'Even though it was caused by the way the tractor had been driven!' The repaired tractor arrived back, with the stipulation that we were not to use it until a specialist from Dagenham showed me the correct way to drive it. The following afternoon a man in a smart suit introduced himself and asked me to hook the tractor up to something that needed a bit of power. Whilst donning a spotless boiler-suit, he watched my every move as I hitched onto a nine tine cultivator. When I was ready, he climbed up, and I drove the short distance to the field, taking advantage to run through all the gears. In the field I dropped the cultivator in some 150 mm and travelled up and down the field twice, running through the lower gears. As I turned to go up for the third time, he said his first word since climbing aboard, 'Stop.' Then, 'Do you always drive like this?' I answered, 'Yes, and he said, 'Well done, you are driving exactly as this tractor should be driven, you will have no further trouble.' And with that, he climbed out to join Jim, who had just arrived in the Land Rover. I re-started the tractor, going into gear with a loud bang! But, by the time I had rushed back to the farm, the specialist had left.

As it happened, that very evening I had been invited to the inaugural meeting of the 'Colchester Machinery Club.' About a score of us attended in a room at the rear of a Colchester pub and, once the agenda of setting up the club and coercing folk into Committee posts – and voting for them – had finished, we retired to the bar. The serious part of discussing machinery could now begin – the Ford Select-O-Matic was quite high on my list! To our collective surprise, no less than four of us had driven 'The first tractor to have a gear box problem.' One had broken down three times within the guarantee period. And a fifth man knew it had happened on a neighbouring farm – and it was all due to our faulty driving! This news was conveyed hotfoot to our respective employers – there must have been some angry phone calls to both Colchester Tractors and Ford's headquarters the following day. Only weeks later, the Select-O-Matic range was no longer available.

The Essex River Board, 'climb down' had brought my name to the attention of another Essex Naturalist Trust official, who was trying to interest members in doing a survey of the county roadsides. Her letter stated that she thought the roadside wild flowers were important, and did I agree? Were they 'holding their own', or were they disappearing? Should Essex County Council be taking more care with mowing and their timing of it? I replied that I had been one of the first to machine mow road verges – Buckinghamshire in 1948 and 49, using a Grey Ferguson tractor with a 'finger mower' – and that I believed the new flail mowers were not only damaging perennial plants by being set too low, but also smothering delicate plants with a rotting mush, further suggesting that many insect species were also affected; butterfly and moth caterpillars in particular being destroyed. Ending my letter with the hope that more care would be taken with the timing of the mowing – and volunteering to keep a sharp eye on the local verges in future. The official was delighted with my reply and, on the back of my letter alone, lost no time in contacting Essex CC!

On our field trips, Caroline – who was small for her age – received much notice, for no matter how many pairs of eyes – or field glasses – were peeled, inevitably she would pipe up, 'Daddy, look at this funny beetle,' or 'Look at this lovely caterpillar,' or 'Is that the bird we are looking for?' On what turned out to be her last trip in September 1972 – to look at fungi in Epping Forest – it was obviously beginning to get to one enthusiast when, for the umpteenth time, Caroline, deep in the bracken, called out, 'Here's a different one Daddy.' 'What can you expect,' grumbled the lady, 'of course she will find the most, she is so much nearer the ground than we are.' But even as she spoke, a voice shrilled, 'Daddy, Daddy. Look!' We followed the line of her finger pointing up into a tree. 'Oh well done,' said our guide, 'come over here everyone, Caroline has found a really rare example.'

9. *Caroline looking for caterpillars in 1975. We got very adept at finding them by following droppings or bites out of the leaves.*

10. *The clump of cowslip seed heads that Caroline saw in 1973 flowered again in 1974. They were the only ones on Wandlebury. I took this photo on a Friday afternoon before placing a notice by them, 'Please leave these flowers for others to enjoy.' By Sunday evening, not one was left!*

11. Tortoiseshell Butterfly.

12. Our first and most spectacular success was in the proliferation of the Peacock and Tortoiseshell butterflies. By placing cages over the nettles with eggs on, and later taking care of the pupae, we changed the near 98% predation to almost 98% survival.

13. 'As we walked on, I explained to Caroline how, at her age, I played
in meadows yellow with cowslips. Pointing to the just harvested field
beside us I remarked, "If the Society allow it, one day cowslips will
cover that field." ' Success!

14. A sketch of the author by Alfred Harwood. Originally featured in
Farmers' Weekly.

7. To Cambridgeshire to Become a 'Full-time' Conservationist

Arrival at Wandlebury

Unbeknown to me, 1973, was to be my 'watershed'! Unfortunately, due to a reoccurring bronchial problem, Caroline had to miss a very pleasant April trip to the Brecklands, and the one to Wheatfen Broad in May. Thankfully, the heavy rain ceased as the coach approached Wheatfen – we were going to be taken round by Ted Ellis, the celebrated naturalist, author, broadcaster and TV presenter. As he met the coach, the sun burst through and with steam lifting from the lush growth we followed him along the lane to his cottage, arriving at a gateway, almost closed by a willow shrub, and filed into his garden. 'You would think he would clear that thing out of the way,' whispered a lady to me as Ted waved an arm towards tables set with cups and saucers, before disappearing into the house. All eyes were looking with some disfavour at the disreputable lawn, but Ted's immediate emergence with a tray of fruit cake, followed by his wife Phyllis bearing a large teapot, put a stop to any comments. Whilst Phyllis kept our cups topped up, and plied us with the home-made cake, Ted regaled us with a resume of what Wheatfen was about, and what he hoped to show us.

I had always assumed that the reason Ted dressed in a pinstripe suit and polished black town shoes, was at the behest of his BBC bosses, but not so, it was obviously his accustomed dress. He did not look at all like the regular country folk I was used to. But the more I heard, the more I warmed to him, rapidly realising that here was someone, not only passionate about the countryside, but with knowledge I would give my 'eye teeth' to gain. How pleased I was, when, after apologising for his lawn being untidy, he then wandered around it pointing out various rare and uncommon wild plants! Once out in the reserve there were those who cut their walk short, even along Ted's so-called managed paths, so by the time we got to where only Ted could hope to know the way – with shoulder high growth brushing us on either side – there were only a handful of stalwarts left. Ted would step off the track – often into ankle deep mud – to point to some insect, or an animal track: then dart back across with arms outstretched to part the sopping tangle, to reveal a marsh plant. I had never had such a wonderful time and was engrossed in every word, pointing out other plants and asking about them too.

We at last regained the mown path and rejoined the rest of the group. 'Capital,' said Ted, 'now we are all back together, I hope to show you something special,' and led us to a clearing in which stood a moth trap. He then proceeded to show us various moths, as he brought out the pieces of egg cartons under which they were hiding. Despite knowing most of the common names, I felt like a kindergarten school boy, as Ted rattled off the Latin names too, but finally, after turning over every scrap of carton, he gave a big sigh. 'Oh well, I might have known that would be the one to fly off.' As he stood up, I pointed out a moth that was new to me, resting on a tree trunk: a delighted Ted told us it was the Lobster Moth that should have been in the trap – the first he had seen at Wheatfen. He fell into step beside me as we walked back to the cottage, and plied me with questions. 'Are you one of the Trust's Wardens?' 'Where did you gain your knowledge?' 'With your visual skills you should at least be leading groups around nature reserves.' After partaking of a last cup of tea from delightful

Phyllis, our trip organiser passed on our grateful thanks, and we followed Ted out into the lane, he calling back, 'Oh, by the way, I believe that willow is very rare, it could be the only one in the country.' I just had to catch the eye of the lady who had been derogatory about it earlier! At the coach, Ted singled me out, and with a broad smile, took my hand and said, 'Now remember what I have said, you are too good to waste your life in farming!'

If I thought any more about his words, it was only with fondness, and regret that Caroline had missed out. I believed there was no way that I could keep myself and my family on the sort of income that went with looking after Nature Reserves. Then only a couple of weeks later a letter arrived for Wendy from her sister Stella, and inside was a short note for me. On a page of bright orange paper was written, 'Just a thought!', and stapled to it was part of a page from the Cambridge Evening News, and highlighted was an advert:

Great Outdoors
Warden required for 110 acre estate three miles from
Cambridge, etc.

Perhaps it was all the spraying that I was in the midst of at the time – May and June was particularly busy with killing aphids on the early potatoes and sugar beet. Despite the meticulous care that I took with protective clothing, respirator, spray pressure, wind direction, etc. I had come to the realisation that I was building up an allergy towards these quite alarming insecticides – even now 40 years on, I know immediately if I am passing a field just sprayed with a systemic insecticide. After much thought I phoned Ted and told him about the advert, and asked him if he really did think I had the makings of a 'Countryside Warden'. He replied, 'Not only do I think you should apply, but I am willing for you to give them my name, and I will give a reference for you'. I thanked him, but declined his generous offer, telling him that I must win the post fairly, and within 48 hours my CV was in the hands of the Cambridge Preservation Society's Secretary.

Things then moved rather swiftly: on June 8th I received confirmation that my letter had arrived, and that I had been shortlisted for an interview for Tuesday 19th. By mid-afternoon of that day I was offered the post, and as I had furthest to travel, the previous Warden's widow, still in residence for another few weeks, had kindly offered to show us over the accommodation. I drove into Cambridge, where Wendy and Caroline were spending the afternoon, and we returned to look at the accommodation. After knocking on a large door in the corner of what had once been the servants quarters of a mansion house, we were shown into a square hallway, with doors to right and left, a staircase at the right rear, and steps going down to a landing, with further stairs going down to a cellar. We stepped into a large kitchen, but although it was a sunny afternoon, the interior was so dark – made worse by smoke leaking from an old cooking stove – that I didn't notice a dog on the chair, and sat on the poor thing! After polite chat to the lady, who was obviously very interested in what sort of person would be taking on the tasks her husband had done for the previous ten years, we glumly looked round the rest of the flat, before returning home, where, after we had visited our son Alan in hospital, recovering from a horrendous motor cycle accident a few days previously, we fell into bed.

The next morning I started work very early – yet more spraying – so that I could snatch an hour or two off to visit Alan, and draft a letter to give my reasons for refusing the Cambridge position. It was actually with some relief, for ten years is a long time to be settled in one place, and Jim, his wife and family, were as much friends as employers, and I knew that Wendy and the children would not look forward to being torn from their familiar surroundings. On Friday morning a letter arrived from the Cambridge Preservation Society Secretary – Neil Clark. He was sorry to hear about our disappointment re the housing, but quite understood, and could I please ring him at his home that evening. That night I was offered the estate chauffeur's cottage, and Neil would take us to view it. As it happened Wendy was indisposed, and I travelled with Neil alone – it was a very educational journey. It was plain, that Neil was a driving force, not only for the Society but for how he thought Wandlebury – as he termed it, the 'Jewel in their Crown' – should be looked after. He lost no time in letting me know that what he was doing would not be at all popular with much of the Committee, and that even if I accepted the house as being suitable, he was going to need to 'pull out all the stops,' to get them to agree to the situation.

We finally arrived at the picturesque cottage of about 1850 vintage. It was in a very poor condition – roof tiles missing and broken gutters leaking down damp walls. Once inside – Neil had to break a window, as the agent had lost the keys – we saw plaster falling off internal walls, and even the sky through the roof in one room! Back outside, two unlocked rear doors, revealed a bucket-toilet, and a tiny – near collapse – cellar. Over it all loomed a large yew tree, brushing against the broken tiles, and on the north side, a four metres thick by five metres high, box hedge leaned against the wall. The area of the large garden was only visible to an enthusiast able to pick out the overgrown, or dead, garden shrubs below the dark canopy of some 25 mature trees. Two tiny squares of grass still existed at the front, and at the rear a stable and trap housing – completely collapsed. I fell in love with the place immediately, but dreaded the thought of explaining the potential to the family!

Neil was ecstatic that I had accepted how things were, and that I would fall in with his plans – if they came to fruition. He told me afterwards, he did indeed have to pull out all the stops. 'Wasn't it stupid to tie up the house that the Agents had said could fetch at least £20,000 on the open market, when the Society was strapped for cash?' 'Was it not foolhardy, to spend money that the Society didn't have, on renovating it?' Etc. I suspected that the agent was also keen on the commission, for he not only urged that the house was far too prestigious for a lowly warden, but later often waylaid the project. Neil was given the go ahead by the Committee on the 6th of July, and I received the contract to sign on the 8th, giving in a month's notice on the same day. On the 10th of August our furniture was put into store at Wandlebury, and we moved into the 7 m caravan, that I had purchased and Neil had parked in the office garden.

Beeches and Battles

On the following day – Sunday – I started my new life as Head Warden of Wandlebury Ring. I patrolled, notebook in hand, jotting down, 'things needing urgent attention'. Caroline joined me for a time, 'Look dad, some primroses.' She stepped nearer to peer at the dozen or so broken stalks, and one tall brown stem with seed heads, 'No they aren't, what are they?' I was in the middle of, 'Caroline, don't tell me you don't recognise .....,' when the truth hit me – hard! Just prior to her ninth birthday, she was looking at her first cowslip plant. I was stunned, and tried to remember when I had last walked among them; During my time in Essex? No. Buckinghamshire? No. Oxfordshire? No. It had to be during my own childhood in Bedfordshire – the ones that I had spread 'Gramoxsone' on. I knelt down to carefully pick off the remaining seed heads, and knotted them inside my handkerchief. As we walked on, I explained to Caroline, how at her age, I played in meadows that were yellow with cowslips. Pointing to the just harvested wheat field beside us, I remarked, 'If the Society allows it, one day cowslips will cover that field.'

We walked on, following the path towards the Roman Road. Simultaneously with me noticing strange wasps flying up, Caroline remarked on the holes that looked like miniature volcanoes in the sun baked path. We discovered two more areas along the same path, each of them with a dozen or so holes, and I later identified the wasps as the interesting Beewolf, *Philanthus triangulum*, said to catch mainly honeybees and some varieties of solitary bees. According to Fabré, she manipulates them to drink their nectar, removing any surplus, as it is of no use to her grubs. We also saw a Speckled Wood butterfly and a handsome Hoverfly which is a Red Tailed bumble bee mimic. Later, in the afternoon, I was treated to the spectacle of one of Britain's largest bats – the Noctule – flying out of a hollow elm beside the Ring Ditch, and languidly circle off towards Cherry Hinton. Already Wandlebury was showing great promise, but I thanked goodness for the rarity of Sparrow hawks at that time!

Living and working in the countryside, it's best to know the trees. Right from an early age I could be found climbing them. Whether it was another boy's kite to be got down, a bird's nest to be looked in, or a neighbour's pears to be scrumped, I was your lad. My brother Bob was more daring, but I had the edge because of my height advantage – there were few trees I couldn't, or hadn't climbed in our locality. I had many a near miss, such as when I reached the summit of an 'unclimbable' 35 metre high elm, to get a rook's egg. Whilst acknowledging the cheers from the lads down below, I put my weight on a dead branch, and fell a short distance before grabbing another branch – only losing a little skin in the process. In order to get a young jackdaw from a huge hollow walnut tree, a bee's nest in a lower hole necessitated a late evening climb whilst they were quiet. Agitated as I scrabbled past, they waited in a cloud for my return! Speeded up by a few stings, my response was to crawl along a large branch that curved out and down towards the ground. But what looked near the ground from 20 metres up, was a different story when I reached the end. I got away with only a sprained ankle from the 5 metre drop.

There was nothing I loved more than the occasions when we visited our nearby woods, either as a family, or just two or three children alone. Depending on the time of the year, we would be seeing buds bursting into life, listening to the birdsong – and looking for their nests – gathering primroses, bluebells or violets, gazing at the autumn colours, and fungi – all of which were 'deadly poisonous' – nut or firewood gathering, or just having fun shuffling through

125

fallen leaves. Later, I occasionally helped my grandfather and one of my uncles to coppice woodland for the provision of thatching spits, hedge-laying stakes and etherings, runner bean poles, etc. I have heard the eery whistling snore of the dormouse – hibernating under the leaf litter – peered inside hollow trees into the eyes of owls; or started back when a score of hibernating peacock butterflies, rustled their wings at my shadow.

Even now, I would swap breakfast at any top class hotel, for a work break in woodland on a frosty morning, mug of tea in hand and a thick slice of bread toasted over the red embers of a fire. During my last twenty years in farming, occasional tree work was engaged in – my foot still bears the scar from a glancing axe whilst pollarding willow trees near Buckingham. In Oxfordshire I trimmed branches off trees around the Duke of Marlborough's estate, and in Essex I 'lowered' a couple of tree tops and did some apple tree pruning. Except for planting an occasional fruit tree and Christmas tree, that was my sum involvement with trees and woodlands, except for those I destroyed during my civil engineering days – which I would much prefer to forget! Throughout that time I also carried out miles of hedge cutting – some by hand but mostly by machine.

Now at Wandlebury, I had 54 acres of very mature beech woodland to care for, with goodness knows how many miles of official and unofficial footpaths threading below the spreading branches. The numbers of folk treading them was unknown, but from day one, I knew that the paths needed regulating, and the people required guidance – and the trees certainly needed some TLC. Many branches were downright dangerous to those walking below – my first contact from a Wandlebury resident, was a complaint about a branch that his wife passed under every day. Half a dozen beech had been blown down in a 1950s gale – the branches long gone for firewood, but the trunks still lying, root plates upturned and not a single sapling planted in their place! At my first CPS Management meeting, I predicted that 50% of the beech could be lost during the next fifty years, and that unless we started a felling and planting programme immediately, there would be too long an interval for carrying over the wildlife that needed the holes, nooks and crannies of ancient trees. A quarter of an acre worked each year, would result in a 200 year cycle. It was then pointed out by member J K Taylor that the whole area was under a Tree Preservation Order, (TPO), put in place by the County Council in 1953. 'Not even a branch can be touched, because of the importance of retaining the woodlands just as they are,' he said. Truly shocked, I remarked, that this was a great tragedy for the future of Wandlebury!

The cottage was still causing angst among the Committee. Luckily, Tony Baggs, the architectural editor of the Victoria County Histories, was a recent and enthusiastic addition to the CPS Committee – and probably the youngest – and he resolutely backed the Secretary during this difficult time, and once the decision was taken, piled in to help. Even so, now a year since we moved into the caravan, the new locks that I had installed, was the only work done so far. Tony was doing much behind the scenes, importantly backing me against the agent's architect – who wanted to do very insensitive alterations to the now named, Jarratts Cottage – and because of the hold-up caused until a new architect was appointed, burnt the midnight oil, whilst helping me strip crumbling plaster off the walls and take down the rotten lathe and plaster ceilings: this was most unpleasant, dirty work, and afterwards, I would step inside a circular plastic curtain, and shower with a hose pipe in a watering can hanging from the yew tree. Once the architect's drawings arrived, we demolished the large chimney at the east end of the house to make way for a bathroom and toilet upstairs, and enlarge the kitchen below. I also did the wiring up for electricity – there was lighting in only three rooms, and just one three-pin socket – in the kitchen.

Tony also made the time to help me dig out the old brick floors – which we lowered to bring the ceiling height to modern standards – and finally concrete through. Once the builders arrived, the first thing I noticed, was that the plasterers kept 'forgetting' to mix in the water proofer – the plaster takes longer to set – so I was forced to be site foreman. At least I was able to use much of this time to clear the garden and remove the trees that had caused so many of the problems to the cottage, though this of course put me behind on the estate work, but again Tony volunteered his services, carrying out much of that winter's coppicing .

Getting the CPS Committee to agree to turning the cornfield into a flower meadow, was not as easy as I expected! The majority of members believed keeping solvent was very important – and rightly so, for the Society was living hand to mouth, and did not want to forego the cash the crops brought in. Even Cambient – now the Wildlife Trust – was unhelpful! I joined their organisation as soon as I arrived, but they were already in close association with the CPS, for they had developed a short 'Nature Trail' around the outer bank of the Ring, and at weekends their volunteers ran a small shop selling Wandlebury Nature Trail leaflets and their own literature – this, I soon found, led to most visitors, and even some of the volunteers, believing Cambient owned Wandlebury! When I invited their committee members for a walk round one evening, expecting some enthusiastic back-up for my ideas, one official was quite adamant. 'Leave things as they are, this place is ideal for soaking up the sort of people we don't want on our Nature Reserves.' My face probably showed my surprise. 'It's my belief,' I said, 'That all the countryside is a nature reserve, and what better place than somewhere overrun with people, to start teaching them how to use it.' I noticed two elderly men nodding in agreement: P J O Trist and Ken Cramp, two botanists who had already made themselves known and were giving me practical help. Ken later volunteered to serve on the Wandlebury Committee when that came into being, and also served on the CPS Council of Management for some years.

With both the Secretary and Tony Baggs believing in the project, I persevered, gaining some sympathy by announcing that some 85% of England's chalk grassland had disappeared – years later, satellite technology proved it was more like 95%! Permission was finally given when the Countryside Commission agreed to grant-aid the meadow, although only on condition that we named it for a specific public use – easy peasy! I named it the, 'Picnic Field'. This approach also brought forth the offer to grant aid my salary – as long as Wandlebury was designated a 'Country Park' – which I privately thought was a retrograde step – but whilst embracing the offer, I always took care to speak of, or write about, 'The Wandlebury Country Park and Nature Reserve': Folk still ask which part is the Nature Reserve. I also heard about The National Association of Countryside Rangers – since changed to Countryside Management Association (CMA) – whilst at the CoCo offices, and immediately joined their ranks.

I was still worrying about the TPO order and with the help of CPS admin secretary, Sally Billing – after a little searching – read a copy of it. And hurrah! Small sections were left out, and neither did it stipulate that new trees could not be planted in the TPO section. At every opportunity I lobbied CPS members who I thought might be sympathetic – 'At least let me clear some trees not covered by the order, and perhaps even plant up new ground.' In Jan 1974 a narrow strip of land along the north edge of the arable 'Shooting Shed' field, was put into my care, and I planted a row of 30 cm high beech, in anticipation of them forming a future avenue with the hedgerow of old trees, and the land between was made into a mixed species nursery. At last we were preparing for the future!

Meanwhile, I was still having problems with the Picnic Field. The Agent responsible for the CPS properties, not content with previously 'pouring cold water' on my ideas, was still trying to frustrate the plan. His approaches to the tenant farmer, to try and 'turn' the Chairman, had fallen on stony ground, and I thought that would be the end of the matter. Hoping to gain a year, I had already asked the tenant if he minded under-sowing his crop of barley, with the grass seed. This was a procedure I had performed many times in the past: the grass sprouts, then almost stands still until after harvest, when it springs into full growth. The seed was delivered to his farm, and on sowing day I followed him to the field, running my fingers through the seed after he opened the first sack. 'This is not the expensive wild meadow grass,' I cried, then we examined the contents label, 'RYE GRASS – PLAYING FIELD MIX,' I, exclaimed 'I'm dreadfully sorry. I shall have to get it changed.' In high dudgeon, I phoned the seed merchant. 'Now just you stop there Mr Clark; I am getting fed up with you Wandlebury people. First you make an order stipulating all kinds of obscure species, then your Agent rings, and says he is in charge of running Wandlebury, and that I must change your order to Playing Field Mix – leaving me stuck with your special blend.' We were sowing the special blend the following afternoon!

The Ring Ditch

Unfortunately other work was piling up for me – literally. I had found a sewage puddle in the bottom of the Ring Ditch – the drainage system was blocked. If it backed up to the dwellings and public lavatories that it served, it could be serious. The extra pressure could burst the old pipes, allowing sewage to leak into the 56.360 metre (186 feet) deep well which served all the estate: even worse, it would be directly in the water table that supplied the City of Cambridge. I made an urgent phone call to the Agents telling them of my concerns, and was told that somewhere on the estate there was a bundle of drain rods for just such an eventuality! Luckily an old estate drainage map was still pinned to the wall in the pump-room, and after deciding which runs were still used by the existing buildings, I started lifting manhole covers. Thankfully all the drains in the courtyard were clear, though I could not find any covers beyond. Having found such things in the past with divining rods, I hurried home to make a pair – they 'indicated' in the centre of a blackberry bush – after clearing the area, and digging more than a spade deep, I found a rusty cover, extremely thin and full of holes; and with that removed could see that the foul water was still below the level of the courtyard pipe – though the depth plumbed to three metres! With my rods indicating further trenches in all directions, I chose the one most in line with the puddle. On the bank of the Ring ditch, the rods indicated a bend – but no iron cover – and I dug at that spot. Although bits of glazed pipe turned up immediately, it was not until 120 cm, deep, that the spade struck concrete. I smashed through, revealing a 150 cm high tunnel, along the floor of which ran a glazed pipe. Climbing in to remove my heap of debris, I uncovered the bend in the pipe which was broken open, and full of bone-dry material – it hadn't run for some years.

Transferring my search to the next line brought me to an iron cover under a thin covering of leaves, full to the brim but less than two metres deep. That evening, having mustered three of the residents together, I tied my new climbing rope around my waist, gave instructions that if I stopped snatching the line once every 10 seconds, to call an ambulance – and try and drag me out. I moved quickly along the smelly tunnel, stopping at the brickwork of the deep manhole blocking three quarters of the tunnel width, and there in the torch light could see relatively new pipe work, constructed in a tight double bend. No wonder it had blocked! And, there was no way that drain rods could pass through it – the old drain had been by-passed. The next day a sewage tanker pumped out both pits, and it then took me all afternoon – employing one hundred hired drain rods – to drag out a tree root and the lost, rotten, estate drain rods, via a third pit, and finally, an unpleasant few minutes to climb down and hook out the blockage in the deep manhole. Job done, I hurled my overalls in the dustbin, washed vigorously under the outside tap, and whilst still in a suitable frame of mind, phoned the Agents to complain about their lack of recording, and their unsuitably aligned drain.

Only days later, a young assistant Agent arrived. After shaking my hand, he said that he too was having difficulties, but he had made a start putting together a 'Wandlebury File,' and he needed my help! Could I tell him which 'Forestry Compartments' I had worked in during the 1973/4, winter, and had I any idea which Compartments the deceased warden had worked in during the 1972/3 winter, as that entry was also outstanding. He then placed a folder on the bonnet of his car, and proceeded to show me various Government forms – no less than eight years before, an earlier CPS Committee had instructed the Agent to sign up for the 'Forestry Scheme Dedication Basis II.' I was in shock! I asked for the file to be left with me, as I would need some time to get to grips with it – there were maps giving ten numbered 'Forestry Compartments' for a start.

More shocks were to come as I read and reread it that evening. First and foremost, the TPO had been made null and void the moment the agreement was signed! Next it showed how little had been done during the first "Five Year Plan", and in the three years of the second one. We were in danger of the grants being clawed back. However, luck was on my side, the trees I had planted in February, were more than should have been planted so far – just not in the right places, and what little weed-tree clearance and coppicing I had done so far, also counted. I would just have to work much harder during the next two years. My dander was up, and with the backing of the Secretary, and Tony Baggs, the Chairman agreed to put my concerns to the next Management Committee.

Many of our visitors look at Wandlebury in an entirely different light, the Ring Ditch is all that remains to be seen of the Iron Age Hill Fort, and is the most visited part of Wandlebury. Despite the inner area bearing the last vestiges of a Mansion and the remaining stables and coach houses – now converted to houses, office and an education centre – a walk round the circumference still has a certain aura, which can be heightened considerably in mist or by moonlight. Since early times there has been disagreement over its origins. Fiction and legend abound. Only days after I set foot on Wandlebury, a Dutchman, Ernst Gideon, wrote to ask if there was a wall on the site – he was doing research for a book about the Trojan Empire. Mystified by his request, I thought a copy of our Nature Trail leaflet should provide all he needed, for on page 4, part of a sentence ran, "to the nearer of the two doorways in the circular brick wall," whilst page 5 provided a stylised map of said wall – and for good measure three pages about the archaeology and recent history. The CPS Secretary was in complete agreement with my solution, and we both thought that would be the last we would hear from Ernst Gideon. Next, only a week or so later, the Secretary informed me that a Tim O'Brien – retired head of an oil consortium – had applied to do research on the origins of Wandlebury, and the CPS had granted permission. He was expecting to take at least three years, and I was told to keep a sharp eye on him – I kept a list of any spot I saw him interested in, taking careful measurements (when his back was turned) and never let him dig or move anything.

Much of this interest, I am sure, was due to a certain Tom Lethbridge! In December 1956, after two years of research and thumping an iron bar into the soil to find the previously disturbed area, he finally dug out a chalk figure. His snap decision was, "It is anyone's guess who this chap is. Mine is that he is a Sun God!" Most press mentions of Wandlebury still insist on using a copy of an aerial photo of Tom Lethbridge's partly excavated 'Goddess' which was printed in 'The Times' in 1956. Because of the trickle of visitors asking questions about it, I had already read up on it, and as many wanted to see it, had also removed the covering vegetation. Gradually it became a magnet for dowsing enthusiasts determined to find out for themselves – is it or isn't it? A popular cry was, and still is, 'Is it on a Ley Line?' The most excited folk found a number of Ley Lines heading straight for it, and I often found myself embroiled in animated conversation! Strangely, although Lethbridge himself had long been a hazel twig dowser, looking for ancient graves and such, and later wrote about the use of the pendulum and paranormal activities, he didn't use these methods to try to locate his figure.

On Dowsing

For a full history of my own dowsing skills, I need to go back to my childhood. I first tried to dowse in the company of my grandfather, who was using a forked hazel stick to look for a lost well. I was useless. Later, I saw a professional water diviner at work. 'You should use a willow stick.' I was still useless! Then in the 1950s, whilst I was working with earth moving equipment, an engineer showed me how to find an underground cable, using a couple of brass welding rods, bent in an L shape. From then on I regularly used them, it was the best grounding – no pun intended – in dowsing that anyone could wish for. At first, I only looked for electric cables – alive or dead – iron, copper or lead pipes, house drains and clay field drains. If any were water-filled I got an especially good 'kick' which led me to believe that I could find water too, and did! A good party trick was to pass them over a glass of beer, and see them clash together. Because I usually uncovered my finds later, I knew for certain what lay below. Once, when excavating low lying farmland ready for a factory to be built, I was puzzled to find nothing where my rods had strongly indicated, until I realised, lines of different soil colour was showing filled in trenches – and I remembered grandfather describing how they used to drain fields with 'bush drains' by burying the hedge trimmings in the bottom of trenches. As I progressed, looking at my surroundings first, often gave me strong clues even before I used the rods.

For some ten years, I had no reason to use the rods, until I discovered that smelly wet patch out in the grounds.

With my brass rods long lost, I made some from the only thing to hand – a length of 5 mm copper brake pipe. Caroline, seeing me testing the rods, asked to try. I steered her to walk over the water pipe to Jarratts Cottage – a metre deep. 'Ow,' she exclaimed, throwing them down as they clashed together, 'A shock went right up my arm!' Needless to say, after putting the drain to rights, I went on to track the other strong lines around the remaining buildings and garden area. Whenever Caroline was with me, our lines where identical, except that her rods gave a more satisfactory thwack – perhaps it was an age thing! Manhole covers along the way, usually told me when drains were below, but others needed a small 'pilot-hole' digging, in order to ascertain the identity. Finally I knew the extent and whereabouts of the foundations of other long-gone buildings, buried gravel paths, early brick drains and lead water pipes – Even the later galvanised-iron ones, running out to both vanished and existing water troughs in the fields.

Ley Lines, what are they? Folk believe them to be geopathic stress lines that emit energy. I can quite believe that there are energies emanating from the earth's magnetic field, both past and present and probably also from tectonic plate and earthquake movements. But I have only seen these people following my known lines of 'dowsing force.' I had to bite my tongue, as compass and map in hand, one said to a companion – marking along a particular drain – 'This Ley Line is heading straight for Kings College Chapel.' On another occasion, a professed expert told me, 'This Ley Line links up with Wimpole Hall and probably Glastonbury' – I had no idea, our old water pipe went that far! Their zenith has to be the gentleman, who after months of research, said, 'I can now reveal that Wandlebury is the epicentre for most of the Ley Lines in Britain!' There was a hole in the centre of Wandlebury Ring on his map, caused by the number of times his fountain pen had crossed through! One enthusiast, living in the Cambridge suburbs, said she had two parallel Ley Lines running through her garden. A glance at the map showed the house had been built on a closed 'Beeching,' rail line. I could easily locate the two lines of rust from the rails, and metal from clattering train wheels, that a century of rain had washed down into the soil. Probably my finest hour, was seeing a JCB digging a trench, and about to cross a line between two sets of distant, 30,000 volt pylons, their cables underground between. My rods nearly jumped out of my hands, just one metre short of the incredulous driver's trench. So, at least for the disbelievers, I should have successfully buried Ley Lines!

But believers will still argue their case and say most of the old tracks, especially Roman roads, are on a Ley Line: I have proved that both dug ground and compacted ground gives a good signal, and our Via Devana certainly has ditches either side and a compacted centre surface – for good measure a steel gas main along it too! Ancient oaks are found on Ley Lines, especially at junctions: I say they were often planted along trackways and at the junctions. Particularly well grown oaks, are often on a Ley Line: I have noticed oak trees grow well along spring lines, these give a very good dowsing signal. One field has many Ley Lines, whilst another none: Few grazing fields were drained, and only the problem arable fields. I remember my father being told by an old man, 'That field has never been drained.' We found a network of three series. Early stone, mid 19C clay horseshoe and end of 19C handmade clay pipes – Ley Line enthusiasts would have had a heyday! I once located straight lines two metres apart over an entire field, the farmer was most impressed. He said steam engines had mole drained the field during his childhood. I am sorry, but I have yet to be shown a Ley Line, that I can't figure out a better reason to make my rods click together. And as for the gold, skeleton and monolith finders – there is most always a dug hole involved! One enthusiast for the hill figure once said, as we battled it out on the Cambridgeshire Radio, 'It's all right for Bill, he will insist on dealing in facts.'

Of seven other 'significant' finds reported to me, two Romano British Temple sites I know to be 18C stable foundations, whilst two others, King Arthur's Camelot and a Wood Henge, are surely figments of expectant imaginations. One old tale, oft repeated, cannot be established by either dowsing or the archaeologists' trowel. It is of Baron Osbert's fight with a ghostly knight who was said to terrorise the area. The accepted mode of doing business with the ghost, was to ride alone into the Ring (when the present circular ditch still had a high bank inside it, and a second ditch and bank inside that) on a moonlight night and issue a challenge. According to who you read, it was either: 'Knight, tonight come forth', or 'Knight to knight come forth'. Shortly after hearing the Norman Knight's ringing challenge, the group waiting outside are said to have heard the clash of swords, soon followed by the triumphant Baron leading out a magnificent horse: he related how he had unseated the rider, who had then thrown his lance and pierced his thigh. The prancing horse was taken in procession to Cambridge, but at sunrise it reared up, broke its tether and disappeared. As for the Baron, it is said that on every anniversary of the fight, his wound would open and bleed. I have often wondered if this story tells us that a bandit once used Wandlebury as a hide-out: and whether anyone happened to hear a shrill whistle, moments before the horse reared up and broke away from its tether?

Jake's Passing

I was no longer taking part in any sport shooting, but I still believed that vermin should be kept in check, in particular, rats, grey squirrels and rabbits. And as I dislike spreading poisons out into the countryside I still shot and trapped. There is a difference between sport and vermin control! It is very unsporting to shoot a, 'sitting duck', so hence the misses and injuries, vermin is given no such consideration, so, 'clean kills' are the norm, putting my dog Jake out of a job. But with fifteen year old Julie taking little exercise, he now accompanied Wendy on her daily walks around

Wandlebury. One morning she lost him in the Dog Run, and it was midday before he slunk back home, and thereafter she wouldn't let the old rascal off the lead.

Then one Sunday our neighbouring farmer called to say, a couple of injured pheasants were in a nearby wood. I took nine year old Jake, and he joyfully romped through the thick ivy undergrowth, bringing me the first – dead and cold – within minutes, and sped off to find the other. Suddenly all went quiet. I circled the quarter acre patch of thick bramble and ivy, whistling and calling, determined the old rogue wouldn't get away this time. Finally, deciding he had evaded me somehow, I turned to leave, but noticed a splash of white. I struggled through the waist high growth, and picked up an unconscious Jake, and carried him out. Laying him down, I ran to get my car, but after a hundred yards or so I looked back, to see him on his feet, walking unsteadily towards me.

Luckily my neighbour Dr Larry Owen, of the Cambridge Veterinarian College, was at home. Larry ran his hands over him, and listened to his heart. 'I think the old fellow has suffered a heart attack,' he said, 'keep him warm, and don't let him exercise. Bring him to the surgery tomorrow and we will have a proper look at him.' A still subdued Jake walked with me into the surgery the following day. Larry took one glance, and said, 'He is very much under the weather, I think we should keep him in; I will ring you when we know more.' He rang at 3.00 pm. 'I'm afraid it's bad news, Jake has had another attack and he is now unconscious. I believe he was in pain when you brought him in, and even if he does come out of this, he will probably have more pain. In my opinion, the kindest thing would be to put him down.' I immediately agreed. Then he said, 'I would be very grateful if we could retain him.' Again I agreed – in fact it gave me a little comfort to think that some future vet, might be all the better for having known Jake.

However, I was due for further shocks that evening, when Larry called in. 'First Bill, many thanks for allowing us to keep Jake. I can also put your mind at rest, as to whether he might have recuperated, the answer is no – in fact, I cannot understand how he managed to survive the attack.' I thanked him very much for all he had done. But Larry had more to say. 'Can you tell me when he had his first attack?' I assured him that he had only had that one. 'In that case,' said Larry, 'He must have had the others before you owned him, for he has had nine and possibly ten – I have never seen so many healed lesions in one animal, he must have had the strength of a lion.'   My memory flashed back to those times when Jake – always in the thickest of undergrowth – suddenly took it into his head to go AWOL. How confused he must have been when he came round, and yet anxious to get back into the action, the moment he had again located us. What a dog!

Grey Squirrels, Rabbits and Moles

I have long regarded the grey squirrel as a tree rat with a pretty tail, and have always been aware of their aggressiveness to the red squirrel, and believed they carry disease to them too. The competition over food is serious, in particular, they ruin the hazel nut crop long before there is a viable nut in the shell, which I am sure is also contributing to the decline of Dormice. The amount of damage they do by stripping bark off young trees is enormous – it can also be quite dangerous for people walking under trees in windy conditions, when the branches they have damaged, shale down – unless foresters make a concerted effort to keep grey squirrels numbers low, there will be no forest sized beech – and many other species – over much of Britain in the future.

As they only stay in their dreys when it is very wet and miserable, it is possible to shoot squirrels all year round. Best time is early spring before breeding starts. Between 8.00 and 10.00 am on sunny mornings, when the tree buds swell to bursting, watch for the discarded sepals and leaves raining down in the sunlight as the squirrels feed – my record, 16 in one hour – but only in my first year at Wandlebury; after that season I averaged three dozen per year – recording only minor tree damage. In a recent grey squirrel eradication scheme – to protect the remaining reds in the Cumbrian region – it has been noticed that woodland bird numbers are rising simultaneously; thus confirming my observations that the grey is also a major plunderer of both eggs and young birds. I have even witnessed one climbing a house wall to take a Swallow's young! After speaking on this subject on the radio, a lady phoned from a London suburb; she was having great trouble with squirrels in her garden. Her neighbour was feeding them and even allowing them to live in her roof space. Was I serious, when I said that they can also carry bubonic plague? I suggested she also tell her neighbour, that there was a good possibility they would set the house alight, by biting through the electricity cables. However, two years later, she phoned to say that her neighbour's roof had collapsed, due to the rafters being gnawed through!!

The rabbit population was also enjoying a comeback – horrible myxomatosis is accounting for an ever smaller percentage – resulting in young trees being ring-barked at ground level. Concerning beech and ash trees, they will attack quite mature trunks. One way to thin them out is to shoot them from a cabless tractor during moonless nights, especially after a period of rain – my record is 25 in two hours. It could have been more, but that is the number of cartridges in a new box! A quieter, more environmentally friendly method, is to use ferrets and nets, however, I still found it imperative that every new shrub and tree had a guard in place. Another problem animal at Wandlebury is the Mole; they breed more prolifically here than anywhere else I have lived. It must be the dry chalky soil! I have no quarrel with them in the right place – they are really woodland animals, and do much good there, helping with drainage, soil aeration, burying fallen leaves and seeds and eating root damaging invertebrates. But out in the grass meadows it is another story! We have all heard of the tale of the 'Little gentleman in the black velvet coat', causing a horse to trip and kill a king; in these days of 'Health and Safety' we would not want to know how many folk damage themselves because of moles – and rabbit scrapes. Their heaps of soil and flints, also cause hundreds of pounds-worth of damage to mowers, and it also gets among the grass when hay making, resulting in poor quality hay, and damaging animals teeth. The bare patches also make perfect starting conditions for blown-in Ragwort seeds. Each winter after trapping some twenty to thirty, I harrowed with a heavy bar behind, which levelled the hills and filled the rabbit scrapes.

A Home for Bats

In July 1974, a scientifically equipped group asked for permission to stay inside the Ring during a full moon and do some experiments and recording. Permission was granted and the group took up position in the Ring. At 4.00 am I tapped on the roof of their car to ask if they had been lucky. Due to the ensuing screams and tumult I deemed it best not to wait for an answer! Then later in the summer, by the sundial, I saw a lady jump as if startled. And when I asked, 'why,' she said she had felt a hand on her shoulder. Twice more during the autumn I observed kindred instances, and got similar answers. I mentioned this to the retired Butler, Fred Reynolds, who had roamed the rooms for many years. 'Well I never,' he said, 'so she is still there.' He then related that on various occasions he had heard ladylike footsteps pacing with him down the hall, close to where the sundial now stands, but each time, before he could light a candle to race down to the cellars, and catch the maid he was convinced was tap-tapping along the ceiling beneath him, all would be quiet. Then in the 1930s an electric generator was installed: 'On the very first evening the power was switched on, I heard the footsteps,' he recalled. 'Switching on the lights I dashed down, but as I ran I realised the tapping was now above me: so, there are two jokers I thought. Bursting back up into the hallway at the far end, I was just in time for the footsteps to pass me by and through the next closed door. I never told anyone, it would only have upset some of the servants: but it did make the hairs stand on the back of my neck.' We then discussed how brickwork can crack, and long timbers and pipes creak in sequence, as boilers hot up or evening temperatures drop, and even how a puff of air on clothing can feel like a touch. I felt I had explained away any mystery. Even when through the years I saw more ladies, and even animals, shudder or gyp by the sundial, I was confident that either cool air eddying off the large stone base, or ground movement in the filled in cellars below, was the cause – the sundial is gaining a definite list.

The eventual clear-up of the sewage puddle, was to prove significant towards my contribution to bat conservation. Even whilst I was sorting out the problem, I was debating within myself as to how I could use the tunnel for bat hibernation – a group of animals I had always been interested in. To make the tunnel 'bat friendly' would need careful consideration, for there had long been an ongoing problem with youths doing damage, and indeed frightening off many families from visiting in the evenings – it had been one of the main reasons why the CPS had chosen an ex-army Military Policeman as my predecessor. These gangs would be highly delighted to find a tunnel entrance, and with little effort, could get inside the occupied buildings. Something would have to be done quickly in the meantime – the concentration of sewer gas at the far end, could kill a person, and if bats entered in the autumn, the same fate would almost certainly be theirs. I constructed a two metre high fence around the opening; and next excavated down to the tunnel roof beside the deep manhole, made a small hole, and fixed in an upright, 100 mm rainwater pipe to stand a couple of metres above ground level. With ventilation taken care of, I next recommended to a resident, who happened to be making alterations to his part of the drainage system, that he brick up the opening that gave access to his cellar. I was thankful for taking these precautions, when only a few evenings later I noticed the fence was damaged, and climbed in to see lights and hear voices at the far end. Needless to say I made sure all were accounted for as they scrambled out!

The next stage was to interest the CPS in my scheme. I needed to construct a small tower entrance which would allow bats in, but guard against casual human access. The Committee members were not at all keen – one doubted bats would use it anyway – mainly because I wanted to spend at least £100. I got in touch with Bob Stebbings of the Institute of Terrestrial Ecology – a bat expert based at Monks Wood – he was so keen he travelled over to see for himself. Upon entering the tunnel he became even more enthusiastic, pointing out open joints in the brickwork with dark greasy edges, saying, 'Bats have been using this tunnel for years!' I was able to tell him, that a former resident had confided that as a child he had often crawled in through a hole in the bank, before it was blocked off in the 1960s.

We also looked at Jarratts Cottage – I had found five long-eared bats behind some sacks in the tiny cellar. In imminent danger of collapsing and taking the corner of the house with it too, it had been condemned by the architect, whilst I, a keen beer and wine maker, looked on it as a very desirable part of the house, and had given my ideas for putting it to rights. Bob thought I should start work the moment the bats left in the spring! I asked if he could send me a letter of recommendation to put before the Committee, and I would also like to know what temperature and humidity the bats preferred during hibernation. He said, he knew of no such research on the subject, then with a laugh, said, 'What an opportunity for you!'

During the following months, whenever I had spare cash – from my own pocket – I bought a Min-Max thermometer, spacing them along the tunnel to take readings. My main stumbling block was the money for constructing the tower, but as I was already mentioning this during my evening talks, I was confident money specifically donated for the bats, would soon be arriving. The price would be kept low by purchasing as much second-hand material as possible; and I would do the work myself. Upon being presented with Bob's letter, and my assurance that it would cost the CPS nothing, the Committee could only give their permission. I now had to overcome problems with Building Regs and the Historic Monuments Commission. I had fun with my planning application to South Cambs, they were continually phoning: 'The building hasn't got a name.' Me, 'Call it the Battery.' 'There is no provision for drainage.' Me, 'That's because it is a drain.' 'There is no rain guttering.' Me, 'Because it hasn't got a roof,' and so on. Permission came through on the 13th of December 1975. I was told later that my original application was pinned up on their office wall!

From Family to Schools

With all but a few cosmetic details to finish, we moved into Jarratts Cottage, and to our delight, Alan, who had decided to stay at his garage job in Essex, moved back with us, and looked for similar work in Cambridge. Once again I thought that I should provide fatherly advice, 'You are capable of much better than the work you have been doing, I can get you an interview with a firm making agricultural equipment.' Alan reluctantly agreed and was accepted. He disliked the work from the start, but I pointed out that he was now in an industry serving agriculture, the factory would always be busy, and there was opportunity to work his way up. He soon left to work in a business providing parts for other firms. To really 'rub my nose in it,' when agriculture went into recession, my chosen factory closed, but as I write, Alan's own choice is still going strong, with him, now at the helm. At least I had the good sense not to give advice to dear granddaughter Amelia recently, in the

144

company of Alan and mum Bea, we proudly watched her receive her BA with Honours.

Things were – at last – going in my favour with the Picnic Field. The barley hadn't been a heavy crop, so the grass had plenty of light, the harvest was early and the straw was baled and removed quickly: a damp warm autumn followed, and the field was soon green from end to end. The mild winter that followed and the 50 mm of February snow that only stayed a couple of days, ensured early growth, and by April I could see a good mixture of wild clovers, vetches and trefoils. Alas the sheep farmer I had booked the previous year – despite my phone messages – had still not arrived and I decided to go and see him. It was obvious he was no longer keen, and I asked what the problem was. 'Well Mr Clark, I have had a visit from your Agent, and he thinks I would be silly to take my sheep to Wandlebury; he reckons if they aren't attacked by dogs, they will certainly be poisoned by the yew trees!' I assured him that I was not only dealing with the unruly dogs, but I would be keeping a personal eye on his sheep too: also that I had already trimmed off all the lower branches of the mature yew trees, and dug up all the seedlings in the vicinity. Satisfied, he shook my hand, and said he would see the Agent and sign up for the grazing. On May the 21st the first sheep to graze on Wandlebury for 20 years arrived. However as it had been a wet spring he was having trouble keeping up with his other grazing commitments – sheep can only do a tidy job if the grass is not too tall to start with – and he could only spare twenty five, the grass grew and grew, and was mostly trampled flat!

My harassment of the CPS Committee regarding trees had apparently leaked out! I received a phone call from the Cambridgeshire County Council's Tree Officer, Reg Chuter, 'I hear you are worried about the Wandlebury trees, when can we have a meeting?' On the morning in question he brought along his recently appointed assistant, Jon Megginson, and after introducing Jon, placed a large map of Wandlebury – showing the parameters of the TPO order –

on the bonnet of his car, and proceeded to acquaint me with its ramifications. After I produced the information they should have received seven years earlier, we walked the estate for some hours, and they both could not have been more helpful, giving much encouragement in what I desired to do; even so, I was well aware that we needed to tread carefully, if we were not to alienate the public – my guesstimate at this time, was that we were well over 70,000 visitors per annum, and rising.

Meanwhile I had managed to talk Wendy into making a start on gathering information, with a view to her writing a history of Wandlebury. Being a busy housewife trying to make time for her own writing – mostly short articles on various topics, which were accepted in a wide variety of newspapers and magazines – she was not at all keen. However, she succumbed to my blandishments – 'Once Around Wandlebury' finally had to go into a second edition – perhaps helped a little by my presenting her with a new electric typewriter, which, I could now borrow from time to time to type up the Forestry Commission's forms, and make some half-decent presentations to the Wandlebury subcommittee! Although I was subordinate to the Committee, they relied heavily on my knowledge as to what needed to be done. At least I was now armed with all the latest information in the Dedicated II project's brochures, and the fact that we could be asked to return payments, helped enormously.

At this time I worried that my title of Warden, was too easily mistaken by the public for certain other folk – I didn't want to gain a reputation for haranguing folk – although I later discovered that the ancient title described what I was doing more accurately than the recent change to 'Ranger'. In fact in my first interview – with a reporter from the 'Farmers Weekly' – I insisted I would be doing much educating. Indeed, this article brought in the first enquiry from a school teacher, and two weeks later, Miss Green entrusted me to take herself and her class of eight year old girls, on an autumn walk along my still being constructed

146

'Nature Trail.' It was a great success; so much so, that she was moved to donate the £100 that I had mentioned was needed to plant a new hedge along part of it.

I had no idea at this early stage, just how popular – and frequent – the school trips would be. My main interest lay in local school children, who were the ones most likely to run amok on Wandlebury; it was also my belief that it was a good way to get the message passed to their parents. The Secretary of a local 'Village College' was the next to make enquiries, and asked if I would take all the teachers on a trial walk after school. Despite one teacher falling and badly spraining an ankle, they arrived back in the car park still very keen, and before leaving they asked if I could give the school's morning 'Assembly,' a fifteen minute taster of what we would be doing. As I had put together a set of slides and bought myself a projector, I jumped at the chance. All went smoothly, and I thought I had left them with a good impression of what to expect.

At 9.30 am the following Friday, 60 excited children arrived on a coach. There then followed a procedure that I adopted for many such visits: I asked them to form two groups – although, thirty children is still a rather unwieldy group strung out along woodland paths, but with the next coach load due in a couple of hours, I would have to manage. I then handed one of the teacher's my written history leaflet and estate map, who was to lead the group to 'do the Iron Age,' whilst I led off the group for the 'Nature Trail.' At 10.30 am we changed over, and at 11.30 am, both groups arrived back in the car park – minutes after the next load had disembarked.

The lesson for me that day was that groups of thirty 12 to 16 year olds, who felt that they were out on the spree, were neither quiet, nor very attentive. In fact if the last, oldest and least attentive group had visited first, I would have found it difficult to continue. Anyway, despite little help or control from the teachers – and by missing out on any sustenance except the odd glass of water, I, and especially my voice, just made it to 3.30 pm, when the last children climbed aboard their coach. I slumped in my chair at home, whilst Wendy put food on the table. Taking a cue from my demeanour, and the fact I could hardly speak, she asked, 'That bad was it?' I just nodded, and later explained I would have to rethink my strategy. Obviously the older, modern school child was not used to paying attention, or that much interested in the countryside; perhaps I had been naive in my belief that I could reach the adults through the children.

On the Sunday – as a warm sunny day was forecast – I hurried to have all in readiness for an influx of visitors – clean the toilets and pick up any litter. By 11.00 am the car park and the roadsides were full of parked cars and I walked the paths keeping an eye on things. Through my binoculars, besides noticing there were more family groups than usual, I espied quite a sprinkling along the nature-trail and resolved to take that path next, but as I approached the car park I noticed a family group looking interestedly at a young man gesturing on the edge of the Ring Ditch bank, and as I arrived in earshot, I heard his father say, 'That was utter piffle. There is no such plant as Stinking Hellebore; and as to its use with cattle in mediaeval times, giving it the name of Setterwort, you are having us on!' I stepped close to the lad; 'Your son is quite correct – and if you would rather he used the botanical name, it is *Helleborus foetidus*, which of course translates from the Latin, as Stinking Hellebore.' Dad swung back to the boy. 'My God, so they are teaching you something in that school after all!' For me it could not have been better, for I recognised him as one of the most vocal and disruptive of the last class on the Friday. In a state of shock, I kept them in sight for a while and he never missed a stop – in fact almost a mirror image of myself – except doing the trip in reverse! For the rest of that Sunday, and a few following weekends, I walked in a happy daze as I passed family groups, often with one young member leading yet another, 'Nature Trail.'

I had already been invited to talk to Caroline's class at Stapleford School – her teacher reminded me in so many ways of my own Miss Arter – and in return I invited the class to visit Wandlebury. We were keen to show off our efforts towards building up the butterfly numbers. In the previous season I had suggested to Caroline that she could make a project out of discovering why, despite these insects laying as many as two hundred eggs, we were only seeing butterflies in twos and threes. Appalled at the losses – Caroline discovered my predicted four or five percent turning into adults, was nearer two percent – she wanted to bring the eggs under our protection. Fortunately during a hospital visit with her, I noticed perforated metal ceiling panels, each about 600 mm square, being thrown on a skip. We were allowed to take all we required; and after buying a couple of dozen small hinges, and a large box of 4 mm pop rivets, we soon had a splendid row of cages!

Later, right on cue, with the buddleia in front of the stable block in full flower, three of the cages of hanging pupae emerged. So late on a sunny afternoon, we transported them over there, opened the doors, and with gladdened hearts saw the majority of the three hundred or so peacock and tortoiseshell butterflies, stay and disport themselves around the large shrubs. However, that was Friday! On Sunday afternoon – another lovely sunny day – I walked into the Ring, to see a child chasing around with a butterfly net, and thought it might be advisable to have a word. Thank goodness Caroline wasn't with me, for as I rounded the building, three more siblings came into view, all thrashing around the buddleia, and close by, one proud mum sitting on a blanket, surrounded by jars stuffed with dead and broken winged butterflies!

My staunch ally Neil Clark, resigned in August 1975, and bought a house in Appleby. Noting my concern, he quipped, 'There is no need for you to worry Bill, the CPS will do whatever you ask. They think the sun shines out of your every orifice!' He was no doubt referring to the Subcommittee chairman's rather glowing tribute in the recent Annual Report. But, they did agree with my next 'Five Year Plan,' at the October Management meeting, helped I am sure by my promise to do everything in my power to alleviate any bad publicity. After the meeting I drove home in some euphoria, although with the Chairman's voice still ringing in my ears, as he called across the parked cars, 'You only have permission to fell 30 trees mind. Not one more!'

8. Mother Nature Upsets My Forestry Plan

The First Storm

For the rest of that autumn – aided by numerous work-parties – I got down to some serious scrub clearance; we were fast catching up. I had even selected and marked the 30 trees that I would fell a year later. Tony Baggs had been appointed Vice Chairman of the Society and Chairman of the Wandlebury Subcommittee which had recently taken over from the Land Agent. During his coppicing help he had noticed that my tools were suffering, being all piled into the small shed that I had brought with me, so he applied for planning permission to demolish the ruined stable and trap shed, and build a workshop. Once permission was granted, we got on with its removal in the evenings. Unfortunately, Tony's own work was pressing on his time, and our last weekend together was spent shovelling concrete for the new foundations, the floor, and a hard-standing for any future machinery. I had to build the shed myself – mostly in the evenings, with the aid of a light bulb dangling from an overhanging beech branch.

So pleased was I with all the progress by Christmas, that I decided to take the family on a break on the 5th of January 1976. With the weather forecast predicting a gale for Friday the 2nd, I spent Thursday nailing the rest of the tile battens over the roofing felt on the workshop roof. By 9.20 pm Friday, the noise was unbearable. Numerous fires glowed, as tree after tree was thrown through the 11,000 volt cables strung through the estate; cutting off our power, and in consequence, the well-water pump, then next the phone lines went – we were to remain in the 'dark ages' for five days. I laboured back and forth checking every new glow, to ensure it was a tree, and not one of the buildings – though how fire engines would have got to them I do not know. One did arrive at one point, for a concerned passer-by had phoned them, but even as I explained the situation, a house fire call came over their radio, and off they dashed. Looking at the devastation in the light of day, I realised that I had been very lucky to survive the night! Over one hundred trees uprooted – and of the 58 large beech down, only two had my red 'felling,' numbers painted on the trunks!

The first need was to get a timber contractor signed up, but being busy clearing the drives and felling leaning trees – plus having no phone – I asked the Chairman to employ Carter-Jonas: which I believed would be the quicker option anyway, as they would have the contacts. By the end of the week I had managed to measure all the trunks and insert the whereabouts on an estate map, in readiness for contractors to view on the following Monday. I was surprised that the first reps sent to view, had no concern as to the quality of the timber we surveyed, with one indicating his fee would be at least £3,000. Time to find the company I remembered from my Topham years! By the end of the afternoon the Home Counties Timber Co.'s buyer, had agreed a Wednesday appointment, and I informed CJ. The buyer arrived at 9.00 am, and by 12.00 pm, he had verified my measurements, but lamented that there were few trunks of best quality 95p a cubic foot timber, and that he could only offer £3,500, to be paid 'up front.' His man could start cutting out the trunks the following week, and would put the 'top and lop' in neat piles for us – which we could sell for firewood – and burn the trash. I asked him to put this in writing to CJ, and breathed a sigh of relief.

However, local reps continued to arrive; most expected remuneration for their services and would be taking every scrap of timber too. I phoned CJ's office to be told they were still awaiting the offers – and there was yet one more to visit. This man was the only one to mention any payment, 'If all goes well, I may be able to offer £500 at the finish. I phoned the Chairman, and he agreed that the agents should accept the Home Counties quote forthwith. And on Friday morning their man arrived at 9.30 am. He apologised profusely for his late arrival, blaming it on having to go out of his way to pick up the promised cheque. By 11.00 am the £3,500 cheque was in our bank, and he had cut out his first tree.

My previous year's fund raising efforts for tree planting, had brought in some forty pounds, we now needed hundreds. Christopher South – who was Deputy Editor at that time – visited, and promised the help of The Cambridge Evening News: and what a splendid job they did! 'Wandlebury a disaster,' ran one heading, 'Plant-a-tree campaign to restore Wandlebury,' read another. Hardly a day passed, without some mention in the CEN; one uprooted tree helped no end by exposing Iron Age Skeletons, resulting in a full page spread. Donations flowed in, and I reasoned that I too should pull out all the stops and get some planting done. This was also a chance to mitigate, what for me had been another disaster! Despite all the care I had given my tree nursery and the row of beech planted the previous season, I only had some 15% left; I was quickly learning that the Gog Magog Hills lay in an especially dry corridor – I still believe that if an official weather station was set up in the centre of the Ring, it could prove to be the driest place in Britain! Even Cambridge, only three miles away, averages 50 mm more rain each year. On measuring out the decimated row of beech seedlings, I was delighted to find that I could plant a one metre beech tree for every person who had donated so far – two or three for those who had given large sums. And there would still be enough to pay for tree stakes and guards, and all the replacements for the uprooted trees – which would be planted in subsequent years.

On the 23 of February over a hundred people turned up to plant their trees, once more the CEN put us to the fore, with a large, delightful photo of two year old triplets, Clare, Faith and Jemma Mason, planting the first one. This of course turned the flow of donations into a flood – tree planting was taken care of for many seasons to come. On the 26th of February, an official from the Forestry Commission wandered in. 'I just happened to be passing; I have been reading all about your problems in the press, and seeing you on TV. When you are ready, send me your next plan and I will help all I can.' My Five Year Plan now needed complete revision, and during the next couple of years, before his retirement, he did indeed give a great deal of help and encouragement. It was certainly required, for my earlier prediction that half the beech could be lost in 50 years, now seemed a certainty.

Heat Wave

The dry summer of 1975 that had killed most of my first plantings, had carried on as a dry autumn and winter, and by the 20th of April 1976, I was writing in my diary, 'Very warm today.'

Although leaves were opening on the old beech trees, the newly planted stood in tight bud, the soil at their roots dry as the proverbial 'shot': by the 28th I dare wait no longer and started to water. I borrowed a 1000 litre water tank from our farm neighbour, and manhandled it onto the trailer. Once filled, two old doors were laid on top, weighted with bricks, and Wendy towed it up to the beech row with the tractor. She then drove in 'creep gear', whilst I tipped two buckets of water round every tree. By the end of the afternoon I was wet through, but so were the trees!

Forty eight hours later most of the buds were cracking open, but already the chalky soil looked dry, so we prepared to do the same again. That done, I looked at the 250 trees that had been planted in the few cleared areas. These also urgently needed water, but were inaccessible by tractor. By parking the trailer as close as possible to each group, I was able to scramble up and down on the trailer, and back and forth to each tree with the required two buckets full. By the end of the following week most of the trees were in leaf, but even by working till nearly midnight at times, the first trees were wilting badly by the time I came round again. I fixed up the tank with a one inch bore (25 mm) hose-pipe, which made things easier and faster. But with so much other estate work, the midnight finishes were followed by 5.00 am starts. A further worry was the fast lowering water in the 186 foot deep well, although the CPS had arranged for the Cambridge Water Co, to bring mains water to the estate, it would not be available until the autumn.

During a check of our facilities the previous year, the fire service had informed me that our silt filled concrete pond was considered an emergency supply – consequently I had cleaned it out, and topped it up from the well during the winter. But even though the fire hazard was now greater than ever, I started to use that water too. By fitting a farm spray pump to the tractor PTO, the tank could be filled as quickly as from the well. As a bonus, by transferring the suction pipe to the trailer tank, I had my own fire engine, and on three occasions I made use of it. On the last occasion, late in the evening, I just smelt smoke, but I had judged the direction exactly. The tractor headlights lit up a tent, with a spreading camp fire just about to engulf it. I aimed the jet first at the tent, and then on the fire. The zip shot up, and a naked couple stepped into the light!

There was no let-up in the heat, and by mid-May my eyes were constantly looking towards the large beech and elm trees, expecting branches to fall. One local WI correspondent, reporting on a talk I had given, wrote, '... and Mr Clark said that the drought is now very serious; large trees are suffering, and only heavy rain very soon, will prevent many from dying. Incredulous editors and radio presenters got in touch for more information, and one national newspaper copied the WI announcement verbatim.

This meant that the derision came down on my head from even further afield! On the thirtieth of May the first branch fell. By mid-June I had emptied the pond and banned BBQs. I continuously patrolled – nerves a jangle – moving folk from under their pleasant shade/my perceived danger!

Saturday the 26th of June – the fourth day in a row that I entered, 'Very hot day', in my diary – was busier than ever; the visitors getting tetchy, even cross, as this ever roving Warden moved them on. A 'Sunday School Picnic' was due just after mid-day, and I met the large group, mostly children, planning to lead them to a safe spot among some elm saplings. But as we arrived in sight of our destination, I noticed a courting couple just settling under a particularly 'worrying' branch in the distance. Hastily pointing, I said, 'Please lay out your picnic under that group of trees, you can play games on the far side, but don't let the children go near any large beech trees – some of the branches are quite dangerous.' I dashed over to the young couple. After seeing them ensconced beneath a 'safe' tree, a further survey through my binoculars revealed a family of four choosing a 'wrong un', and they too were moved to a safe tree – thank goodness my trusty old Raleigh bike was holding up.

Finally, I returned to check on the Church Party. To my dismay they had hardly moved a dozen steps, and were busy spreading their feast under just about the largest branch on the estate. 'This is a very dangerous spot, you must move at once,' I cried. And against a background of agitated mutterings, I bent down, grasped two corners of a cloth and dragged it – with angry ladies hovering – to the far side of the tree. With not a sandwich spilt, I stood up and remarked, 'There, that wasn't too bad was it, we'll bring all the others over too.' With a little louder grumbling, including, 'We'll be sending a letter of complaint to your employers,' the picnic was at last out of my perceived danger zone. 'Please make sure no one even walks beneath it,' I called, as I cycled off, giving the branch a wide berth myself. Seconds later a loud 'crack' rang out, followed by a thump. The tree sized branch lay on the ground, a huge white scar on the trunk, and equally white faces almost in the leaves on the far side. Dashing back I scrambled towards an ominous red glint – it was a drinking cup, and then another. Standing to climb over the trunk-thick centre, faces came into focus, and I realised they were calling to me. 'It's all right, no one is in there.' 'But there are two drinking cups.' 'We know. They dropped them, as they ran back.' Almost in tears with relief, I clambered out, only to have the man who had grumbled most hurl himself at me – he was in tears, as he threw his arms around my neck and hugged me!

But there was no time to bask in their accolades. Only stopping to point, and say, 'You can help me by going over to that lady leaning out of the window, she is the CPS Admin. Secretary, tell her I am closing and clearing the park immediately – and I am sure she will welcome any donations!' The family so recently moved to a 'safe' tree, came hurrying by, the mother called, 'Thank you so much for the wonderful care you are taking, but we really do think you should shut the park before someone is killed. That branch has fallen that you moved the young couple away from, they were very shocked – they said they won't be coming here again!' It seemed my afternoon could have been much worse. But I was well aware of the troubles to come. With the park cleared, and the gates chained shut, I rushed home to make up a notice. Eventually at least ten would need to be posted at all the official and unofficial entrances. In those days, many cars parked all along the roadsides, and the passengers scrambled in wherever they could. By eight o'clock Sunday morning all the signs were in place – more professional ones could be made later. People were shocked, but not too surprised, and the day of manning the ramparts went quite smoothly, helped by the fact that I kept quoting the rising number of falling branches, thirteen in less than a week.

I could close the car park and the estate grounds, but the Public Footpaths could not be legally closed – only the County Council could do that. And they needed to make an application for a 'Temporary Prohibition of Use' order, which could only be granted by the Secretary of State for the Environment. This could take weeks, and until then I was on my own. (It was in fact August the 27th before it was in my hands, but dated to start on the 6th of September, for three months only!) The Society backed me to the hilt. Our solicitor was appalled that I had 'admitted' that Wandlebury was dangerous on my signs. 'If anyone is hurt, it will be the Society's fault for not removing the known danger.' The park's insurer was also unhappy, 'Admitting there is a danger could make it very difficult for us. Whatever you do, you must keep the people out Mr Clark.'

At 10.00 am on Tuesday I heard vehicles arriving, and dashed to investigate. It was an ITV film crew in two vans and three cars. 'I am sorry we are closed,' I puffed. The cameraman ignored me, continuing to unload his equipment, but a man detached himself from an assembling group, proffering his hand he introduced himself as the Producer, 'Are you the Warden, Bill Clark? Wonderful, I thought we might have difficulty finding you; you don't have to worry about us, we are all fully insured. I understand you can show us the next branch that is going to fall. Once my cameraman is ready we will film it.' I stifled a chuckle, but said I would show them a dozen that in my opinion could soon fall, but as to whether it would be today or next week, was quite another matter. A loud crash then echoed nearby. 'Hurry, hurry, that's one we've missed,' cried the Producer. We stood first for an hour at this branch, three quarters of an hour at that; the time shortened at each. Next a wide angle, to take in as many trees as possible, but to no avail. Despite cracks and crashes during the day, all the branches I pointed out stayed attached. They filmed dying trees, broken stubs, fallen branches; me using the chain saw, and quite a lot of me talking about the summer's effects. Unfortunately – at least that is what was blamed – I took them a glass of my home-made beer each during the afternoon, and soon after, as the cameraman unloaded the can of film, he dropped it on the courtyard cobbles, splitting it open, and that was the day's work ruined. Another film was loaded, and we did most of it again, this time taking only an hour or so – and still not a 'falling' branch!

Day after day I ran hither and thither, cajoling, entreating and sometimes shouting. One lady I met knew her rights! 'I am sorry Madam; the park is closed due to the danger from falling branches.' 'I am on the Public Footpath, you cannot stop me,' she snapped. I moved in front to block her way. 'Stand back,' she shouted; and gripping the hands of her two small children even more firmly, stepped around me. I fell into step beside them. She querulously said, 'If you lay a finger on us I shall sue you for assault.' The little chap next to me wailed, 'I want to go home.' 'Nonsense, we are going for a lovely walk, and this stupid man is not going to stop us.' At that moment a loud crack rang out, and one half of a double spired top swung over, toppled into the next tree, then sprung back to thud across the track just ahead. I turned to speak, but the lady was scurrying back as fast as her children could run. I followed behind to get my chain saw. She stopped as she reached her car, 'I am so sorry for being such a nuisance,' she called, 'I thought it was a trick to keep us out for good.' Oh, if only I could have done that demonstration for everyone!

It was the last week in June, yet the roadside beech trees were all in autumn colour, many of their branches hung over the road. Even a small branch could cause carnage if it fell into the double line of evening traffic travelling homewards at 60 mph plus. The Chairman agreed, this was not the time to wait for a Committee decision, 'Get on with it Bill, we will find the money.' The County Council and Police pulled out all the stops, and by 8.00 am on the 30th the road was coned down to one lane, and Town and Country Tree Surgery were able to spare me two men. By taking on the clearing up myself, it was possible to fill all the roadside gaps with the branches – and keep costs to a minimum. By the end of the third day, the quarter mile of trees was no longer a danger, and folk could only enter by the main gate.

Probation Service

Back in April, the Probation Service had approached me, and asked if I would be willing to take Community Service lads for one or two days' work each week, on a regular basis. Once on site, they would be in my care and under my control, however, any nonsense, I was to phone their office immediately, for anything worse I was to phone the police. Unless unsatisfactory, each lad would work out his entire hours with me. The first two cycled in together – one suffered from asthma, and the other was a right little skiver – but by choosing suitable tasks, and working with them, they worked well; the skiver finished his 50 hours first, as the asthmatic one sometimes couldn't make it – though he was the one who introduced me to his parents, volunteered for further work – bringing a friend to help too! This success placed me on the best of terms with the Probation Officer.

My next C S lad was of the type, my father would have said, 'Don't trust him further than you can throw him!' I never once let him out of my sight – always working alongside, pleased to be getting some useful work out of him. Then the Probation Officer phoned, 'D***** has worked so well, I think we can let him have next weekend off, he wants to go to London to buy his mother's Christmas presents.' I asked if this was wise. 'Oh I am sure he has learnt his lesson this time,' came the reply. The next phone call was to inform me, 'D***** is in a London Nick!' She was more forthcoming than usual when she phoned about the next candidate, 'He should never have been given community service!' Then gave me some lurid history. A hard drinking Scot, working on rail-track maintenance, he constantly got into trouble at weekends; on this occasion, and not for the first time, he had punched a policeman. She seemed surprised that I was still willing to take him on, and insisted that at the first hint of trouble, I should dash to the phone.

A couple of days later, a small, thick set man, climbed out of her car to be introduced, and as she drove off, an admonishing finger wagged, 'Remember. No trouble,' she called. I instructed him to climb on board the trailer, he must have felt quite at home on seeing a couple of 14 pound sledge hammers, two crowbars – one an extra-large, early 'plate-layers' model, and a couple of heavy duty, 'navvy's' digging forks. Hopping off the tractor at the work site, I explained that we were going to dig round the foundation of a long-gone stable, break it into sections, load them into the trailer, for me to tip them in a nearby pit. We soon had an open trench all round, and it was then just a case of donning our goggles, and thumping and levering, until sections broke off, when we lifted them into the trailer. We got on so well, that we had time to spare, and finished the day splitting logs.

The following morning Wendy called me to the phone, 'It's the Probation Officer!' 'Good morning Mr Clark, what on earth did you do to poor J**** yesterday? He is with me now, in tears; you should see his hands. He cannot possibly go to his work. He says he has never worked so hard in his life, it is impossible to keep up with you, and he doesn't want to work at Wandlebury again.' I asked her to make my apologies for providing such fragile work gloves, and she could assure him that further tasks would be much more reasonable. A tentative J**** was delivered again the following week, and from then on, he arrived on his bike, on time, every Tuesday, and worked with never a grumble – often unsupervised – until his order was finished. But that weekend, did he celebrate! His antics – including hitting at least two policemen and getting down on all fours to bark at a police dog – earned him another term in Bedford prison.

With all this contact with problem lads, I now believed I was quite adept at picking them out at other times, whether in a group or by themselves, but at 9 o'clock one morning, two young lads forced me to take my skills to a whole new level! One cheerily called, 'Hullo,' as the other got hot drinks from our machine. Lifting the bag of used cups from the nearby waste bin, I peeled another from

161

my roll, inserted that, and carried on my way. Hearing the clink of dropped coins as they walked off, I glanced round, but they didn't stop to pick them up. Turning back to investigate this strange phenomenon, brought the office window into my view – it was slightly ajar; A glance inside revealed open drawers and a bone-handled dinner knife on the window ledge. The miscreants, meanwhile, had vanished into thin air. Whilst pondering which way to go, rustling sounds came from nearby bushes, and I called, 'Come out of there, I want a word with you two.' They crept out, still holding their drinks. 'You have been in our office and taken the change, haven't you?' The lad with the bulging jacket pocket nodded, and said, 'Sorry.'

During the next half hour, their replies to my questions were quick and varied! They lived in Cherry Hinton – Fulbourn – Stapleford – Great Shelford. Their parents knew they were here – didn't know – would thrash them – didn't care what they did. They were brothers – cousins – in the same class at school – and only the lad with the coppers had broken in. Then noting the other's jacket hung lopsided, a pat from me, elicited, 'Yes I took all the silver.' Next, I noticed a sly glance back to the bushes – there lay a pile of goodies from the gift shop. 'Is that everything now?' 'Yes.' But an involuntary hand movement caused me to look in an inside jacket pocket and find a bundle of notes. Right, now everything is sorted we will go to my house and call the police.' But another look flashed towards a large box bush as we trudged past, and I finally loaded my double bin bag to bursting point. A Sawston police sergeant soon arrived, 'Well hullo Mr **** and Mr ******.' Totally different names to any told to me! 'We have been looking everywhere since you climbed out of the Home's window this morning. Now, before I take you back, are you sure Mr Clark has got all the stuff you have taken from his shop and office? QUITE SURE? Right, come on then. I'll be back to see you later Mr Clark.'

With a cup that cheers, I settled down to list all the loot; I had just reached the end, when the sergeant returned.

'The housekeeper found these items in their trouser pockets. Oh and she asked if you would mind letting her have her kitchen knife back please.' We decided it would suffice for the police to make their report to the relevant County Council body in charge of the Home, and that would be an end to the matter. However, on the following Sunday, the sergeant was at our door at 7.00 am. 'Sorry to bother you Mr Clark, but could you keep an eye out for the Messrs **** and ******, I've taken a look round, but it's only half an hour since they were missed.' In the afternoon he called to say they had been found, 'The young beggars thumbed a van driver within minutes of hitting the main road, spun him a story that their mother had left them, and they were trying to get to their grandmother in Brighton. By eight o'clock he had given them breakfast at a transport cafe, and put them in a lorry heading for Brighton. At midday, a policeman, noticed two boys in badly fitting shoes – their own had been locked away – trying to get onto the pier without paying!'

Winter Battles Indoors and Outside

By September, with the rain at last falling, I felt the most stressful time was over. Then the Secretary called me into the office. Looking very serious, he asked if I was absolutely certain of my facts regarding the tree problems. I said I would bet my life on it – if I lived through it! 'Well, I'm sure you know what you are talking about, and I will back you all I can, but you will have one hell of a task at the AGM. Dr Roughton, one of our members, has complained that you are keeping Wandlebury closed unnecessarily, and is going to bring that up, and Oliver Rackham, has written a letter to the Chairman voicing similar concerns, also disagreeing with your predictions published in the Annual Report, and he too will be at the AGM.'

On the evening I sidled into the meeting with two plastic shopping bags; one contained twigs, the other pieces of wood. A Committee Member gave me a quizzical look as

I took the vacant seat beside him, 'I hope you are not going to use those as missiles Bill!' The assembly was eventually called to order, and the Chairman moved smoothly through the agenda until he came to, 'As you all know, it has been an unprecedented year of disaster for Wandlebury ... valiant efforts from the Warden ... Footpath Closure Order, has been granted for three months ... the Warden believes we need to ask for a further closure to take us into the spring.' ending with, 'However. Dr Alice Roughton and Dr Oliver Rackham have written letters disagreeing.'

Dr Roughton was invited to speak first, and she eloquently gave her concerns culminating in her thought that Wandlebury had already been closed overlong. Dr Rackham was next invited to speak, but declined – content to have the Chairman quote his letter. After which, the Chairman asked if I would like to reply to these concerns. First putting the emphasis on the near misses to visitors, from the 80 boughs that had fallen so far, and that even though I was constantly watchful, had myself been struck three times, I next commented that the recent heavy rain had indeed ended the drought, but it was only making matters worse. Dead branches on dead trees were soaking up water like a sponge, and in a softened state, the extra weight was bringing them down too, at least another 200 were still likely to fall. Worse, four large trees had toppled over, as dead roots were acting in the same way, in the now soft soil.

To answer the more serious accusations – that I had removed gale blown and desiccated trees that would eventually recover – I stepped up to the front and asked the Chairman if he would like to give a view as to whether the twigs in my carrier bag were dead. He thought they were, but invited me to hand the bag to Dr Rackham, and ask his opinion. He agreed they were dead, even rotting, but further said, 'I can pick up twigs like these under any beech trees in any season.' 'Of course you can,' I answered. 'That is why I climbed twelve beech trees this morning, and picked these from the tops.' A murmur ran through the assembled Members – Dr Rackham was obviously taken

164

aback but not beaten yet. 'I have known many stressed trees with dead twigs, and they throw out new growth when rain returns. I think you should wait for a year or two, many of them will recover, especially with the amount of rain that is falling at the moment.'

Lifting my second bag, I lined up the 24 pieces of sawn timber in a row along the front edge of the Chairman's table. And said, 'The sections numbered 1A to 12A are pieces from the base of the trunks of those same twelve trees, and 1B to 12B are from the largest branches. It is plain to see that the branch sections have fungus stain rampaging totally through, this attacks and rots dead beech wood extremely fast. In ten of the trunk pieces it is already into the timber, and on the last two, it is evident as patches just under the bark. These trees, and dozens like them are dead and dangerous – Wandlebury must stay closed whilst they are standing. And another consideration is that at this moment, the best timber is worth 95p per cubic foot, which will pay for the felling and removal, and may even make a small profit. Wait another twelve months, and that fungus will ensure we will struggle to get 20p.' Quite a hubbub ensued as I returned to my chair. Then the Chairman pointed to the back of the hall, 'You have a question?' The familiar voice of Reg Chuter said: 'Mr Chairman, I am the County Council's Tree Officer, and I can report that we fully support all that Mr Clark is doing, in fact we are full of praise for all he has done so far.' The Chairman thanked him, and looked around for other hands, relief showing on his face as he asked if there was, 'Any Other Business? No!' – I had won the day.

Although the County Council had got the closure order on the footpaths, they refused to include the bridle way on the south side of the estate. Unless we carried out surgery at once, they would get the job done and send us the bill! Nearly half the length was owned by our neighbour – who they had failed to inform – and he agreed for us to include his section. Town and Country Tree Surgery were not available, and I had to phone around – there were quite a few, 'tree surgeons' in the Directory, who I thought would be better named, 'tree butchers' – but after viewing the work of several I engaged Mick Bandorski, working under the name of, 'Oaktree Surgery'. We made a start on the 9th of September, with me again doing the clearing up. We got along fine, once I had impressed on him, that his ugly dead stub needing removal, was my lesser stag beetle habitat; and to look for bats before cutting into any hollow branch, and even then leave as much as was safe, for their living quarters. I was later most impressed by the way he treated the CEN photographer's requests to make as much saw dust and smoke as possible, whilst leaning at impossible angles, 10 metres up and with no safety line. Even more so after the man had left, and Mick came down the ladder to ask if I had some rag, as he needed to stop the bleeding where the chain saw had 'nicked' his thigh!

The autumn and winter tree felling was much more traumatising than the storm; at least that was over in an hour or so, and it wasn't I making the choices. To make matters worse, the timber merchant's excellent contractor sent in January, was on another job, and they sent a great bear of a man, who swung his huge chain saw around like a scimitar, and drove his Drott Skid Shovel about with no care of his surroundings whatever. His two labourers cutting and piling the cordwood, and burning up the trash, were bullied unmercifully – both of them injured themselves! Anyone else involved received his ire too; every day we shouted and swore at one another, as I fought to keep him from damaging other trees and the Ancient Monument. Things got a little better after his machine broke down and I fixed it for him; but he was a man who would always blunder through life, and to hell with whoever got in his way.

We started in the quarter mile avenue towards the Roman Road. Although some of these trees had survived the drought, my scheme was to 'clear fell', to enable complete replanting – scheduled for the spring. I was standing with the feller discussing which direction to fell the third tree, when one of his two men cutting the branches off the

166

previous tree, shouted 'Bats! Bats!' and started to dance about. I rushed over, but he had already stamped on one, luckily the other had crawled back into the hollow branch. The big strong man was shaking, and almost in tears! He wailed, 'It was terrible – terrible. I cut through that branch, and out of the end jumped that great bat, and clung to my coat; uuurh, uuurh.' I thrust my arm up the branch and pulled out the other Noctule. With the men now sharing a comforting flask of tea, I took the opportunity to give a lecture on bats, and the great trouble I was having with their conservation. At least from then on, I was always called when they found a hole in a branch or trunk – often before felling took place.

Thankfully, they worked a five day week, so every Saturday and Sunday, various youth groups arrived to help me. All were welcome – and useful – thankfully the Community service candidate during that time was a much tattooed Hells Angel. Built like the proverbial 'brick shed', I made full use of his muscle power to heave logs onto the trailer – by the end of his 100 hours he treated me as if I was a member of his Chapter, looking out for me if any gang of youths dared to be a nuisance during his Saturday stints. However, I turned down his generous offer of getting the Chapter to act as guards during Bank Holidays and weekends when we reopened!

By the 11th of November we were ready to fell the diseased elms on the Ring Ditch banks, unfortunately I was ill with flu, but struggled out at 7.30 am to show them the access to the trees – giving strict instructions not to do any damage – and almost fainting, returned to my bed. At around 12.00 pm, I heard the big 'self-loading' lorry grinding towards our cottage gate. The driver of it I had known as a lad at the little Colmworth school and I also knew that he would drive out – come hell or high water – taking up the total width of the road and both verges for some two to three minutes, as he juggled his long load round and off towards the A11. I dragged myself downstairs, threw on my bright yellow waterproof, picked up a white towel, and arrived on the crown of the hill as the lorry appeared in the gateway. Thankfully, only one car was climbing the hill toward me as I stepped into the middle of the road madly waving my white flag. Only at the very last second did I jump clear, turning to see smoke pouring from the tyres, as it slid towards nine elm trunks travelling on 14 wheels. The lorry driver's foot never wavered on the pedal, as head out of his window – cigarette dangling – he gunned his cab round off the far verge and back onto the road. The driver of the car – now at a halt and almost touching the rear wheels – must have been mightily relieved he was in a low slung car, as the overhanging butts, with two yellow and black triangles attached, swung round over his roof, with only millimetres to spare!

Due to bad weather, the last tree – our biggest and probably oldest elm tree close to the Cupola building – had to wait until the 29th of November. As most of the other old elms had rot at the base, a winch lorry was hired, whilst I pushed with the their Drott to ensure no mishap – as it happened the wood was sound, enabling me to count the rings to a reasonably accurate 285 years! It was the 9th of December before the feller next arrived – in great excitement – to tell me he had won a contract to fell trees for the Queen at Windsor, but he must start, 'next Monday,' he needed to go and spend the next three days getting ready. He then offered me money to clear the last of his tops – in my spare time!! So glad was I to see him go, I would have worked through the night for nothing. 'Poor Queen,' I thought, as his crawler trundled onto a low loader that afternoon.

It was as well that I had asked for an extension to our Footpath Closure Order in good time, for even with Mick Bandorski back, dropping the rest of the unsafe branches, we were to have a hard time being ready for the 'Official Opening' on Sunday, April the 3rd – I had judged it wise to avoid the 1st! One bit of luck, although I didn't know it at the time, was noticing an abandoned Mini-van on the Roman Road some weeks earlier – the police had arrived in time, to not only see a second van, but the youth about to dismantle them. The outcome ensured that he was sentenced nicely in time to become one of my most useful CS lads, for he was an expert mechanic: never was our machinery so well cared for. I just made sure to refuse his continual offers of cheap parts! And much to my pleasure, he gained both a second and third stint with me, although I am sure his probation officer didn't look at it in the same light. My second piece of luck was with the County Council making some teachers redundant. One happened to be Netherhall Geology Teacher, Bill Scoble, who in his younger days was a forester – if he hadn't volunteered his almost full time help, then I am sure I would have had egg on my face. Even so, we were working until dark on the Ring Ditch path on the Friday – with me out again at first light on Saturday to clear the last branches – to be ready to welcome in the Great Shelford Junior School. Although the, 'Official Opening' was to be Sunday, their sponsored walk had been booked some nine months earlier, and I was determined not to let them down!

Plants or People?

I had managed to plant another 500 trees, but summer droughts were now the norm – storm after storm would skirt round us, often leaving a distinct cut-off line across the road halfway up the hill. The consequence being, that even trees planted in previous years dropped leaves if watering was delayed too long. Another of my farmer neighbours, seeing my trailer tank slap slopping its way along the tracks, offered the loan of his 200 litre, wheeled tanker for a while. Besides being able to travel much faster, I could see other possibilities too, and decided that I should – with some urgency – look for one. I asked my sheep farmer if he knew of such. 'Get in touch with Chafer the spray contractors, they are always buying new sprayers, they must have redundant tankers,' was his reply. Within an hour, I had located no less than ten 325 litre tankers at Downham Market – they were changing over from galvanised to stainless steel – I drove over and selected one with all the spraying equipment already removed. A snip at £30.

Back at Wandlebury, I grumbled to Sally Billing our admin secretary, about the long day I had set myself, driving our little Ferguson 35 tractor to pick it up – and on the notorious A10 too. An hour or so later she rang to say her husband Roy, could borrow a large box trailer from his work at Colchester, and collect the tanker early the next morning – if I wanted? The following morning – with only millimetres to spare – we loaded the tanker and brought it home. By the end of that day, what Wendy said looked like the world's largest watering can, was ready for use. From the tractor seat, using a rope through a pulley, the spout could be raised and lowered whilst driving along rows of trees – and fifty trees could be watered with six and a half litres each in half an hour. To water a group of trees, the old hose, housed on a reel at the rear, was pulled out and attached to the lowered spout. Magic! From that day the planting losses fell to one percent.

Out in the Picnic Field, the few clovers and delicate grasses that had survived into the spring of 76, had just about been scorched to death during that summer, nevertheless the wet autumn had regenerated the surviving grasses, and by the 77 spring the field was reasonably green again. Then in April, I was surprised to see the sheep farmer's brother driving a tractor out of the field. I saw he had a mounted fertiliser distributor, and empty 'Nitro Chalk' bags on a trailer towed behind. The chalk grassland of the past was so floristic, because the thin soil, of poor nutrient value, grew mostly dwarf grasses: which allowed all the various wild flowers to grow unhindered – the Babraham area used to be recognised by beekeepers as an area for high quality honey. The explosive nutrients of Nitro Chalk were the last thing that was needed and I phoned the grazier to voice my displeasure. He was surprised that I was upset. 'The annual 'Grazing Licence Agreement' that I have signed, says that I must keep the land in good order, and in fact the Agent has urged me to fertilise it and take a crop of hay this year.' I was devastated. Showers ensured the grass was – to quote a popular song – as high as an elephant's eye'! Later on the rain really set in, the grass went down, and the chance to make hay was lost; the large flock that finally arrived did a grand job of treading most of it into an even thicker mat than the one in 1975; this rotting carpet destroyed just about every vestige of the original planting.

Permission for the 'bat tower' had arrived from the Historic Monuments Commission, but I still hadn't raised the money – and was wondering how on earth I would find the time to build it – when 'Lady Luck' took over! The Headmaster of the Great Shelford County Primary School asked if they could again hold their annual, 'Sponsored Walk', followed by an afternoon BBQ in the grounds, adding, 'We would like to donate half of the money to Wandlebury this year, it should be over a £100.' I thanked him profusely, suggesting it could be specifically towards our bat conservation project, and promised to show the children the site, and talk about it during their visit.

Next, only days after the cheque arrived, a County Council officer rang to ask if I had any small building projects in the offing, as they had a group of youths on a government Job Creation Scheme with a builder in charge, and had run out of tasks, 'You can have them for free,' he ended. On the 3rd of November I selected and bought all the materials. On the 7th they were delivered, and I constructed the wooden door frame. On the 8th the group arrived and started on the foundations. I next fitted the door frame, and welded up the roof bars from a SH metal corn-bin ladder on the 14th, which the gang cemented into place the next day. And on the 16th they tidied up the surroundings – just in time for the Cambridge Evening News photographer to take a photo for inclusion in the following day's CEN. During the next couple of weeks hardly a day went by, without some media presenter knocking on our door. TV, radio, newspapers and magazines: all wanting to

171

look in the tunnel, and view our single Common Long-eared resident, obligingly hanging only a few metres from the entrance.

Come the 1978 spring it was obvious that the prickly seeded barren-brome, an absolute weed of a grass, had taken over the Picnic Field, in fact the field was a wreck! At least the Management Committee agreed that I could remove the grazing from the Agents books, and in future let it out on a, 'donation' basis, completely under my control. Besides my conservation friends not being too keen on my seeding of the new meadow, they did not agree with moving wild plants – even on the same site. Dr Walters was aghast, when he found out that I had moved the last two pyramid orchids growing along a path edge, to a safer place after five had been stolen – I got their number back up to eleven before I retired, but sadly, later management has lost them all! William Palmer, who I could call a friend almost from the day of my arrival, once told me what he thought in no uncertain terms. Hurrying towards me, he called, 'Bill, Bill. You have had the vandals in again! Next to where you have been tree planting, they have dug up every one of the 39 belladonna seedlings that I counted the other day.' 'It's all right William,' I replied, 'it was me, they were too close to the footpath – you know how poisonous they are – I have replanted them out of sight: hopefully most of them will survive.' A look of anguish came over William's face, 'Oh Bill, Belladonna is so rare; and there are more than enough people in the world.'

Apropos the trouble I so often had with people, I suppose I should have agreed with him. One early incident concerned a man thieving from the parked cars. Despite chasing him on foot, then trying to block in his speeding car, which bounced off mine, leaving a large dent and scrapes all along the side of his, he got away. Because of my detailed description he was later picked up by the Suffolk Police, to whom he confessed to some years of breaking and entering vehicles. Up to the end of the 1980s in particular, gangs of rowdy youths were still causing mayhem. One such was well after midnight – for the fourth weekend in a row – the noise of screeching vehicle tyres, shouts and screams were coming from the car park. Leaving Wendy to phone the police, I raced down, and was just in time to see three sets of rear-lights disappearing through the trees. As I dashed back in for the tractor keys, Wendy called, 'The police are on their way.' I drove the tractor out into the reserve – lights off – to look for the cars lights. Gauging their route from the distant beams, I reversed the tractor into some shrubs at the side of a track; zooming out, as a Mini sped along. It hit the big back wheel of the tractor spot on! Pandemonium ensued as three cars tried to reverse, turn, and get away, hitting trees, and probably one another. The first police car arrived as I drove into the car park, and I informed the constable that the, 'birds have flown,' and confessed to my 'accident' with them. His face looked serious in the light of my headlights, then, grinning from ear to ear, he said, 'Oh Mr Clark, I do wish I had been there!' It was most satisfying in the light of day, to see the amount of headlight and rear light glass, strewn along the path.

A School Visit

School visits to Wandlebury, and invitations for me to visit schools, began to take on a momentum of their own. One reason was that nearby Homerton Teacher Training college did regular visits; then later when on a tutorial placement, the young hopefuls recalled their day with me at Wandlebury. One such visit, involved a school from a London borough. The head teacher phoned to say that their trainee teacher had recommended that they pay us a visit – was it possible on a Saturday morning. A week or so later, I stood at the entrance gates, awaiting the promised double decker, and only minutes beyond their ETA, an ancient blue vehicle ground its way up the hill, streamers and balloons hanging from every window. With the aid of a pole – which I had ready – the bus slid under the telephone and electricity cables; and a noisy crowd spilt into the car park. I tried to make out which was the young teacher. Fortunately, one shell shocked looking, pasty faced young man, stepped forward to introduce himself, but I barely heard him above the din. I was pleased when he pointed out that the couple of cars just parking, contained the head master, and more teachers – who had wisely followed behind.

The Head entered the scrum, profusely apologising for disrupting such a lovely place, before weakly adding to the noise whilst trying to introduce me, and in an aside to me, saying it was probably only to be expected, as most of his pupils had never visited the countryside before! I jumped onto the top step of the bus, and bellowed, 'QUIET PLEASE,' quickly explaining that they were now in the countryside, and as the noise bubbled up, again bellowed, 'QUIET PLEASE. I am going to lead you to the toilets first, people live nearby and they like the quiet countryside, so please, NO NOISE there. Next I shall lead you round our footpaths, out in real countryside, to show you all manner of things. When I walk alone, I see badgers, foxes, deer and rabbits, even stoats catching rabbits; but when I walk round with a group we rarely see an animal. I would like to show you a fox or a deer – is that understood? And lastly, if anyone runs ahead, they will frighten away what we are hoping to see, and if anyone takes a different path, it may be a day or two before we find them again!'

A reasonably quiet group eventually followed me out into the trees. I had decided to take them round the outer perimeter in the hope that I would tire them out before the more mundane ancient history. I could not believe that some 70 children could be so well behaved and attentive: I had already pointed out squirrels, sundry birds and even a deer, when one boy – who had been 'in my pocket' the whole time, not missing a single word, and shushing any who interrupted – suddenly pointed to an orange glow beneath a shrub, 'Mr Warden, what's that?' I stepped off the path, bent a branch to one side and held forth. 'This is very interesting. What you are seeing here, is how the whole world keeps on regenerating itself – all things, including us, finally come to an end – and if it wasn't for the likes of this fungus, breaking everything down into the original components, we would not be able to walk along this path today, for there would be hundreds of dead tree trunks piled one above the other, still here from thousands of years ago. As a result, this dog mess deposited last week, will be food for the surrounding plants when the next rain washes the remains into the ground. Meanwhile, these thousands of orange spores are already floating off to find more dog mess to colonise.' The head teacher caught up with us and pushed through the throng, 'What is so interesting?' he enquired, 'Dog shit sir,' answered one helpful lad. I hastily moved on, the only loud noise was my own voice, and the occasional, 'BE QUIET,' from my 'shadow', as we progressed along the paths.

Finally back at the centre, I felt it was safe to venture into the, 'Iron Age' – that subject went so smoothly that I still had time to fill before heading back to the bus. I called out, 'Who would like to see the biggest tree in the world?' There was a chorus of, 'ME! ME! ME!' 'And so would I,' I answered, 'luckily, I do have one of its seedlings close by, so we will look at that instead.' We walked the few yards to our 30 metre high Redwood; and whilst I arranged them in an ever larger circle around it – with even the teachers joining in – I explained its origins and why it had such a variety of names: finally satisfied with the diameter of their circle, I asked them to put their hands out, palms forward, 'You are now all pressing your hands against the soft bark of the mother Redwood.' There was a hubbub of Oohs and Aahs. 'But I expect you would also like to know how high it is too? For this I need you to imagine that I have a chainsaw and some fast setting glue. First I must saw down another tree like this one, and glue it on top.' Faces upturned. 'And yet another on the top of that one. Still it's not high enough! I will now cut half a tree, and glue that on the very top of the other three. We now have the mother tree standing in front of us, one hundred and seven metres high.' All faces craned skywards, and a lone voice shrilled, 'B***** Norah!'

There was only the murmur of voices, still trying to assimilate the news, that there were trees in the world that dwarfed the beeches they were walking under, as we trudged to the bus. Quite a few crowded round to thank me or shake my hand, before they climbed on board, whilst the teachers just stood numbly in the background. As the last child disappeared, the Head leapt forward and clasped my hand. 'Mr Clark, I, I,' the words caught in his throat, 'That is, all the teachers and I, just cannot thank you enough. We never, ever, thought that our ragtag mob was capable of giving anyone such attention. Oh if only you could stay with us.' 'Or better still,' interjected one of the others, 'We could teach among these trees, instead of our dingy classrooms.'

A further rise in school visits was caused by the County Council's, Advisor for Schools! He came along with one school, and liked what he saw. Afterwards, saying that he would like to help us update our facilities, and ensure that all the Cambridgeshire schools were aware of what we had to offer. I envisaged having to work to a mandatory curriculum, rather than what I desired to impart, but he assured me that I would still have full control. I informed the CPS, and they agreed that I should follow it up in the hope that money would be forthcoming. When the CCC, only offered the help of the Work Experience, youth group – who had worked on the bat tower – to do the internal alterations to the small asbestos-clad bungalow, the Society became cautious, afraid that I might commit them to spending money they could not afford. But the widow of CPS secretary, Philip Clarke – previously Director of Education for Liverpool – heard what I was trying to do, and she volunteered the £500 I needed, dedicated in Philip's memory – a few years later, her daughter paid for new floor covering, in memory of Mrs Clarke.

The bungalow, once on show at a 1930s Daily Mail Homes exhibition, had been a gardener's home and was in poor condition. In the evenings, I stripped off the asbestos exterior, repaired the wooden frame, and recovered it in tar paper and metal mesh, before engaging a builder to plaster it. I worked with him too, throwing on the 'pebble dashing' to match the neighbouring bungalow. The Work Experience lads managed to put in a second toilet, washing facilities, and a kitchenette, before the CCC recalled them – leaving me to do the inside painting and decorating. Finally fifty second hand metal chairs, three tables and some curtain material – to allow the windows to be blacked out for slide shows – were provided by the Advisor from a council store, to make it all ready by mid April 1978. He had also been busy in other ways, and on the 8th of May – after welcoming Miss Green and class as the first over the threshold of the 'Schoolroom' – I joined other providers, the RSPB, the National Trust, etc. in the Brunswick Teachers Centre to give an afternoon presentation to head teachers from the region's schools. After we had all spoken for our allotted ten minutes, tea and biscuits were provided, and teachers crowded round asking questions. Even before the Advisor phoned to say he would like to arrange a further session at Wandlebury, the bookings were pouring in!

9. Bees, Birders and the Picnic Field Begins to Bloom

Beekeeping

Three gales during January and February 1979 dumped the next lot of hard work into my lap. Fifty eight beech to clear up, and of course the dying ones with broken branches, still standing 'four square' to the wind. It had also been a cold wet winter, persisting into late spring – the worst kind for honeybees – and I remarked to Wendy Reynolds, my keen gardening neighbour, who was also Librarian for the Animal Research Institute, that the half dozen wild colonies in our few hollow trees seemed to have died out, this would be a disaster for pollination in our area! I also mentioned that I had had a yen to keep bees since childhood, having devoured every word of 'Teach Yourself Beekeeping,' by Norman Schofield, many times; and despite the price of a Second Hand hive filled with bees now being in the region of £50, it was perhaps time I made a start. The following weekend she called to say that a researcher moving abroad, had pinned on her notice board – "Three hives of bees for sale" – and further mentioned that she too would like to start beekeeping. Could we go into partnership, she buying the hive, and me providing tuition?

Knowing that being a paid up member of a Beekeepers Association gave free insurance cover against claims from the public, on the 19th of May I wrote to the

179

Cambridge Bee Keepers Association's Secretary for details. His answer arrived promptly, with a PS: Our first demonstration of the season is this Saturday, 26th May at 3.00 pm in the Cambridge Botanic Gardens. Fortunately Wendy R had asked a local dealer to call that Saturday morning, so that we could fit ourselves up with protective clothing and the necessary tools; also a very capable young volunteer was helping me on the estate and he was delighted to be put in sole charge for a few hours. I resolved that I should turn my, 'paper' expertise, into 'hands-on'. By 5.00 pm Saturday, I had handled my first colony of bees – under the tuition of appropriately named expert, Bill Mead – and was a fully paid up member of the CBKA. I found them a friendly bunch, and although they had collectively lost a lot of colonies during the previous winter, they would let me know of any swarms and suitable Second Hand hives and equipment. The beehive arrived on Sunday the 3rd of June, but expecting an influx of visitors, I apologised to Wendy R, explaining we would have to leave the bees alone until another day.

That evening, Ken Taylor visited, and having noticed the beehive, related a story that made me pleased that we had not interfered with the bees that morning. He said that in 1939 his wife had decided to keep bees in case sugar was rationed. She read up on the subject, located a beekeeper and ordered two hives of bees. They were duly delivered in the sidecar of a motorcycle, and after lunch – and a bit more reading of the finer points on beekeeping – she fixed herself up with a straw hat draped over with net curtain, and wearing a long beige warehouse coat, hied off to the bees. Minutes later he heard her shouting 'Run the bath, run the bath,' and looked out, to see her running towards him, throwing off her clothes. He said, 'I got to the landing as stark naked, she rushed in, and I spent the next hour spraying flying bees and removing all her stings. After dark the beekeeper took the wretched bees away.'

Wendy R and I at last looked inside our hive, and I immediately knew by the lack of bees and some sealed

180

queen cells, that a 'prime swarm' had left the hive in the previous days – and as we tried to put the home-made hive back together, also realised it hadn't been made by the best of carpenters! I was later pleased to see the swarm had entered a nearby hollow tree, and was busily clearing out the remains of the previous colony. It was probably as well for my helper, that the hive was now short on bees, because there is nothing more daunting for a beginner, than opening a strong colony – though we were not to be single hive beekeepers for long.

On the following Wednesday, I happened to see some boys pushing over four hives in a nearby field. I arrived to find live bees in one, and a sheet of paper with the name and phone number of the beekeeper, among the debris of one of the three containing only dead bees. I dashed home and phoned him with the news, he said that he was sorry, but dare not go near! I 'hurrumphed', saying, 'There is only one live colony to deal with.' – I was already thinking that they had not been left with enough stores to see them through the winter, and my opinion of him, was getting lower by the second. He then explained that during the previous autumn, he had been stung and had an anaphylactic shock. 'If my wife had not seen me fall, I would have died. Whilst I was in hospital, she arranged for someone to remove them, and I have promised her I will sell them.' I remarked that I understood his wife's concern, mine too, was apprehensive about my recent start in beekeeping. His voice went up an octave. 'Do you mean to say you are keeping bees on Wandlebury? Oh Mr Clark it would make me so happy to know my bees are in your care, please take them, as a gift!'

I installed the colony on new combs and fed them with some sugar-syrup – with the intention of cleaning and sterilising the other three hives as and when I had the time. A couple of days later, the phone rang as I arrived for my midday meal. Lifting the receiver, I could only hear sobbing. 'Who is there?' I asked, in some alarm. A lady's quavering voice, asked, 'Are you Mr Clark, the Warden at

Wandlebury?' My heart sank – she has been assaulted. Assuring her I was the Warden, brought further tears. Trying to calm her down, I said, 'I am sure it is not as bad as you believe.' 'But it is, it is,' she sobbed. 'You should have called the police,' I said. The sobs died down. 'I did, they were useless; they told me to phone the City Council.' 'And what on earth did they say?' I asked. 'They just gave me the number for South Cambridgeshire Council, who told me to phone Rentokill, and theirs is only an answer-phone, please help me,' she wailed. The penny dropped! 'Have you got a swarm of bees?' Louder sobs issued, 'My kitchen is full – thousands of them.'

This was quite exciting, and they were less than a mile away! Dinner was put on hold, and I arrived within minutes. A lace curtain twitched at a window and a hand beckoned me down the path. A finger pointed to the left. Around the corner, the hand waved me on from another window, and upon turning the next corner of the L shaped building, I could see a half glazed door, partly opened inward, with bees on both the inside of that and the closed windows either side. On a flowering currant bush, a couple of steps in front, hung a small swarm; which I shook into my special collecting box, put the lid on and waited a few moments for them to settle down. Next I opened the small bottom entrance, and out some streamed – if the queen was inside they would start to fan their pheromones at the entrance to guide the others in. All indications were that the queen was in the box, so I fully opened the kitchen door and windows, and fanned the bees from behind the glass, satisfied to see the box getting ever more covered in bees as the kitchen emptied. Finally closing up a bee-free kitchen, I walked round to the front door. It was opened a crack, and I explained, that in order to take away every last bee I must leave the box in position until dusk. That evening, after closing the entrance, I carried the box to my car, returning to inform the lady. As I lifted my fist to knock, the door swung wide open and a pair of arms encircled me whilst my face was covered with kisses! She pulled back, still gripping my arm. 'Oh thank you, thank you. You are my Knight in Shining Armour,' then letting go. 'What am I thinking of, keeping you like this, when you have had such a busy day.' And giving a cheery wave, she closed the door, and I dizzily walked to my car.

The following morning I tipped the swarm in front of the hive I had hastily made ready – there is nothing more satisfying than to watch a swarm of bees march into their new home. Next, during the afternoon, a second swarm left the 'bought' colony, causing me to rush another hive together, only for a beekeeper to then offer a 'big' swarm for £9 in the evening. This I tipped in front of the last, even more hastily prepared hive – I was now getting quite blasé with my swarm technique – except that this swarm decided they didn't like the smell of fresh creosote, and decamped to another hollow tree the next day. If I had thought that I could now ease off on my beekeeping, a visit from the Vice Chairman of the CBKA that afternoon should have forewarned of a different outcome! 'We are so pleased that you have decided to keep bees at Wandlebury Mr Clark – you are just the sort of person we need to help us in our fight against poisonous sprays. Would you be willing to act as our Spray Warning Liaison Officer?' My answer had to be yes, for I had already had confrontations with spray operators damaging wild bee populations: this was also to be the start of my continuous membership of their Committee, in various posts until 2010 – and still in charge of their equipment loans in 2012! My high profile with spray problems – I was probably the first to get a spray contractor to admit his guilt, and pay a beekeeper compensation – resulted in being interviewed on TV, radio, and in the press.

Young Helpers

At least those spring gales blew some good my way – except it didn't come about until almost the last day of the clear-up.

A shy young lad walked over, as I picked up roots from the cultivated ground between the stumps in readiness to start planting. Hesitantly, he asked if it was possible to volunteer for work. I smiled, and answered, 'When can you start?' And with that he began picking up roots and throwing them on the trailer. Richard Finnigan came at every opportunity – wet or fine – from that day onwards and for some years. I am sure there were times he neglected other things, perhaps even his school work when he first came. I would be using the noisy chainsaw, and suddenly realise logs were being pitched onto the trailer, or hear the smack of my pickaxe whilst I planted a tree, and turn to see the next planting hole being dug.

Richard boarded with an Aunt, and occasionally had holidays with his father who worked in Jamaica. After one – lasting some weeks – he arrived back, and finding Wendy busy in the greenhouse, immediately asked where I was working, but still hung around, acting as if on 'tenterhooks'. She asked if he was well. 'Of course I am well, whatever makes you think I am not,' was the indignant reply. Wendy persisted, 'Richard, if you are worried about something, I am sure we can help.' Richard shuffled, his face colouring up, 'Well actually, I was wondering why you are growing cannabis?' Wendy now coloured up, and pointing, said, 'Oh good gracious, do you mean that row of plants?' Richard looked even more embarrassed, 'Oh dear, Bill hasn't told you!'

I had found fifteen pots of tiny plants and a trowel hidden in the undergrowth one showery afternoon, and assumed it was the work of some well-meaning person – other garden flowers had been planted around the new trees from time to time. Not recognising these, I had asked Wendy to plant them in the garden. 'They must be something exotic,' I had remarked. Wendy sent Richard 'hot foot' after me. I jogged back beside his bicycle; Richard apologising profusely for causing such a kerfuffle, and surmising – although he had seen the plants all over Jamaica – that he could be wrong. At home – looking in the correct book – we could see the now quite large and handsome plants, were indeed cannabis. I looked aghast at Wendy. 'Can you remember if any policemen have driven round here since you planted them?' Neither of us could be sure, for they came fairly regularly. Not always because of Wendy's 999 calls, sometimes bringing information, or hoping for some, about local, 'bad lads' – and also, just in case Wendy had her celebrated honeyed scones in the larder. It was no good, I couldn't take the chance and just burn the plants – we could already be under surveillance – I would have to phone up and confess. It quite amused our local bobby, but to Richard's anguish, the 'Narcotics Division' still arrived with sirens wailing and blue lights flashing.

By the time my first Merrist Wood Agricultural College student, Carl Wright arrived in April 1980 – to work the nine month practical part of his four-year Countryside Management Course – the barren-brome covered Picnic Field was interspersed with large patches of sage-green ground ivy. He thought it looked 'quite reasonable,' and by mid-July when the ground ivy was in full flower – and smothered with bees of all descriptions – he expressed the opinion that the field was, 'quite beautiful,' and even though it was way short of my aspirations, I had to agree. With no possibility of a second grant, I was using my initiative, whenever I was out and about, I filled my pockets with grass and flower seeds, later scattering them as I walked about the field.

Wildlife and Birders

I had recently been asked to give a display entitled, "Notifying beekeepers before spraying insecticides," at a national demonstration for farmers growing Oil Seed Rape, and Carl was most impressed with my three panel folding display board – opening to four metres – made entirely from the scrap someone had dumped in our lay-by. But his enthusiasm didn't include my rather wordy display: his suggestions – and help during the following evenings – turned it into a tableau, showing beekeepers and farmers working together to protect bees. I was next invited to display it at the East of England Show, when it stood for three days in the 'Farm Safety Arena' – for the next six years it stood at any show that farmers might visit! Whilst at the show, I also discovered the 'Cambridge Bat Group', who were manning a stand, and I invited them to come along to Wandlebury to check the bats in the tunnel during that winter. We were having difficulty finding the time and also the protection of bats had been beefed up with stricter legislation. Unless I went through the procedure of getting a licence, or was in the company of a licensed worker, it was possible I could be prosecuted for going down to look at my thermometers!

One of my first actions upon arriving in Cambridge had been to join the various wildlife organisations. Although it was a struggle to fund the membership from my now lower salary – some 30% less than the farm – I regarded it as essential to learning about the local environment, as well as somewhere I could appeal to for help, if need be. I quickly learnt how their officials and many of their members regarded Wandlebury. One of my first contacts with the RSPB Cambridge Members Club was to invite them for a 'Walk and Talk', this brought forth the comment, 'I will put it to the Members, but I am afraid we usually recommend they give Wandlebury a miss – unless it's midweek and they have nowhere better to go.' Of the twenty or so RSPB members who eventually came one evening, most continued to be regular visitors – probably helped by seeing three pairs of nuthatches and a couple of lesser-spotted woodpeckers. They also spread the word to the Cambridge Bird Club – which was just as well – for after one of my midnight sorties pursuing marauding youths, I came across a Manx Shearwater toddling along a moonlit path – and three

CBC members, volunteered to transport it to Hunstanton the following day.

The local RSPB members especially, raised funds and made up work parties to help clear gale damage and plant trees and shrubs. Their blackberry and wild rose plantings to block off some of the miles of unofficial paths, not only raised the numbers of nesting whitethroats and yellowhammers, but as the bare areas behind filled with grasses, nettles and thistles, the number of woodland ground-nesting birds, such as chiffchaffs and willow warblers went up. Another important factor was the extra eyes and ears, for although I tried to cover most of the estate each day, with all my other work I could not hope to know all that was happening. It is not surprising that they listed some 80% of the interesting or first of a season's migrant birds – on occasion almost getting me out of bed to rush off with them! Common Buzzards, Bramblings, Golden Orioles, Great Grey Shrikes, Honey Buzzards, Nutcrackers, Peregrine Falcons, Pied Flycatchers, Redstarts, Ring Ousels, Rock Partridges, Spotted Flycatchers and Wheatears – even my old friend the Osprey passing overhead – to name but a few. If a bird visited Wandlebury, there was a good chance it would be noticed.

Their finest hour – to get them national recognition – was the morning of the 24th of June, when CBC member Dr Rathnell knocked on my door to inform me that an Icterine Warbler was singing near the car park. I was pleased by this, because on the 16th, I had heard strange warbler song: but upon returning with my books and binoculars, I heard it no more. I walked down with the excited Doctor and we stood listening and confirming with our books. The next few days brought a trickle of bird watchers and I thought that I should prepare for a flood! Fortunately Carl pitched in – he was nearly as excited as Dr Rathnell – and warmly met and conversed with the 'twitchers', but looked askance at my unusual reticence. I told him of my past problems with the Osprey at Wivenhoe, and that we must have ropes, posts and signs, ready for the worst.

By the 30th, the constant attendance averaged a score from dawn to dusk. Very conveniently the bird spent most of its time in a couple of spindly ash saplings – the only tall trees left on the north side of the car park – all the birders had to do, was park, set up their telescopes and cameras, and watch. Unfortunately there was an argument raging and this was bringing in even more punters: most thought it was an Icterine Warbler, whilst others argued for Melodious Warbler. I suggested it may be a 'Meloderine Warbler' – receiving some pitying glances. On the 1st of July, Carl and I were waiting in the car park for a school bus, and I remarked, 'Someone of consequence is about to arrive, see how the twitchers are all looking at every car that turns in the gate.' Sure enough, minutes later a car drove in and parked among them, causing some cameras to turn towards the car!

The 'royal' personage stepped out, gave a smile and a nod towards all and sundry, lifted his car-boot lid, and proceeded to fit telescope to tripod. I muttered to Carl, 'Try and find out who he is,' for by then I was no longer on the twitchers Christmas card list, having forbidden them to enter the woodland to search for a nest. Our bird was pouring out its song almost directly above the great man, as he leaned back in the car and retrieved a camera, hanging it around his neck before straightening up and swinging round. With a broad smile, he called out, 'Good afternoon everyone, has anyone seen it yet?' Carl was not at all impressed, especially when he learned the man was the editor of a prestigious bird magazine!

On the 7th of July, Rosemary Jellis, the author of 'Bird Sounds and Their Meaning', arrived to play some recordings to the bird – it was still singing non-stop – and she confessed she didn't recognise the song purely as one or the other. It completely ignored a Marsh Warbler's song – stopped singing briefly at the sound of a Melodious – but upon hearing the Icterine, dashed down and flew at the loud speaker, before agitatedly hopping from twig to twig around it. After a second playing gave the same results, Rosemary switched off the equipment: 'That settles it, it's definitely an Icterine.' But it was not cut and dried! The 'experts' were measuring the tertials, primaries and scapulars on their close-up photos, coming down on the side of Melodious: whilst others compared photos of Icterines, and argued for the wing length, leg colour and wing panel colours. Perhaps it was fortunate that the bird left us before there was open war, or the suggestion that it should be captured. Later, when a draft of an article was sent to me by the 'British Birds' editor, for my approval – I was amused to read the hypothesis, 'the possibility that it was a hybrid Icterine x Melodious Warbler, however, might tenuously be suggested.'

Bees and Negligees

Carl's main task throughout his stay was to make a list of all the plant species on Wandlebury – which is still being added to. I had already put together a reasonable list using mostly common names, now at last a College educated plants-man was getting to grips with giving them all their Latin names, and in some cases his checking proved the actual plants were rarer relatives! We were both amazed at just how many species there were. One issue we had, was whether to include the flowers of the 'lost' gardens, and 'escapes' from roadside dumping; we decided we would list them as groups, such as: Snowdrops, *Galanthus* sp – little did we know that these alone would put Wandlebury on the world map of places for gardeners to visit. I was later quite overcome, when Carl visited and presented me with two expensive books on Fungi and Plants, saying that his nine months with me had surpassed his college education – which he had passed with honours!

Despite all the extra tree work on top of the normal Wandlebury management, I was still keeping up with my beekeeping. The success of the Spray Warning Scheme meant that I often had farmers phoning for advice, and our

189

visitors saw my beehives, or bought honey in the shop with my name on the jar, so in next to no time, I was the 'Bee Expert' to call when folk had a problem with anything that looked remotely like a bee – even beekeepers were asking advice. Looking back, I wonder how on earth I coped, especially as Wendy R had decided beekeeping wasn't for her after all. Certainly it could never have happened without Wendy – my wife – fielding all the calls, and before the arrival of our pocket radios, often chasing all over Wandlebury to find me if it was an emergency, and concerning bees, it usually was. I have removed swarms from every kind of building: large ones, such as churches and Wimpole Hall, down through farm houses, barns, council houses, thatched cottages, pig sties and even a dog kennel! One swarm collecting exploit – in the lion's cage at Linton Zoo, was written up in the Beekeepers Annual. The Editor enjoyed the article so much, she arranged for her artist son to illustrate it with humorous drawings.

I believe it is important for all beekeepers to dash and help members of the public who have a problem with bees – if the beekeeper is able. For most people, a swarm is an alarming circumstance, and by taking the swarm, the beekeeper is indeed their 'knight in shining armour'. Picking it up promptly prevents it from choosing a new home in such as a chimney, and causing even more alarm, thereby giving bees and nearby beekeepers a bad name. Above all, it is important to save the bees, and get them into a beekeepers care, for seldom do more than one in three swarms survive in the wild. Of the hundreds of swarms and established colonies I have dealt with, I have only had to kill two lots. One was my first Wimpole Hall incident. It was the Easter holiday, the season's first opening of the house, and the housekeeper had entered to find bees everywhere. It was an early call, with my own busy day about to start. 'Is there anything at all you can do Mr Clark, we shall lose thousands of pounds if we have to keep closed.' Upon my arrival I found three rooms full of bees. They were coming down two, back to back, chimneys. I asked for old blankets, and an industrial vacuum. After stuffing up the offending chimneys above the fireplaces, I whizzed around the rooms sucking up bees with the vacuum. The last bee was going down the tube, as the first visitors walked to the door!

One call was from the ambulance station at Addenbrookes Hospital. 'There is a large swarm hanging in the leylandii hedge outside our front entrance.' I unloaded my swarm box, stopping briefly to pull hat and veil over my head, then shook the hedge vigorously over the open box – praying that the queen had fallen in. With the lid replaced, box and I smothered in bees, I moved it from the hedge a few paces. After opening the entrance, I stood up to watch events, and realised that a row of shocked looking faces were peering out of the windows, and I hastily held up both thumbs to indicate all was well. Within moments bees were leaving me, to enter the box, as more and more fanned out their pheromones denoting the queen was inside. Soon afterwards, free of bees, I called in to say I would return that evening, to take the box away – receiving a round of applause.

One swarm-collecting foray brought the colour to my cheeks! Wendy had told a lady I could only get there late in the evening, and on arrival I walked round the back as instructed and knocked on a door, whereupon it was opened by a housekeeper type lady, who said she was just leaving, but that I was to go up the stairs, and knock on the second door on the left. Swarm box in hand, I climbed the carpeted stairs and knocked, and upon hearing a chirpy 'Come in Mr Clark,' walked in. Finding myself in what I can only describe as an OTT lady's bedroom on an American film set! Sitting up, surrounded by silk covered pillows, was a buxom lady of about 60 years, in an extremely revealing black silk negligee. If it wasn't for the fact that I could see bees flying around the open window, I would have fled. As nonchalantly as possible I walked over to the window. Although there was no swarm, I could see one had been there by the flecks of wax on the pelmet. I placed my hand out on the tiled roof still baking hot from the sun, turned –

the negligee was now covering even less – and said, 'The swarm has left, these few bees will return to their original home shortly. What happened is that they went up into the casement roof to live – probably yesterday – but today's hot sun roasted them out and they have gone to find another home. It would be a good idea to get a handyman to block up the hole before another swarm arrives.' 'Oh Mr Clark, you are so clever, I love listening to you on Radio Cambridgeshire.' She patted the coverlet, 'Come and sit down and tell me more.' I said I would love to stay and chat, but unfortunately there were more swarms waiting – and escaped from the room.

Caring for Wild Plants

Ivan Perry, a Cambridge entomologist, who had discovered the larva of the rare hover fly, *Calicera spinolae*, in the interior sludge of one our hollow beech trees the previous autumn, visited in September, arriving at the precise moment, to record an adult, egg laying – on the outer bark. This was one of the trees a Forestry Commission officer, who was checking up on work in progress, had insisted should be felled and cleared away. Thank goodness I had stood my ground, and said that I would rather lose the grant, than fell trees that were important for the wildlife. A year or two later, a CPS Chairman also took issue with me over a hollow beech, his argument being that the wet-rot inside it, could spread to the buildings. I again held forth on the reasons for keeping it: then later Ivan Perry, accompanied by noted entomologist, Graham Rothery, collected a pupa from its watery depths, and hatched out an *Ethelurgus vulnerator* – an insect only recorded three times before in the whole of Europe!

Another tree that I set great store by, was our only Cedar of Lebanon. Not liking dry, chalky, Wandlebury, it probably had more dead branches than live ones; each season I threw a rope over them, tugged hard, and any that broke off I stood upright nearby. Why such concern for dead cedar branches? I saw more adults of the Greater Horn-tail, *Sirex gigas*, Lesser Horn-tail, *Sirex noctilo*, and their imposing predator, the Ichneumon, *Rhyssa persuarsoria*, emerge from holes in this one tree in 1977, than I had seen during the whole of my life up to then. In common with other forested areas, we are losing too many of our largest and oldest trees with rot holes and other nooks and crannies, and it will be many years before similar trees are available again: one of my solutions was to interplant with Silver Birch and Cherry. These short lived trees will at least provide insect larvae and woodpecker habitat, long before the beech and oak I have planted get to that stage. Another of my solutions, which needs to go on for many years, was to hang up 'Rot Botts' – consisting of plastic buckets of various sizes, some designed as bird nesting boxes too, but all filled in the lower section with sawdust from our woodcutting activities, and kept wet in order to simulate rotting trees. These were well used by many of the common insects. I even sawed holes in selected young beech, to start off the hollowing process.

Alan Dixon was the Merrist Wood student for 1981, one of his tasks was collecting and sowing flower seeds, delicate ones put in pots in the greenhouse and some 600 pots of cowslips outside – descendants from the plants that Caroline first saw. Wendy took them over after Alan left, and by the time student Hugh Roberts arrived the following year, many were ready to plant out. As I was to be busy at Bourne windmill on the chosen day, I hurried to the Picnic Field with Hugh and a school boy volunteer, and demonstrated my method of planting. Removing a small square of turf – to ensure the plant didn't get too much competition at the start – I dug a hole in the centre, put in the plant and firmed it with my heel. Hugh's planting of the second one was quite satisfactory, and I left them to it. Upon arriving home at 6.00 pm, I was surprised to see them only just putting the tools away. They had decided to finish the task as the weather forecast was for rain to water them in the next day. After tea, I walked over to admire their work, but before I got near, noticed a problem. During the next couple of weeks, Hugh wandered over the field each morning, picking up every plant that had been pushed out of the ground, to replant them in a different place. During the original planting, he had decided the mole heaps were a ready prepared spot!

I was apprehensive as to how much damage the sheep would do to these newly planted cowslips, but I needn't have worried, for only days later, I was informed that the grazier had sold up and retired. And so I flail-mowed the field myself, and with the aid of some horse keeping friends, carted the hay off. My associates on other reserves, must have thought, 'Ha, Bill is coming round to our way of doing things!' However, during the twelve years since I had told the Essex Naturalists Trust, that I was convinced that Essex CC were damaging roadside sward and invertebrate life with their flail mowing, I had seen nothing to change my mind. Through the years there have been many mutations; large hydraulic machines that can reach up and mash 100 mm thick branches to a pulp, down to tiny hand-held strimmers. Though why anyone should want to use a strimmer with all the noise and fumes they have to put up with – and all the safety gear that must be worn too – is beyond me! Much to one salesman's chagrin, I was able to scythe faster than his, 'Professional,' strimmer – and in today's jargon, I could also have pointed out my, 'low carbon footprint!' Although I did mention that I could listen to the birds singing whilst I worked.

Thankfully, I found another grazier and during the next four years, we gave the lawns an early graze to encourage the dwarf grasses, clovers and bird's-foot-trefoil, then when the seed was ripe, I scythed and spread that too in the Picnic Field. The grazier – Mick Mellows and his son Roy – could not have been more enthusiastic and helpful, even though my set-up meant that they had no security of tenure and must allow me to move the sheep to wherever and whenever I wished. They provided the batteries and

194

electric netting, and though I carefully hid the expensive batteries from view, some were stolen – even the energiser and a complete length of netting on one occasion. They voluntarily tidied up after the sheep with their own tractor and mower – which gave me a small problem! I have never expected – even the most careful wildlife enthusiasts – to be able to notice everything whilst working with machinery: so I examined every area prior to their arrival and flagged up any plants I needed for seed, those with butterfly and moth-caterpillars or eggs on the leaves, or the occasional ground nesting bird, or leveret in its form: in order for them all to be given a wide berth. One afternoon, I failed to notice the pair waving for my attention. 'Huh,' remarked Roy to Mick, 'We should have been a couple of b***** caterpillars!' The Picnic Meadow was still short of my vision, but because of the thin grass cover and the activity of moles, many of the arable plants still flourished, so there was always plenty to interest the school children: White campion, Venus's-looking-glass and heart's-ease. Wild mignonette and red dead-nettles – especially loved by the bees, and stork's-bill and crane's-bill providing the food plants that caused an upsurge in Brown Argus butterflies.

WAC oog

10. A Police Sergeant Advises – Wendy Receives Gold – I Upset the Top Brass – Doctor Varley's Bequest

Bruce

I was suffering yet another spate of evening problems – some thirty lads in cars and vans came careering round this Saturday at midnight. The police, as usual, were very prompt, and after all was quiet, the Sergeant said, 'They were a very rough lot Mr Clark: it worries me the amount of time that you are alone confronting these yobs, I wouldn't care to do it. You need a big dog, have you thought of a German Shepherd?' I confessed that I had, and added, that if they hadn't been so expensive, I would probably already own one. In fact, I had been apprehensive for some time about Wendy walking through the woods alone, accompanied only by gentle old Julie and latterly Jake. And therein lay another problem: I needed a dog with a bit of 'presence' when dealing with unruly youths of an evening, but Wendy could only handle a gentle dog, and neither of us wanted to intimidate the thousands of visitors we met. A few days later the police sergeant in charge of the Dog Section phoned. 'I have been told you require an Alsatian. I believe I know of the very dog for you – he is too docile for our needs.' He then gave me the details of Joe, owned by a man working at Sibson airfield who was about to go abroad. I thanked him profusely, and phoned the chap immediately.

The following morning I arrived at the airfield in my little Citroen C4. Joe's owner had already left, leaving instructions with an office secretary to give me the collar and lead and the key to a large warehouse – I was expected me to take the dog immediately! As I unlocked the door I made suitable calming sounds and slid in quickly peering into the gloom. A very large white Alsatian was standing in an alleyway between piled up desks, tables and chairs, he gave a couple of 'woofs' but stood quietly whilst I put his lead on. We walked a couple of times around a large empty car park, before I returned the key. The couple inside the office said they were so pleased that I liked the dog as his owner had been going frantic with worry. I arrived home, drove up to the kitchen door and pressed the hooter. Wendy's face was a picture! She hadn't dreamed that I would bring him back immediately, and the colour white had been the farthest from our minds. Before I let him out, I stood in the kitchen doorway to view the spectacle. He filled the entire back of the car, drooping his head over the front passenger seat to see out! We both agreed Joe was no name for a dog of ours, and promptly renamed him Bruce which he took to with alacrity.

A couple of evenings later, as I walked him through the car park, I came across five noisy youths sitting in a car, with a circle of cans, bottles and take-away cartons scattered around it. The driver answered my 'request' with. 'Pick 'em up yourself.' Bruce, noting the tone of his voice, growled. 'All right, all right, I was only joking.' the driver said, quickly climbing out to pick everything up. But I still wondered whether Bruce would stand firm if we were actually attacked? The next weekend I had my answer. An elderly Wandlebury resident, saw me remonstrating with a group of youths in the car park as he drove home, and walked back down to see if I needed him to phone the police. But they had already left, and I explained how my life was suddenly so much easier now that I had Bruce, and how he growled when they raised their voices at me. 'How clever of him: I expect if I was to try and strike you he would attack me?'

And he jokingly raised his walking stick. Thank goodness I had the lead on Bruce, but it was all I could do to hold him, as his teeth grazed the man's sleeve. 'Oh dear, that was rather stupid of me wasn't it,' he remarked, as he retrieved his hat that had been sent flying.

I Upset the 'Top Brass'

In July 1984, I very publicly upset the Chief Superintendent of police, and probably the Chief Constable too. A sunny Saturday usually promised a busy day. But with a large contingent of Girl Guides booked in – expecting input from me at various times – and my assistant having a weekend off, hectic was probably going to be nearer the description. I hurried home to get in a tea break before the coaches arrived, and noticed the car park was full of police cars. A sergeant I recognised stepped over to say there was, 'an incident,' and they were only using our car park to rendezvous and would soon be leaving. Later, after spending the morning with the Guides, I was heading home for lunch only to see yet more police cars, just queuing to leave. I asked the nearest driver, 'Are you still on this morning's incident?' 'No idea, I have only just come on duty,' he replied, and followed the others out.

After lunch I traversed the estate on my mountain bike, making sure all was well with the numerous groups of girls – now amusing themselves – and in particular, that there were no 'undesirables' around. Then soon after 4.00 pm, I noticed police cars and a large motor van in the car park. After climbing the steps at the rear, I was introduced to the, 'Chief Superintendent in charge of operations.' I was horrified to hear, that two men – probably armed – had been loose in the area for most of the day! But as the Golf Course had been surrounded, it was only now deemed necessary to clear our park. I immediately cycled to the top of the hill, and could see constables at intervals, from just below my house, to the Hinton Way crossroads; but along the estate boundary from my house to the Roman Road, not a single one. I returned to the Chief somewhat miffed! 'There is not a single man across country on our boundary.' 'I am well aware of that Mr Clark, I would need at least a hundred men to seal off that woodland area and I haven't got them available.' 'I could have stationed only three men along there, and they could tell you if as much as a hare came out of the Golf Course.' He stepped from his desk, and called to a nearby Sergeant, 'Quickly. Get three officers to go with Mr Clark, he will show them where to stand.' And by about 4.45 pm, not only had Wandlebury been cleared of visitors, but no one could cross between the two areas without being seen.

After a late tea I strolled out, expecting the police operation to have long been abandoned, only to see the nearest constable still standing where I had placed him. I expressed the opinion that surely the two men had long gone, and he agreed, but that his instructions now were to watch for the miscreants trying to get back to the golf course. Officers were about to sweep the cornfields from the A11, back through Wandlebury to the golf course! I dashed down to the van, and informed the only constable there, that unless the sweep started much closer to Wandlebury, it would be too dark to see under the trees. He thanked me for my concern, but assured me that the Chief would have taken this into account – he expected the men would be moving quite fast. Needless to say, the hunt ended in complete disarray as they entered Wandlebury in the gathering darkness.

Late Monday afternoon, only minutes after my reading the Cambridge Evening News front page headline: '60 POLICE IN ARMED MANHUNT', a reporter phoned to ask, 'Did the police hunt on Saturday affect you at all Mr Clark?' This resulted in the Tuesday edition's headline, 'SIGHTSEERS 'AT RISK' IN MANHUNT,' and in lower case: 'Police failed to clear park – warden.' The rest of the story was about my grumbles, and police denials that anyone was at risk. Soon after reading that, Wendy dashed to find me,

'You had better come home,' she panted, 'The Chief Constable has been on the phone.' I agreed to visit the police station the following morning, and arrived to find some half dozen 'top brass' gathered round a table with a large map of the area laid out on it. After being asked if I preferred tea or coffee, the Chief Superintendent introduced me to the others, including the Assistant Chief Constable, who apologised on behalf of the Chief Constable, as he was going to be late. Everyone was surprisingly friendly – I was expecting a drubbing for sticking my nose in. Once the Chief arrived, he asked for my view of the operation. One outcome of the morning was that I provided them with an up-to-date, large scale map of Wandlebury – they had used a ten year old, countywide one. We parted on the best of terms – though I was extra careful with my driving for some time afterwards.

Dr Varley's Bequest

Doctor J F Varley died in 1981, he was a life Member of the CPS, but other than that, no one in the CPS knew much about him, and it came as a surprise to hear that he had left one third of a large bequest to them – two other recipients being the National Trust and the RSPB. Some £110,000 was paid in 1982, with a further £35,000 or so in 1985. Even disregarding money from the sale of a house and reparations for land taken for the M11 motorway at Coton, this immediately put the CPS on a more favourable financial footing; the hand to mouth existence of former years should be no more. I saw a, 'now or never' chance to get Wandlebury's last 18 acres of arable put down to flower meadow. However we had a very cautious Treasurer – he had had to be – and I knew even now, he would not be keen to lose the income from this land. I suggested to Steve Donoclift – that year's Merrist Wood student – that he could draw up my plan as part of his College dissertation. (We couldn't have dreamed that 28 years on, he would be visiting with his two sons – my grandsons – to play in the field!) I later approached CPS Vice Chairman, Gwyneth Lipstein with the first rough proof. She was very enthusiastic, but thought we should enlarge the small tree nursery at the north end, into a commercial venture. Realising we needed to make both a good business plan, as well as a pretty meadow, I spent any spare minute with Steve, honing the presentation for the future Committee meeting.

By the time we had finished, the field plan looked quite handsome. A nice curved hedge snaked across the centre of the north field. Behind the hedge – besides our tree nursery – were thousands of Christmas trees. In the first season we could sell hundreds of half to one metre trees, then as the years progressed, four or more metre trees would be available too; the enterprise should eventually equal the farming income. Regarding the flower meadow, grants were attainable from the Countryside Commission, City Council, South Cambs and the County Council, keeping the cost to a minimum for the Society. Although Gwyneth liked the plan, she was not at all sure the vote would go our way, 'Can you give a forecast of the profits to come on the Christmas tree venture – should it be on an even larger scale, perhaps the whole of the north field?'

On the morning of the meeting my final inquiry was answered. My profit margin on the trees held good; the bad news being that year on year, people were turning away from real trees. I closed my folder with a sigh; 'Oh Dr Varley,' I thought, 'Why didn't you make yourself known to me, I could have encouraged you to fund your own field.' I jumped to my feet to answer the phone, 'Ah, hello Bill,' said Gwyneth, 'how are things going?' 'Well I am ready for the meeting, but still apprehensive as to the outcome, might it help if we named it, 'Dr Varley's Field?' 'Bill, you're a genius, see you shortly.' During the meeting Gwyneth introduced my proposal for taking in hand the Telegraph and Shooting Shed fields, and Chairman Sir Desmond Lee, invited me to talk it through. I placed our field plan in the centre of the table and proceeded with the explanations, putting emphasis on the future income; leaving Gwyneth to come in at the end with the idea of the name change.

One of the three members I feared would be against it, spoke up, 'I am afraid I am not in favour at all; why on earth make yourself a lot more work by growing and selling Christmas trees?' 'Exactly,' broke in another of the trio, 'Take away the commercial venture, and it is a good scheme.' 'It is obvious that it should be one large flower meadow,' agreed the third, 'However, I am not at all happy with the name, Dr Varley's Field sounds a bit of a mouthful.' 'Varley's Field sounds much better,' said a fourth member. A mutter of agreement from all and sundry ensued, and in a daze I heard the Chairman say, 'Well that's settled then Bill, when are you going to start?'

The last crop grown in the field was winter barley – not a crop that could be under-sown as I did with the Picnic Field, and so it was a case of waiting until the harvest was off. As it happened, things had moved on since I planted the Picnic Field, not only were there even fewer wild meadows to harvest seed from, there were less, 'seed houses' in business, but more folk – from Prince Charles to City Park Managers and Coal Tip restorers, all wanting seed to create 'Conservation Areas.' It was to be September before I gained delivery, of what I discovered afterwards was just about the entire UK quantity of many varieties! Of the five companies I contacted, only one could supply enough for more than one hectare, and even by rounding down the area with my tree and arable plantings, I still needed to plant just over six hectares. Another shock was that rarity had pushed the value sky-high; even if those firms could have supplied my needs, we could never have afforded to buy. The whole field price for 320 kilos, varied from £500 through to a massive £16,500. Fortunately the one firm that said they could supply my needs, was the second cheapest, but for weeks they continually phoned to say certain species were unobtainable, could they change for this or that – even from foreign climes, and the problem there was aliens, but I could weed them out as they grew – one or two did turn up. Another worry was that a grass acclimatised abroad, could have difficulty when sown in our dry, chalky soil, but as this could be a problem from another part of Britain, I allowed the changes.

Unfortunately, due to rain the harvest was late, so no chance to sow before the winter. The heavy crop had also laid in many areas, leaving much straw behind. The Merrist Wood student, Edward Wills, needed tractor driving experience, and he certainly got all he needed – as the cultivator blocked every few feet in places. I reluctantly decided to join the stubble burning brigade – at least it would be the last time that I would ever need to do it. As it happened, it also turned out to be one of the last seasons in the country before it was outlawed altogether! Once the deed was done, the cultivating was an easy task, if a little on the sooty side for Edward, and he soon had a fine tilth encouraging the weed seeds to grow, he was even able to cultivate the first flush before he finished his time with us.

Protecting Rare Farmland Weeds

One innovation was a small arable plot at the top of the field, to show the school children the sort of weeds that used to grow in the farmers' arable fields. I already cultivated a small plot at the top of the Picnic Field. Only owning a cultivator meant that few seeds got buried deeply – as originally used to happen with the plough – to be brought to the surface in later years. And so the harvesting of some seeds was needed. Plants such as scarlet pimpernel and Venus's looking-glass were usually few and far between, whilst poppies, spring up, flower and seed, at the 'drop of a hat', but others need help if there is to be a 'show' during the time most schools are visiting. The cornflowers, corn-cockles and corn marigolds were collected as they ripened, and then in late summer, the plot was flailed and cultivated a few times over the course of a few dry days – to frizzle up

the grasses, docks and thistles. In the autumn or spring –
during a dry period – the plot was cultivated again, and the
gathered seeds broadcast and harrowed in. with a final
firming down with the tractor tyres – in lieu of a roller – as a
final touch. Over the seasons there was always a profusion
of flowers, and I found that autumn cultivating and sowing
favoured the Corn-cockles, and in spring, the Poppy. The
Corn Marigold would not have grown in this area, as they
prefer sandy soil, so they needed constant help to survive.

That plot had sat a little like a fish out of water in the
Picnic Field, so a band of trees and shrubs would separate
this new plot from the rest of Varley's Field. Because of the
mild winter, I was able to cultivate out a second crop of
weeds over the whole field in mid-February, before getting
on with this planting. I was rushing to finish, before
promised rain or nightfall overtook me, when through the
gloom, I spied a couple of regular visitors hastening along.
'Look dear, isn't that Mr Clark?' 'Of course not silly, Mr
Clark doesn't work, he just walks about,' said the husband. I
straightened up to tread in the tree, 'There, I knew it was
him,' said his wife. 'Oh dear you are planting trees, who on
earth decided that?' 'Yes indeed, what bad planning, we
always stop here to admire the view across this field,'
interjected her husband. 'It was my plan, I will argue the
reasons with you another day,' I said with a wry smile, and
turned to plunge my spade in the next spot as they went on
their way, still grumbling. I had just two or three plants to
go, when I heard, 'There's someone digging over there.'
And a lady came quite close as I bent down to place the tree
in its hole. 'Oh, how marvellous, come and look darling,
Mr Clark is planting trees; you have no idea how many times
we have stood in this corner and said how bare it looks. Are
you going to plant the whole field, it could certainly do with
it!' The following day I was able to hand broadcast the corn
cockles and various other flowers and the, 'Arable Plot' was
done and dusted.

Except for cultivating out another crop of weeds, it
was April before the rest became dry enough to think about

seeding. With the forecast for only three more dry days, I decided to get the job done. At 6.00 am on the 23rd I was driving the little Ferguson 35 tractor up and down – with a home-made levelling bar fixed behind the spring-tine cultivator – and by 8.00 pm I had driven over every inch of the field in three different directions leaving it reasonably level and firm. The following day, as soon as it was daylight – headlights are not much help when not leaving a mark – although it was really too windy for seed sowing with the borrowed machine, I made a start on the sheltered side of the field. Luckily the wind dropped away, and I carried on sprinkling the fourteen varieties of grass and flower seeds until by evening I had broadcast two thirds of the seed in two directions. Unfortunately the TV weather forecast brought the next lot of rain forward from the following evening to midday. I had planned, whilst broadcasting the last seed in the third direction, to hook up harrows behind to cover the seed, then finish by rolling the field. So, at 3.00 am I coupled up the roll behind the harrows behind the drill behind the tractor, and although having to drive in a lower gear, I had a good mark to steer by in the headlights. At 11.00 am I pulled my 'train' off the field as the last specks of seed scattered into the gateway, and rushed the borrowed seed-drill back to the farmer in Stapleford – getting caught in the rain as I drove back up the hill!

Wendy's Gold

I was sitting at my desk on March 21st 1985, perusing a catalogue for wild seeds and plants, when I heard a knock on the door. The lady apologised for being a nuisance, but explained that she had come on behalf of her son, Joe Sharman, a horticultural student at Writtle Agricultural College. 'We believe a rare snowdrop is in the grounds here; could he have one?' I said that it was usually not our policy to allow plants to be taken, especially rare ones, but we could at least have a look. I collected a trowel, and as we walked along I was acquainted with a little of her son's history. Joe was a keen member of various horticultural groups, one of which was concerned about the loss of old varieties, and as a hobby, he searched the vicinity of old houses and gardens, and had already found some rare and uncommon plants, but he was especially keen on snowdrops. I soon realised that we were heading towards a group of yellow centred snowdrops, and remarked as such. Mrs Sharman stopped in astonishment, 'Good gracious, how long have you known about them?' 'About 11 years,' I answered, 'My wife and I usually make a point of looking at them each spring – the clump is particularly good this year.' As I knelt to dig a bulb from the edge of the clump, Mrs Sharman exclaimed, 'Bless my soul, there is Joe!' I stood up, in my hand a large lumpy bulb with three flowers attached. I was introduced to Joe, and he was informed of events so far. He turned to me, 'You knew they were here, and never did anything about them?'

I explained that I was restoring a remnant of Cambridgeshire's chalk grassland, and only gave the garden flowers in our grounds a cursory place in my species list – at least he was able to see that I still protected them as enthusiastically as the wild ones. Any knowledge I lacked about this snowdrop though, I was hoping to now put right. 'Joe, this is about to split into three bulbs, yours with pleasure, but the price is – all that you can find out about them, they may get a special place in my plant list yet!' Payment arrived on the 26th of March! After extensive enquiries, he had found information of a similar snowdrop in the 1920s, the nearest location being the Cambridge Botanic Gardens. All had been lost – probably during a botrytis epidemic in the 1940s – he thought that the Wandlebury group were the only survivors. Surprisingly, any name had been lost too. He described how I could name and register them, and if I spent a couple of years building the numbers up, there was a good possibility that they would sell for more than £6 per bulb. However – Joe's letter went on – you will need to hide them and take great care of them.

Only a day or so later, I saw an elderly man diligently quartering the snowdrop areas: I immediately dug them up and hid them in my garden. At the next management meeting of the CPS, I spoke of my snowdrop problem and suggested we should sell them to a bulb growing company. Agreement was given, and I posted off blooms to likely firms. The 'Procurement Manager' of the Horticultural Marketing Arm of Geest's, replied the following week. Later, as we looked at the pot of bulbs, he remarked, 'Your flower caused quite a stir when I showed it to my colleagues.' I explained that I did not want to be accused of losing a rare snowdrop by taking it from the home where it had thrived for so long, so one bulb was to remain with me, and it was to be understood that Joe Sharman had potentially three bulbs, and could do as he wished with them: also if Joe and myself did successfully increase our bulb numbers, we would give Wisley and Cambridge Botanic Gardens samples. And finally, the snowdrop was to be known as, 'Wendy's Gold' in honour of my wife, who had given me so much help and encouragement in looking after Wandlebury. Without a quibble he made an offer of £250 for the 27 remaining bulbs and said good-bye.

An expert from their 'Quality Control' department was next to arrive, wanting to examine the bulbs for disease. He gave an enthusiastic appraisal, mentioning that his boss had flown to Holland with the flower. I expressed my disappointment at the low price being offered for such a rare flower. A few days later a letter arrived giving three alternatives. A £1,000 outright payment, a £250 payment, with a five pence royalty per bulb over five years, or a £500 payment plus £500 worth of trees and shrubs for Wandlebury. I had at that time planted all the trees I needed, and being a firm believer in the, 'bird in the hand' theory, I accepted a £1,000 cheque on behalf of the CPS.

Brewing Mead

Of all the, 'small' gales, the Christmas Eve one in 1985 was the most upsetting for we always had a lot of visitors during the Christmas holiday. I cycled round at daybreak, expecting to have to put out the closed notices, but finding only two trees – out of the seven down – blocking paths, and a single hanging branch, I dashed home for my equipment. By midday, exceedingly sweaty, dirty, and feeling guilty that Wendy was having none of my help with the family 'get-together', I dragged the last trunk off the path with the tractor. Seeing a family group approaching, I jumped down to hurl a couple of small branches out of their path. One lady stopped briefly as they passed, and loudly exclaimed, 'You would think that he could leave his blessed chain saw alone on Christmas Day of all days!'

This was the time of year that my wine and beer making efforts bore fruit! My occasional gallon had long since built up to as much as thirty eight in one year! The reason being, that I could give my long term volunteers a nicely presented bottle – or two – and on some tasks, whole groups could be treated to a glass of cider or beer. To prove to the recipients that they were getting something a little special, I attached a copy of my latest prize card. I was now judging wine at village shows – and of course could no longer enter my own! I could still enter my beer in one show – where I often got first – as they had a separate beer judge, but on one occasion, when he didn't arrive, I was requested to take his place. I asked the steward to taste too, who thought that some were undrinkable. When he turned over the cards, he said they indicated that I had won the 'panful' – but I just gave myself a 'First', and left a note to say that the rest of the entries were, 'not up to standard!' At least my efforts were rewarded by hearing the comment – at the Wandlebury Cupola, topping out ceremony – 'Bill's champagne is better than that stuff we had at the wedding last week!'

When I joined the Cambridge Beekeepers Association in 1979 their Honey Show was held in conjunction with their AGM. It covered at most, four tables; later, in discussion with the Secretary – both of us having been voted into Committee posts half an hour earlier – we agreed that more should be made of the show, especially inviting the public to view: not only would it promote beekeeping, it could also help honey sales. Year on year the One-day Honey Show steadily grew. We moved it around various villages, in order to gain a wider audience – though opening to the public for only the afternoon, still didn't give us a very wide, 'window' The catalyst for really doing something special was our 1981 centenary. And what a display it was. On a splendid site – Our President, Mrs Townley's lawns at Fulbourn Manor – and not only a two day show in a marquee, but demonstrations too. Alas it was also very expensive – even though it was in conjunction with the Fulbourn and Teversham Garden Society – and we returned to our previous format.

A week previously to our Centenary Show, I had attended the East of England Show with my 'Spray Warning' display, and spent the between times helping the Peterborough BKA in their marquee there – the outcome being that I promised I would try to get the CBKA to take part and help in future. Then only weeks after the Centenary Show, CBKA Publicity Officer, Bob Lemon, asked if I could help, as he had been invited to stage a beekeeping exhibit at the first 'Fenland Fair.' The stage was set to require my presence at three annual beekeeping shows, fortunately, Richard Steel, another beekeeping stalwart, threw himself into making permanent show equipment and helping set up – often providing 50% of the exhibits! In 1988 – the now fully fledged 'Fenland Country Fair' considered the, 'Bob Lemon' beekeeping exhibit warranted its own marquee, and the CBKA arranged to move the Honey Show in too – Saturday for the beekeepers, Sunday and Monday for the public – and very popular it proved to be.

Most years I constructed the 'theme' exhibit – this was not too onerous, as it was used at all three shows, and I also helped fill space at the Cambridge Honey Show with a Wandlebury exhibit, which first did duty at the Cambridge Converzatione. At least I could enter my theme, in the "Z Class" of the CBKA show, so I often won a Rosette for something, other than my mead entries! One successful theme was mead making – complete with tasting. The first airing was at the East of England Show. There was much interest in the three laden tables of bubbling jars, possible ingredients and information. Even Cecil Tonsley, a beekeeping magazine editor and honey show judge – famous for his own mead-making – volunteered to man it for a while. In the dying minutes of the final day, a group of men wandered in, and despite intimating 'home-made' was not for them, asked to taste – and then commented very favourably. I noticed them in a huddle outside, as I started to pack, then one strode back in and offered £6 each for all the remaining bottles, upping his offers after each of my refusals. After his final offer of £30 was refused, he said, 'I am a BBC Producer, we have been celebrating the successful conclusion of a series and at the end of our dinner last night, we still had money in the pot, so I decided to treat us to a once in a lifetime toast, and bought a £300 bottle of wine; we are of the opinion that yours is equal to it!' As I finished my packing, an elderly Peterborough beekeeper, having collected her own mead and honey exhibits, paused by my opened bottle still on the table, 'May I have a taste of your Black Mead?' She held up the glass to the light, 'Hmm, it's clear!' Took a tentative sniff and then a sip. A look of anguish came over her face. Spitting it out, she snapped, 'Absolute rubbish,' and swept out of the marquee. By the time the Fenland Country Fair moved to Quy in 1989 and provided us with an even larger marquee, the PBKA no longer needed our help. Happily, our helper numbers had grown too and I was now only involved with one 'Honey Show'.

211

15. The author standing under the first beech tree that he planted at Wandlebury in 1974 - replacing one blown down in the 1950s. The four metre tree was dug up and transported in a wheelbarrow.

11. Damsels in Distress – The Ivy and the Holly

Damsels in Distress

Ladies needing my help seemed to happen fairly regularly. Most of those on the phone were quick and simple to deal with: 'The organisation you need to speak to is ...' Or, 'take the baby bird back to where you found it – no not the middle of the road – close by in the hedge, the parents are searching for it as we speak!' Constant alertness for the wellbeing of our visitors is a necessity, a snap decision can become quite involved. A lady gathering up her accoutrements was being harassed, and seeing me dashing over, called, 'Please help me, this horrible man has made my visit here an absolute misery!' By the time her husband had convinced me he was her husband she had driven off in their car, leaving him to walk home!

One midmorning as I was hurrying home to get tea for a volunteer group, I passed a lone lady who looked upset. I stopped, introduced myself, and asked if she was lost. Bursting into tears she leapt forward and threw her arms so tightly around my neck that I could hardly breathe, and between breathlessly kissing my face, sobbed that she was in a terrible state, and just did not know what to do, and what a wonderful man I was to stop and help her! After going up various 'blind alleys' in an effort to help – and not wanting to walk round for the rest of my life, with her arm tightly round my waist – I deemed it best to take her to the Police Station, and get help there. Making sure the child-locks were on I went inside, pleased to see an elderly sergeant behind the desk who I always found very helpful when I took in abandoned animals. 'Hello Mr Clark, what have you brought in today?' 'Well.' I hesitated, 'It is something a bit different this time, I am sure you can help, but you need to come to my car.' He followed me outside. 'I have picked up this lady in Wandlebury, who is in a bit of a state,' I explained. And whilst he stood at the driver's side, I unlocked the passenger door, and helped my passenger out. Worried that she might freak out at the sight of a policeman, I held her arm and chatted merrily to her. 'Would you believe it, this must be your lucky day, this nice policeman has said he is willing to help you.' With one bound, she was out of my grasp, and had her arms tightly round the sergeant's neck raining kisses on him. 'Oh well,' I said, 'that is good, she has taken to you, I will leave her in your capable hands.' 'Oh thank you Mr Clark. Thank you very much,' he called, as I quickly jumped in my car.

Ladies who had lost their dogs were legion – despite our policy and notices that dogs must be kept on the lead – one lady with an unruly couple, got very annoyed when I demonstrated, that with some firmness, hers could behave whilst on the lead, and suggested she should go to training classes. That I was, 'a cruel, unfeeling man,' was one of the kinder things she said during our continual confrontations. Then one cold February Sunday evening, there was a hammering on our door; and there she stood – in floods of tears. 'Oh Mr Clark, please, please help me. I have lost both my lovely dogs.' And off she dashed. Throwing on a coat, I caught up with her at the car park as she opened the back of her car to reveal the sopping wet bodies of both dogs. She had lost them during a walk by the river in the morning, and with the help of her family, had finally found them – floating at the base of a much scratched wall. The help she wanted from me, was to bury them in their, 'favourite place.' At least I would know where they were in future!

Another lady had lost her beagle, I finally found him – chomping down a long dead rabbit – She was sorry she had let him off the lead, but bone cancer and pain made it difficult to hold him. I could see by her stance that I was being told the truth, and as a concession, asked that she walked him – early or late – when few other folk were around: at least he mostly kept to heel. Just after dark one evening, I saw her car was still parked and I immediately cycled along her usual route: only to find her sitting on a tree stump. Nearby, the dog was chewing on the head of another stinking rabbit! Smiling with relief, I said, 'You seem to have a problem?' 'Nothing like the problem I shall have later,' she grimaced, 'he was sick in the car last time.' Bending down I grasped the dog firmly by the back of the neck, then with one foot on the rabbit's body, I lifted him sharply. Despite snarling, he managed to keep his teeth clenched tight enough to keep what was in his mouth. I put her lead on him, and walked with them back to the car.

As her illness progressed, a chain-smoking, overweight gentleman transported her and waited in the car for her return. After her death, he gave a donation for a group of trees to be planted in her memory, and took over walking the dog. Unfortunately the animal kept pulling him over, so I gave him the same privileges – which ensured I had to make two more rabbit chomping rescues! A couple of years after I last saw him, the CPS secretary, asked if I had any idea why £15,000 had been left to the Society specifically for Wandlebury. Fortunately, I remembered the man's name from his tree planting donation. Finally – soon after my retirement – I was told a lady was giving a handsome donation, on condition that her dog was interred at the spot her brother's ashes had been scattered: 'did I know where that was?' I was honoured to dig out the last resting place for the 'tad' overweight beagle, who had set off the train – and he was now among his first owner's memorial trees.

215

A goodly number of mothers managed to lose their children – how different the reactions in such circumstances. A mother without an 'H' in her vocabulary, but a few crude additions, who had earlier ushered her brood off the bus, was absolutely frantic, demanding that I ring the police. I refused, but said that I would cycle round to look for them. I arrived back at the car park with them as a police car drove in! After assuring the busy constable, that they were indeed the, 'lost' children, and getting a promise from the children that they would stay put, I cycled off to find mother – which was no problem – I just rode in the direction of the shouts and screams. With mother and children reunited, her final expletives were directed at me. 'I shall be writing to the f****** office, regarding your f****** unhelpful behaviour.'

The exact opposite was represented by a mother who arrived in a large car and unloaded an elegant picnic basket and half a dozen children. It was obviously her own child's birthday. Late in the afternoon I saw her glancing at her watch, as she calmly sat on a blanket and asked if she had seen her children recently? She admitted it had been some time, but expected it would not be too long before they returned. Remembering my last sighting of them, I followed their possible route out onto Roman Road: a good mile later, I was about to turn back, when with a last sweep of my binoculars, I espied a head moving above a low hedge in the distance. The birthday boy was adamant they were not lost, even when I pointed out that their every step was still taking them away from Wandlebury. We trooped along together, until I deemed it safe to go on and inform their mother. 'Oh well done Warden, I was just beginning to think I ought to contact the other parents,' she said, languidly moving her position on the blanket. I strongly suspected later, that the £10 pound note among all the two and ten pence coins in the, 'Honesty Box,' may have been her doing.

Ladies having problems with cars came my way quite often. One such incident was on a lovely summer's day, with the car park full to capacity. At such times I

216

passed through regularly to deter thieves, and seeing a lady throw her hands in the air, I dashed over, only to find she had locked up and left her keys in the ignition. At my offering to get my tools to open it for her, she looked uncomfortable, and said that she would rather get the AA – could she use my phone. I pointed out that it could be some while before they arrived – meantime I would have done the job. It was a very new looking car, and my mention of tools probably worried her: however, she agreed, adding, 'After all we can still phone the AA.'

I arrived back with my home-made bits and bobs, to see mother conversing with her daughter. whilst her young son dancing round chanting, 'Daddy is going to be very cross, etc.' I started to operate, and as the lock gave a satisfying click, mother turned and saw my metal device wrapped in a tea towel, tucked in the door. A look of horror came over her face, 'Oh no, you mustn't do that, my husband will never speak to me again if you damage his car.' I tried to explain. 'No. No. Please, just get away from it.' She turned to her daughter, 'It's no good, I shall have to phone daddy.' I opened the door, took out the keys, walked round and handed them to her. 'I don't think the AA could have done it more quickly.' Her mouth fell open; she looked at the car door standing wide. 'You can't have taken a minute.' 'The latch was an unusual one,' I explained with a smile. She spoke to her daughter, 'Oh my goodness, whatever is Daddy going to say when I tell him?' Then turning to me, 'His last car was stolen and he went to great trouble to get a car with thief proof locks!'

One especially memorable occasion occurred on a cold and misty November day. Cambridge and Oxford students were about to battle it out with a series of running races around the paths – A little akin to the University Boat Race, but with a much smaller audience. On a couple of previous occasions runners had collapsed, so I cycled around in case I needed to dash off to phone for an ambulance. I noticed one girl walking unsteadily through the woods, and when I saw Wendy walking the dog, I asked if she would mind keeping an eye, 'I think that girl is drunk!' However she returned immediately to say she was now sitting on a bench, and we both went our separate ways. As the last race came to a conclusion, I noticed Wendy franticly waving and pointing. I dashed over, to see the girl now lying down, with vomit dribbling from her mouth. Wendy was already running! I immediately went into 'First Aid' mode, placing the girl in the recovery position. I was pleased to find a pulse – though weak – and see pieces of white pills dribbling forth. Inside her handbag was an empty vodka bottle, and two empty aspirin bottles. The ambulance soon arrived – with Wendy in the passenger seat directing the driver. I later remarked to Wendy, 'Let's hope she considers we did the right thing.' A few weeks later a letter arrived – profuse thanks for saving her life.

It might seem strange to some people, but I have often had to go to the aid of plants too. You only need to look at the bark of any tree near a footpath, to get some idea of the number of folk I have spoken to, who walk along bashing at trunks and stems with sticks – and probably a similar number thwacking flower-heads off. But one needs to take care in one's approach to such people, as an elderly visitor discovered. He had seen me remonstrating with a lad striking off the cowslip flower-heads. So, when he saw three boys – and their father – acting similarly on the verges of the Roman Road, spoke to them. The angry father turned his stick on him – leaving him lying with a fractured skull!

A Good Word for Ivy

From time to time I go into print to help the ivy – usually in answer to published letters and articles wanting a purge on it. Despite the popular conviction, I have never seen a mature tree killed by ivy! Of the 250 huge Beeches that died on this estate during the 1976 drought – when I reckoned that the ivy must be competing with the trees for water – no dead trees were ivy covered: but among the

1,700 that remained, many of the healthiest had ivy covered trunks. I decided that the ivy had protected these thin barked trees from sun scorch. Of a further 3,000 mixed species lost in various gales, only four were heavily ivy covered – even I had thought that an ivy covered tree would be more vulnerable in a gale! Of our 600 Elms that were lost to 'Dutch Elm Disease' I noticed that the ivy covered ones were the last to go – I believe the ivy camouflaged the trees from the causative beetles (mainly *Scolytes scolytes*) which seek out the living trees by scent in order to feed on the young shoots, thereby introducing the fungus. In really hard winters, ivy covered trees did not suffer from frost crack – which spoils the timber for future marketing. (Ash trees are still being cut down with ancient frost crack present.) Continuous observation shows that ivy spreads vigorously over dead and dying trees after leaf loss lets in more light – the casual observer then believing the ivy caused the tree's demise. On many dead trees, branches that could be dangerous, are held in place by the ivy, so gradually disintegrating rather than crashing down – which is good for the 60% of woodland wildlife that depends on rotting wood in part, or all, of its life-cycle!

Ivy provides nest sites in one way or another, to a greater variety and number of birds than any other shrub; helping to make up for some of the thousands of miles of lost hedgerows. Similarly, because of the loss of hollow elms to disease, many of the larger birds that nested in them, now frequently use the thickly ivy covered crutches of trees. It is also our last shrub to flower, providing heavy yields of nectar and pollen – a final and often only food source – for a variety of insects, including bees, beetles, hoverflies and butterflies. In fact, butterfly species such as Comma, Small Tortoiseshell, Large Tortoiseshell, Peacock and Camberwell Beauty – many of whose last broods go into winter as butterflies – search for ivy flowers because they need to build up body-fat before they go into their winter torpor: interestingly, you can look at ten ivy covered trees in the shade and not see a butterfly, look at the next in full sun –

when it smells most honey-like – and count them by the dozen! I believe some of the visiting Red Admiral and Painted Lady butterflies – two more ivy nectar imbibers – are now managing to hibernate here because of our milder winters. After feeding up on the nectar and pollen, many of these insects then snuggle under the ivy mat on tree trunks and walls – especially lacewings and ladybirds which devastate the hated aphids the following year. Ivy is also the last of our berries to ripen, and coupled with the insect life hiding in its depths, feeds many birds just when food is most scarce – at winter's end.

It can also be linked with the Holly – besides in the much loved Christmas carol – through the Holly Blue butterflies, *Celastrina argiolus*, which emerge in April/May from chrysalides attached under the ivy leaves: they mate and then the females search for a holly tree, and lay their eggs on the flower buds. Once hatched, the tiny caterpillars start by devouring the opening flowers, later eating the developing berries – those that get laid on the male flowering trees, have to move onto tender young leaves – eventually pupating in chrysalides attached under the holly leaves. This brood emerges in July/August, when after mating, the females go looking for ivy flower buds on which to lay their eggs – so giving rise to the caterpillars, which after finishing on young ivy berries, will go into pupation and start the cycle once again the following May. I have also seen them laying eggs on Spindle and Dogwood flowers, and others mention Snowberry, Buckthorn, Furze and Bramble. In some areas, it is known only as a single spring brood, which makes me wonder if there are two distinct families, with only the single brood one managing to survive where there is no ivy! There are times when their numbers crash. Ted Ellis was overjoyed in June 1974, when, just as he had decided that this time they could be extinct, I phoned him, to say I had just seen two flying around our holly trees.

If ivy is allowed to grow on young saplings it can strangle and smother them – on large trees, the growth just

220

bursts the ivy apart, but a continuous canopy of ivy can cast so much shadow below, that ground flora struggles to survive. A carpet of it over the woodland floor can certainly cause the demise of most other woodland plants! And left in a hedge, even an annually trimmed one, it can smother that too. It can be both, 'good' and 'bad' on buildings! Growing on old brick or stone walls, with poor, or none existent mortar, ivy will creep between, and lever them apart as it thickens up. But on house and barn walls in good condition, it is a good insulator and keeps them dry – allowed to creep up under tiles and guttering though, it will lever those apart too, letting in the weather. Folk mistake the suckers that hold the ivy to its support as roots. However, if any is growing through trapped rotting leaves or on a permanently wet wall, it will very quickly develop roots at that point, and cause big trouble.

In my dealings with ivy, each and every case was carefully assessed before deciding whether action was needed – much damage can be done to tree trunks by inconsiderate use of chain saws and axes. Every last root has to be severed before it will die, for the vines will be fused together, so forming a common nutrient supply across the network – once dead, it falls away without damage to bark or wall surface. I never cut offending vines against the tree trunk, but locate them at soil level, wrenched them out or cutting through with a stock axe. Using a heavy duty 'navvy's' fork, I have levered and rolled patches of it up like a carpet on the woodland floor, and cleared acres using a small tractor and spring-tine cultivator – adjusted to just scratch the surface. It was quite gratifying to see the variety of woodland flowers that appeared after such treatment.

Similarly, after cultivating Varley's field, just about every variety of weed imaginable appeared there, although we must have thinned them by the fourth cultivation – One botanist has estimated that over one hundred million poppy seeds can be lying dormant in one acre of land, and I know from my own observations, that they can remain viable for well over 60 years. The most prolific weed was 'fat hen', and after flail mowing the thickest patches in June, I moved the sheep in during July, and they gratefully removed the tender regrowth in days. Unfortunately, the half kilo of cowslip seed that I had ordered separately – at a cost of £65 – had arrived too late to go in the drill, and so after vernalising them in the freezer, I sowed them by hand – some three seeds to every square metre. Now, in the following spring, I was quartering the field looking for any sign of them – they can lay dormant for two or even three seasons – when a lady visitor called out to say that she had a present for me. Handing over a litre sized yogurt pot, she gave a quizzical smile, as she waited for me to open it. 'Cowslip seed!' I exclaimed. She had collected them from her own meadow. I thanked her profusely, and raced home to put them in the freezer. A day or so later, I threaded a string handle through two holes in the top of the pot, made another tiny hole in the base, and once in Varley's, hung it from the handlebars of my cycle, and rode around until the pot was empty.

I also continued hand planting another sixteen varieties of grass and some thirty varieties of flowers – quaking grass for instance would have cost £150 per kilo to buy. I have always been a bit of a thorn in the sole of the 'PC' brigade. They peer at the replaced flowers and grasses wanting to know if they are indigenous – and if they are not locally sourced, they prefer not to have them at all. Some ninety-eight percent of Wandlebury's original meadow flora had gone by 1973. Even if it had been allowed, I would not have dreamed of taking plants from nearby reserves, SSSI's and such like. I made friends with the head green keeper of the nearby Gog Magog Golf Club – he was very keen on keeping the wild flower content of the 'rough', and he allowed me to collect many varieties of seeds from there in 1974-5 when it shone blue with wild flax. However, most of those areas of flowers have now disappeared because of the present, more frequent mowing regime. Whether on the Golf Course or any other permissive area, I still passed very rare seeds by, though I did purloin five seeds of Pasque flower from the Devil's Ditch, and Wendy grew four plants from them, later supplying me with dozens of plants grown from their seeds – although rabbits and thieves have successfully ensured not one plant has survived out in the meadows! On July the 7th 1977, I counted no less than 68 pyramidal orchids flowering on the Roman Road, just the other side of Worsted Lodge, but as there were still two on Wandlebury, there was no need to return for any seed.

One or two 'CAMBIENT' members still grouched about the 'new' plants growing on Wandlebury, and Terry Wells, a noted ecologist based at Monks Wood, visited me on a few occasions during the 1970s and 80s and gave words of caution – later he too was an enthusiastic sponsor of rehabilitating flower meadows, also getting grumbled at by the purists: I would like to think it was I who helped change his mindset! Wandlebury would certainly be much different if no reintroduction's had taken place – although I must confess, I do dig up those coloured cowslips that occur from time to time, because some errant bumblebee has visited our neighbour's polyanthus first. But who knows what we should expect to be native once all has been lost? Which period in history should we choose? Many people have suggested that it would be nice to favour the Iron Age period for Wandlebury: that would mean getting rid of practically all of the woodland, certainly the beech, and cultivating much of the rest!

Fagus

For nine years Bruce had been a great favourite with most of the visitors whenever he was out walking, as well as a friend and guard to Wendy – and the near neighbours – when I was out at the many evening talks and meetings. Then one day he started to limp, and a visit to Larry acquainted us with the news that he had, 'hip dysplasia.' Drugs kept him going for his last two years, before, once again, Larry had the unpleasant duty of telling us our dog was in pain, and it was time to let him go. A police 'Dog Section' sergeant said he would keep me in mind, but the weeks went by: so we discussed buying one, but felt guilty at not giving a deserving dog a fresh start, and decided to visit a well-known dog's home. Among the dogs we thought suitable, were two pups – but with the condition that they must stay together. We had plenty of room for two dogs, but jibbed at the thought of the extra bills, but by the time we had patrolled past the appealing pair a few times, we were ready to sign all the necessary papers, and returned home to await their inspector's visit.

A couple of days later a lady called, I recognised her immediately as a visitor who gave me trouble from time to time; refusing to only let her dog off the lead in the 'dog run'. My heart sank when she said she was the Inspector come to look at my kennel facilities. Then, squaring my shoulders, I thought, 'There is nothing she can find fault with here.' How wrong I was! Our kitchen was too small for starters! As was the two metre high, by just over two metres square, outside kennel, built with 12 mm marine ply. 'Most unsatisfactory; the poor things will be frozen in the winter.' I triumphantly swung the door open, to show what had been Bruce's purpose built hospital quarters – a fully insulated inner room, with a suspended ceiling, and 'walk through' plastic curtain. And to silence her totally, I swung up the curtain to show the electric heater. She sniffed, bent down and examined the heater. 'Just as I thought, utterly useless, only 500 watts.' Outside again, she glanced around the large sheep-netting run. 'And as for this run, nowhere for a dog to get out of the wind and far too low. I am sorry Mr Clark, but I am going to have to refuse permission for you to have our dogs.' I thought to myself, 'I may be a little firmer with you the next time we meet,' but sadly she never gave me the satisfaction.

That weekend I located a dog – eleven months old and last of the litter – a bit boisterous, but we fell for him immediately, paid the £100 asked and, large though he was, he travelled home cuddled up on Wendy's lap. We named him Fagus – the Latin name for the beech tree family. He proved more difficult than Bruce to train, and probably due to two loose dogs attacking him on one of his first walks, I was never able to stop him from trying to get in the first nip; so we always needed to be watchful.

Some of his stroppy manner may also have been sparked off by a police dog during his second week with us! Steve phoned to say he had just seen someone climb over the wall round East House garden. As I ran to the scene with Fagus, a car without lights raced towards me. I flashed my torch – stepping smartly to one side as it swept past – but getting the registration as it roared off. Two figures then loomed out of the darkness. Switching on my torch, revealed Steve seemingly about to grasp a man's arm and the glint of a long knife in the man's other hand. I shouted, 'Jump away Steve, he's got a knife!' At the same time, pulling Fagus into my light beam. I had left Wendy dialing the usual number, so all we needed to do was slow him down – he was now in whining mode. A police car at last turned in and the man's demeanour instantly changed, ranting and raging until he was handcuffed, when he quietened down again. I had seen his knife fly into shrubs as the police arrived, and this was soon retrieved. Luckily a second car with two more policemen arrived just as the car that had sped out returned, and a huge bruiser of a man leapt out, and dashed among us.

All hell now broke loose, as, shouting and bawling every obscenity, he demanded that his partner be set free. Fagus alternately acted nervously and excitedly, his excitement notching up a gear, when a large, snarling Alsatian leapt out of the next police vehicle to skid to a halt. I moved away, but Fagus still had a very exciting time before the drink and drug crazed men were loaded aboard a police van. Even then, we could hear banging and shouting until the van was some distance off. Fagus went on to save my hide on a number of occasions, and was especially on guard when staying in the house. If I happened to be out, woe betide any family friend that visited. Fagus would tell

Wendy – in the strongest terms – that no one must be allowed in when the 'Master' is away.

He got quite adept at leading me to anything that he thought needed my attention, and would look at me in disgust when we were elsewhere, and I declined to pick up any litter he had noticed! His most memorable accomplishment was on a very frosty night, when he refused to go past a large blackberry bush. I pulled at him and told him not to be stupid. 'Probably a fox, or a mixey rabbit,' I muttered, and tugged more forcefully. Again he refused, trying to go under the bush: so I got down on my knees, shone my torch, and there in the light was a small boy, curled beneath a plastic mac, and shivering violently. I radioed Wendy to have a hot drink ready, and after putting the lad at ease, took hold of his freezing hand to help him out. His only clothing being a light tee-shirt and short trousers, I wrapped my own heavy tweed jacket around him and hurried home. Fagus had a good life until arthritis caught up with him, though due to the expertise of Larry, he still enjoyed further pain-free years – but soon after my retirement he deteriorated, and Larry volunteered to take care of him so he would not have to leave his home patch. I learnt afterwards that it was Larry's last veterinarian 'act'.

16. Young Bill looking over to Cambridge - showing a class the joys of the countryside.

17. Wandlebury in Autumn 1983 - A reminder of what much of the Wandlebury woodlands once looked like.

18. Wendy and Bruce about half way down the Roman Road Avenue of four metre high trees. Most of the tall trees on the right crashed onto it in the October 1987 gale.

19. Roman Road Avenue 2008 - checking for grey squirrel bark stripping damage.

20. *Putting the etherings on the first hedge I had laid since helping my grandfather in the 1940's. Cambridge Evening News.*

229

21. Drawings for the 1991 Beekeeper's Annual, illustrating my tale of taking a swarm of bees out of the lions' cage at Linton Zoo. Drawn by Luke.

12. The Worst Storm Since 1703 and a Roman Ghost

The Great Storm

Much of my early tree planting was now getting tall enough to deflect the wind, and I took to mentioning this in my talks, slotting in slides showing how this led me to believe that fewer of the old trees would fall, even though I expected more frequent gales. On Thursday October the 15th 1987, I took a whole day off! A fellow member of the Arboricultural Association had phoned from Sussex, hoping that I could look at the Jockey Club's beech trees alongside the old Bury St Edmunds road at Newmarket, to see if they were starting to drop 'mast' (seeds) yet. They were a registered seed stand, and he had a gathering contract. I had a good idea at what stage the mast would be at, for the soil and weather conditions there were similar to our own, and I hoped to gratefully seize the opportunity to gather some for Wandlebury. By 10.00 am Wendy and I were walking beneath the fine canopy. The trees were much younger than those at Wandlebury, yet collectively, nearly all as tall and straight as our very best tree. Whoever planted them had not only purchased good seed, but taken extreme care in the weeding, thinning, and branch trimming during the formative years. Seed was falling from about one in ten of the trees, and we rushed back to the car for broom, shovel and sacks. With Wendy holding the sacks open, we had

231

three filled to the brim within half an hour. Back home, I phoned to say – weather permitting – a start could be made in a week's time, but I would check again the following Wednesday.

That evening I attended a Management meeting – reporting that we were at last on top of the woodland management and in my view, the place had never looked better, though cautioned that there was a forecast for strong winds and, because we had recently had some 15 mm of rain, there was the possibility we might lose a tree or two overnight. After watching the late weather forecast, and listening to Michael Fish reassure us that we were certainly 'NOT in for a cyclone' – it even looked as if East Anglia could miss it all together – I climbed into bed and slept like the proverbial log. At 4.30 am, hammering and rattling on the windows woke me. I sat up and listened for a moment and decided the wind sounded fairly strong. 'Damn, we are going to lose some trees,' I thought, and drifted back to sleep. The next time I woke the whole house was shuddering, and a bright glow emanated through the drawn curtains. I leapt over to the window, calling, 'Wendy, there is a fire outside!' What a sight met my eyes as I threw back the curtains and the daylight streamed in. Our house, surrounded by trees, often needed a light to read by, day or night, but not any more! The only three trees still standing close were the ones on the side that would have crashed on us in bed if they had fallen!

Remembering what happened after the 1976 'blow', when all the local machinery sales people ran out of equipment and spares, I rushed into my workshop to assess what was needed to keep the chain saws in continuous operation for weeks ahead. Whilst I was doing this task, I had Wendy's little battery radio with me, and it was soon obvious that 1976 paled into insignificance. In fact the media insisted on calling it a 'hurricane'. Certainly this gale covered a large area; the whole of southern and eastern England seemed to be at a standstill – and in deep shock. Having completed my list of needs, I removed the one small plum tree blocking my way out onto the road, and drove to the home of the Duxford Hire and Supply proprietor. Apologising for my early intrusion, I handed him my list. Giving it a cursory glance, he said he was just leaving to open early, and invited me to accompany him, but I explained that things were needing my urgent attention, and I would pick up my order later.

Back at Wandlebury I clambered out into the park to decide which road needed the least clearing to allow staff and residents safe passage, and left my assistant Steve Donoclift with a group of volunteer residents – who, like thousands of other folk, were going nowhere – cutting and dragging away the branches of Wandlebury's biggest – and probably oldest – beech tree, currently blocking all the routes. The same tree that only a month before had been featured, with me standing beneath, in a two page spread in the Cambridge Evening News, entitled: 'Leading the 'Good Life' as beauty spot's keeper.' – The same tree that I often paused under, describing to children the different people and vehicles that had passed below its spreading branches. The same tree that after an earlier storm, one child had asked, 'Why is this tree still standing Mr Clark?' And I had patiently explained how it had grown so large because it was in some of the best and deepest soil on Wandlebury, this meant that it had grown a massive root system too, ensuring it found enough moisture even whilst others suffered, making it the healthiest tree on the estate, and giving it a strong anchorage. In fact, I had said, 'This tree is so strong, it will only die of old age many years from now!'

I needed a rough idea of numbers of trees down, but it had already taken half an hour to scramble the distance of a previous five minute walk, so I made my way to a tall fir tree that was still standing, but with the top blown out, and climbed that. Through my binoculars I could see devastation in every direction! Certainly over 300 beech down. I could now give the timber buyer a rough idea – he would need to act quickly to sign up a contractor. With Caroline's car blocked in, I was hoping that, in return for driving her to Mills and Reeve Solicitors – where she worked as the receptionist – I would be allowed to use one of their phones. Despite my dishevelled appearance, I was taken straight into one of the Partners' offices and, to my surprise got straight through to the timber merchants. Then I eventually got through to the power and phone engineers and, after giving my profuse thanks to the concerned solicitors, returned to my car. As the engine started, the radio also sparked into life. A BBC Radio Cambridgeshire announcer was speculating on the damage in the area, and realising they had probably been trying to contact me, I drove into the radio station car park, close by the Mills and Reeve offices. I was immediately ushered into the studio where Christopher South was about to start his broadcast. It was a highly charged interview. Christopher had passed by Wandlebury and, having seen fallen trees from the road, wanted a fuller account of the devastation. Although I was having some difficulty speaking, I said that there must be over a thousand trees down, and that people should keep away because of all the danger – broken branches were still dropping in every breeze. We would be closed for some time. Many folk said afterwards, that that interview affected them more than the television pictures they saw later.

I next drove on to Duxford Hire, acutely aware it was now after their Saturday closing time, only to find a long queue aligned out into their car park. As I walked past, all was a hubbub of, 'my neighbour's car,' – 'barn roof gone,' – 'a huge branch,' – 'a massive tree,' – 'lucky to be alive!' Many had chain saws in their hands needing urgent maintenance. I walked to the counter, a harassed face smiled in recognition. 'My goodness Mr Clark, you knew a thing or two this morning!' He retreated through a door; returning with a large cardboard box and heaved it onto the counter, then passed over the invoice to me, commenting, 'You are a very lucky man, that chain saw is not only my last one, it is the last in East Anglia.' As I checked through the list, his wife called to him, 'The phone for you.' He stepped into his office, spoke briefly, and returned to me. 'I would like to rephrase my last remark! There is probably not another new chainsaw available in Britain, certainly not a Husqvarna.' I thought I had better get out before I was mugged by an angry crowd.

Back on home ground, a quick assessment showed that the route along the phone line was mostly fallen saplings – the easiest to clear – and by 3.00 pm, all was ready for the maintenance crew. Moving over to the more difficult task of clearing a track for the 'power' workers, I found that the 'big beech' had snapped the 11,000 volt cables at the terminal pole and decided to start there, clearing a straight line through the twenty or so beech tree tops, using the further poles as a sight line. I first cut forward as far as the saw could reach on my left, then similarly cut through a metre or so over to my right. Constantly stopping to throw these short pieces from under foot gave me a nice clear pathway and allowed the new saw to cool down. The aluminium cables lay in the mess somewhere, and although they were now scrap, needed to be located; the steel core would destroy my cutting chain in a split-second. It wasn't until some twenty metres of path had been cleared, that a loop came into view and, about to pull on it to find the broken end, I had the ludicrous thought, 'This could still be live.' So instead, carefully cut round it, watching out for the second cable. After another two or three paces of sawing and throwing, my visor began to fog over – well I was working hard – and I swung it up out of the way. To my astonishment, steam was rising from the ground, and my feet were getting hot inside my rubber 'chainsaw' boots. Just under the next branch lay the end of a cable, glowing red and gently sizzling!

Against all my expectations, a phone-line repair crew was on the scene at 8.30 the next morning with the electrical engineers arriving soon after. It was then all that Steve and I could do, to keep ahead of them. Just after midday, Lou the timber buyer – who had come out of retirement – called in to look round, and give me the good news that he had signed up a contractor to start on the

Tuesday. Though my heart sank to my very boots when he said that, despite contacting a long list of contractors, the only one available was my old adversary from 1976. However, I was too busy in my workshop straightening pylon cross bars and making old bolts reusable for the electrical engineers, to dwell on that. As a result of our efforts, just after 5.00 pm Wendy was astonished to hear the purr of the freezer motor – although there was also a down side for her. With the phone back on, she was constantly interrupted by concerned friends and well-wishing strangers: especially on Monday morning, when by late lunch time, she had managed to slot in – and keep happy with tea, coffee and scones – local and national newspaper reporters and photographers, television, and radio presenters, whilst I struggled to give each individual attention. Her last call that day, was the welcome news, that the County Council had granted a temporary footpath closure order – with none of the kerfuffle of the 1976 occasion.

It was a continuing surprise to me at how much love and concern was directed at Wandlebury from such a wide area. Entire schools and individual classes, youth groups and adult groups of every denomination, as well as families and individuals, were raising funds. And more than once I was told, 'We said prayers for you in our church Mr Clark!' Even poets put pen to paper. Of the poems sent me, the one that still stirs me, was from Wendy's brother in law, Denis Griffiths, who visited just after the storm.

WITH THE WARDEN

I follow Bill the Warden
On slippery mud
Through darkening trees
Stricken by the storm
Drought and disease
Denuded as if
By a bombardment.

Beeches and elms
Fallen and felled
Are everywhere:
Dead monsters, dragons
Weighty and grey
Efficiently dropped
In their deep tracks.

I stick to Bill:
He deals with dragons:

Or are they shafts
From flying saucers
Circling the earth
Whose data registered
This habitat
2,000 years
Or more ago?

Somewhere around
The ancient figures
Of Gog and Magog
Look up in chalk
Look up and wait.

Wandlebury darkens:
Bill points to trees
Yet to be felled:
Trees he knows well
As friends old friends
Talking to them
Even in the damp dusk.

His world is falling:
Wood stacks abound
Cut from the dead:
Smoke rises, drifts

And the saw screams:

I follow Bill closely
Avoiding dead dragons
The length of trains
And heavy as hell
Stumbling over mantraps
Of stiffening branches

Hoping to see soon
The warm light
Beckoning from Bill's house.

The feller didn't arrive as promised. As things stood, I was confident the timber would pay for the clearing, but any delay could jeopardise that. With so much timber coming onto the market the price could fall. At last I managed to contact him. He apologised. He was awaiting the delivery of a Bray loader, and would definitely be with us on the following Tuesday. This new tractor was good news, for it was his use of his Drott that had caused most of the damage on the previous occasion – slewing huge holes in the ground, and bruising nearby trees. Meanwhile I had set the crews of three log merchants as well as five individuals collecting their own fuel, clearing logs and tree tops along the road and tracks. I assessed the quantity of logs in each top or group of tops, we agreed a price, and I collected the money before the work was started. It was essential they only cut logs they had bought, did no damage to any trunks, and only drove along stipulated routes – so I kept my eyes peeled. And by the end of the first day – after one crew 'lost' a brand new log splitting axe – I also put them to work at good distances apart!

On Friday morning, our neighbour phoned to say that he wanted to start sugar-beet harvesting at the end of the following week. With nine huge beech trees lying on his field, he was worried that he could miss his loading dates at the factory. As it happened, these trees were next to the avenue we had cleared and replanted in 1976, and desiring to keep to a similar order of clearing the estate, they were first on my agenda. Minutes after the call, yet another firewood merchant arrived to enquire after timber. In the field, I told him, that providing he started work the next morning, and cut up all nine tops, and stacked the logs neatly along the hedgerow before Thursday, he could have one top for free, and me and my volunteers would burn all the brushwood.

I still had my father's – now heirloom – sugar beet fork, and topping knife; and rushed to the field, to lift, top, and throw the beet into heaps ready for the farmer to collect, working from the gateway and along the headland towards the first tree, then under and around it. By nightfall it was ready for the merchant to start in the morning. Luckily the trees had all fallen obliquely onto the field, but it still meant that I had lifted half an acre by the time I finished. If my father was still around to read this, I can just hear his comment; 'Only half an acre, you don't know you have been born!' Sadly, the large beech trees on the other side of the avenue were all now laying on the four metre high, 1977 planted trees. Bill Scoble and I scrambled the quarter mile length, and to our surprise, discovered that only one tree was completely destroyed. Bill volunteered – with his family often helping too – to do the delicate clearing. All the feller had to do, was cut off his trunks, and drag them out to the side track. Six months or so later, after my team had picked up all the logs, and I had 'guyed' up three badly leaning trees, the young avenue looked unscathed.

On Tuesday morning my pulse calmed a little, as a noticeably mature feller climbed out of his van, helped further, when I could see no sign of a monster chainsaw! He apologised for the lack of his two assistants, they were still finishing his last job, and walked over to meet a low-loader just arriving with the enormous Bray – once used for compacting and levelling rubbish, and still bearing a 'City of London Corporation' logo on the cab. He joyfully leapt on board and off-loaded it, then jumped down and circled it, chuckling like a child with a new toy, only to climb back in again, and with a shout to me, 'Right now let's see what she can do,' roared up the car park to the big tree trunk blocking the back road and still attached to thirty tonnes of root system. The tractor's fork tines rammed under the trunk, lifting it a little, before the rear wheels started to come off the ground. I waited with baited breath for a hydraulic hose to burst: but he lowered the fork, and grinning from ear to ear, yelled, 'What about that then?' Then reversing out, attacked it again – closer to the sawn off end – and with a lifting, a roaring, and a skidding of wheels, the mighty Bray swung the massive trunk off the road. That done, I led the way over to the sugar-beet field. With the first trunk trimmed, severed from its roots, measured and tagged, he trundled off with it like a dog carrying a stick. But as he thumped it down, the tractor lurched up, and the radiator cooling fan snapped off with a bang!

Leaving him trimming out trunks, I went off to locate a mechanic and when the fellow arrived the next morning, I introduced him and left them to it. Marshall's at Cambridge Airport, had offered to fly me over the estate on the next available sunny day to photograph the damage, and this was it. I was hoping a series of photos from the air would allow me to make a better count of trees down. Alas, despite many photos, it couldn't be done. Back with Jepps I noticed water dripping from the Bray. The fan had damaged the radiator when it snapped! He drove it to my workshop that evening, where I spent till late, constructing and soldering. A pleased Philip lifted the remaining trunks off the beet field, unfortunately, he thudded the last trunk down, again giving the tractor a large jolt. I heard a ping like a bullet, and a jet of water spurted out – a piece of the welded fan had shot into the radiator. I spent another evening soldering and re-welding the fan. It was going to be a long haul.

240

Better Communication

During visits to other venues with the Rangers Association, it was noticeable how much use was made of small pocket radios. But despite inviting some 'big name' firms to demonstrate, the sets were useless at Wandlebury. One Rep – from a firm specialising in dealing with parks and zoos – barely moved from his car to give the briefest of demo's, before handing over three handsets, and saying he would be back in a week. These were excellent – as long as we didn't walk further apart than we could hear by shouting! When he returned – to be angrily informed of their uselessness – he calmly replied, 'Yes, I thought they would be. You will need at least four of our very best models – there is a waiting list, and the cost will be £600 each.' Now, with most of the largest trees down, I thought perhaps the situation had changed and with so many helpers in dangerous situations, I deemed personal radios to be essential – perhaps a local firm would be more helpful? A flick through 'Yellow Pages' turned up the name Bancom. And on Friday the 13th, the Rep knocked on our door. After explaining the radio's workings, he fixed a holster to my belt and asked me to call in from as many locations around the estate as possible. I cycled off, whilst he sat in his car with a similar set. Upon my return he explained that due to our undulating terrain and the trees, the pocket radios with their tiny aerials, were having difficulty bouncing the signal to one another; it needed a 'repeater station'. This would magnify the signal but it needed an aerial as high as possible. He then proceeded to climb a beech tree at the rear of my workshop, and stuck an aerial out of the top! On Saturday morning he set up the station in the workshop, and again asked me to cycle around the estate. With that done, he announced that the signal was now much better, but with some 'dead' spots. Then handing me his own pocket-set, said, 'At least your wife will be saved a lot of chasing about to find you now. You will have to manage until I can make improvements.'

Over the ensuing days, the Rep – I now knew to be Tony Sayers, owner of Bancom, and also the engineer, linesman, and office manager – was seldom off the estate. First Wendy was interrogated as to exactly where she would like the repeater/base station placed, and shown how to operate it. It needed a mains socket – two hours later one was in place. A fibreglass aerial attached to our chimney was said to be the best option and by midday Sunday it was up, cabled, and plugged in. The new system, serving four hand portables, was soon up and running and I thought it was excellent, but Tony continually popped in to tweak things – finally admitting defeat. There would always be some dead spots, he glumly told me, it required an aerial at least 30 metres high which would cost hundreds, if not thousands of pounds.

A couple of days later, about to step out of the Ring Ditch, I saw a known thief watching the car park through his binoculars. Unable to move for fear of being spotted, it soon became clear that no one was answering my calls, I was in a 'dead' spot. The thief eventually decided to depart, and I later asked Tony if a tower really was the cure-all. 'On this hill top? You would be the envy of every taxi firm in Cambridge, but the authorities will surely never allow one here. If you ever did get permission, I could also use it, fund the building work and provide your radios for free.' I put the scheme before the CPS Committee at the next meeting. The offer of a free radio system helped, but there were still those who didn't want such a thing standing in Wandlebury. Having seen a 30 metre mobile mast being used by the Cambridge Amateur Radio Club, I asked Tony's opinion of borrowing it for a trial. In next to no time Tony had transported it in, and we set it up. The test transmission was excellent and none of the invited Committee Members spotted it as they drove up – from every direction – and their opposition crumbled away. The planning application was sent off to the South Cambridgeshire District Council forthwith. With only one dissenting voice – from a member of the Stapleford Parish Council – and almost exactly a year from the day that Tony first arrived, the mast went up. It still took another five months for the Inspector to arrive from the Department of Trade and Industry, to test all the equipment and hand over Wandlebury's Broadcasting Licence, with our own, 'Fagus' call sign.

The change the radios made to our lives was incalculable – I believe I could not have survived through 1987 – 8 without them. Folk at work now always had a radio, so my rule of never allowing a person to work alone was relaxed – only to be reinstated a few weeks later, when a young man scything the footpaths was attacked by a naked pervert. (A pervert who will never again attack someone with a scythe!!) Being able to radio Wendy, meant that police or ambulances arrived in less than half the time of previously. And being able to pass on messages, or direct people to me, instead of chasing all over the place, gave Wendy back a large part of her life, although there was a downside. She had to take notice whenever a radio was used, and even if the message wasn't for her could be burdened by anxiety. For example, she could hear the shouts and threats from the confrontational gangs, and once as Steve and I searched the woods for the driver of a car left overnight – 'Fagus-one to Fagus-two, I have found the body of a man in Compartment One!'

After the mast was built, I was amazed to receive a crystal clear message from Wendy whilst I was inside the RSPB building at Sandy, and a query from Steve, when I was giving a talk to beekeepers at Silsoe. Although the cause of the most, 'air time' the one person not entrusted with a radio, was the tree feller – it would have been lost, buried or crushed within hours! I just had to stay around him as much as possible. I later heard that he had made such a mess whilst working at Windsor, that he was being sued by the 'Crown'. The one time that the Queen and I have dealings with the same person, and it is nothing to boast about!

A Drott Eases the Clear-up

A machine was urgently needed for clearing and preparing for planting, after the tree trunks were removed. Enquiries as to hire costs came to a minimum of £5,000. I made a case to the agencies giving us grants that buying our own second-hand machine would save money. Given the go ahead, on Monday the 2nd of November I visited the famous Cambridge Machinery Sale. As an adult I had continued to visit auctions – during my farming days it was mostly to sell cattle and pigs, and much of our earlier furniture was also bought that way. But now all memory of the tractor drawn Claas combine harvester in perfect working order – worth in excess of £300 – that I had bought for £16.50p in a Colchester auction – had to be expunged from my mind; serious dealers from all over Europe were at this sale. Among the hundreds of tractors, there were only three machines of my choice – Drott Four in One Shovels – all well used, and only one 'sweetly' ticking over. As I went to climb in the cab, a man introduced himself saying, 'Some clumsy oaf has broken the throttle lever.' This meant that I couldn't do a proper test of the machine, but he promised that it was reliable – working right up to being brought to the sale yard.

The auctioneer at last reached 'my' Drott, and only one other person in the crowd bid against me, but as he bid £2,600, a look flashed from him to the owner still standing near me: I quickly turned, 'If your mate bids once more I drop out.' It was knocked down to me for £2,700! I removed the broken throttle and the battery and returned home. Thursday was the soonest the Drott could be transported, and by 9.00 am I had refitted the repaired throttle lever and fully charged battery. Despite my apprehension, the engine started at the turn of the key. But as I speeded it up, I heard a loud and ominous rattle! Removing the side panels, and holding a metal tube to my ear – taken along for such an eventuality – I placed the other end against the engine and finally decided the noise was in the radiator cowling. With the aid of a mirror on a stick, all was revealed. Beneath the fan belt pulley, six stud bolts were dancing around in time to the rattle, leaving only two holding on the quarter tonne cowling. At home, it was fixed in a couple of hours, and except for the problems of working in our exceptional conditions, it did all that I put it to.

With this logging contract the feller also had to load the lorries, and he wanted to get them away as fast as possible. I wanted him running about with trunks as little as possible, so it was in both our interests for the lorries to drive close to the felled trunks. In consequence, most of his ire and bullying was directed at the poor lorry drivers. One owner-driver was near to tears, when suddenly the rear end of his wagon was lifted – wheels spinning – and slung into position by the Bray. Despite my rush to get the buyer on site before prices plummeted, he had not been near or offered a price. Meantime I was hearing of thousands being spent on clearance at other places, and the timber being trashed. After threatening to stop timber being loaded, I was told that we would get 40p per cubic foot for the first couple of loads, and would have to accept payment on a load by load basis – it could go as low as 5p. Then through a friend, I heard of a furniture factory whose buyer would like to purchase English beech: I got in touch. The manager sounded quite shocked, when I suggested he could have all the trunks he wanted for 40p per cube, plus delivery. 'But I get it delivered from France, sawn, and kiln dried ready to use, for 40p,' he cried. I stopped fretting after that.

Despite a strong wind felling half a dozen on the 6th of January, the last trunk was loaded on the 19th, and the feller was off my back. I now knew that the final tally of beech trees lost in 1987 was 380. Counting all species, we lost just under 1500. Now we could start the final clearing, and look towards getting the estate reopened. Even though only heaps of branch-wood lay in place of the beech trees, there was still a phenomenal amount of smashed shrubs, broken branches and timber the merchants didn't want. Despite turning much of it into firewood logs to sell direct to the public, and making 'eco' heaps, there was still much to burn. A large old oil tank or such – fixed on runners – was needed. Dragging the fire site round the trash would save much walking to and fro, and also eliminate scorched areas all over the place.

I had noticed some tanks whilst buying the Drott at the Cambridge Sale, and drove over in the hope that more would be in this next sale. Alas, none were suitable, but whilst walking back through the lines of machinery I noticed a large horizontal, drum-like manure spreader. The lid was rusted shut, but levering it open a crack, revealed the chain covered shaft which flailed the muck out was all but rusted away; and for good measure, the power-take-off gear box was rusted solid too. I couldn't believe my luck! About a score of 'bidders' still following the auctioneer when he at last called out: 'What will you bid me for this fine muck spreader?' Titters rippled through the group, and my bid of a fiver brought forth outright laughter. But a dealer had kicked the two heavy duty tyres, and he ran me to fifty pounds. It was still a bargain, because the wheels would fit our trailer, which had very poor tyres. As I radioed Steve to tell him the good news, a concerned local farmer hailed me. 'My word you have bought yourself a load of trouble there, Bill.' 'I don't mind betting a tenner, that it will be doing all that I want by this time tomorrow,' I replied. 'I wouldn't take your money,' he chuckled, 'but you can plant a couple of trees in my name with my winnings.' The next morning, I cut off all the extraneous gear – the lid lay nicely in the rather rusty base – and changed the wheels over with the trailer. By 11.00 am, Steve and a couple of volunteers had lit a fire in it, and at 12.30 pm a visitor was hammering on the door, to announce that our trailer was on fire!

A Roman Ghost

Most school visits went smoothly, even when I had an entire school – it was only me that suffered! On one such day, a

246

coach was doing a shuttle service – some sixty pupils at a time – the first load arriving at 9.30 am, and the last at 3.00 pm. Each load would be split to enable me to give one group a half hour tour of the Nature Trail whilst the other visited archaeological sites in the charge of a teacher using my script and map. All went well until I was departing with my fourth class. The other group had just walked off when screams came from their direction. I raced through the trees, and found them crowding round a crying girl. 'Whatever has happened?' I panted. A pupil pointed to the trunk of a large beech. 'She said a man wearing a grey anorak stared at her from behind that tree.' I ran ahead to the main path, but seeing no one, returned, and assured the group that all was well. Whoever it was had gone in the direction of the car park, and I made a mental note to make sure a vagrant was not camping in the area. Thankfully the rest of the event went without incident. Then a day or so later an excited teacher phoned. Following a hunch she said, she had taken the girl to a museum, and upon being shown a waxwork of a Roman Centurion, the pupil had immediately exclaimed, 'That's the man who looked at me from behind the tree at Wandlebury!'

Meanwhile my efforts with conservation work were bearing fruit, and as the shrub-layer thickened up, I hoped to see the badgers return to the abandoned sets. Muntjac and Roe deer were already being seen, which I was positive was the reason for the age-old stories of, 'huge ghostly dogs crossing the road over the Gogs,' resurfacing. I had all but forgotten the episode with the possible vagrant, when a family said they were visiting for that very reason, the mother said she knew about such visitations and wanted to see the exact spot. I was rather busy, but with a wave of my hand indicated the woodland they should walk through. A short while later, two excited children hurried toward me, 'Mum has seen the Centurion.' As we met mother, she gasped, 'I am so thrilled. He is definitely a Centurion.' And she led me to the beech where I had found the school group gathered, 'As my family caught up with me, he just seemed

247

to dissolve into the side of that tree!' Two years passed before my memory was stirred again; it was a sunny Sunday afternoon with lots of people around, and one family who regularly visited, pushed a hesitant mother forward. 'Mr Clark, I know you are going to think this is a stupid question, but have you heard of a ghost in broad daylight in these woods?' 'It has been brought to my notice from time to time,' I said. She turned to her husband, 'There! I was not imagining things. Hurry Mr Clark I will show you.' We ended up at that same tree!

Of Rangers and the Importance of Boots

The first one or two meetings of the Home Counties and East Anglian branch of the National Association of Countryside Rangers (since renamed, Countryside Management Association – CMA) that I attended, took place at the Countryside Commission headquarters in Cambridge (later Countryside Agency) but the idea was to mostly meet at one another's work places, where we could use the collective expertise of the Ranger/Wardens, or invite in authorities on subjects. It was at least comforting to know that I was not the only one with problems, and quite an eye opener to find that although most of the Epping Forest Rangers were ex Guardsmen, it was deemed unsafe to patrol alone, or even out of a vehicle after dark! One Country Park had nine torched cars in a month: and one Ranger spoke of losing some thirty sheep to dogs, during his summer 'up north'. With Wandlebury being fairly central for meetings – helped I am sure by my midday beer and Wendy's honey scones, we became a popular venue. My own input ranged through tree surgery, tree planting, re-establishment of wild flower meadows, grassland management, safety at work, etc. And with the Newsletter editor continually badgering us for material, I contributed from time to time. The following being a précis of one such article entitled: Of Boots and Pedometers.

During my schooldays my poor mother was always complaining that our boots were worn. It was common in those days, to buy children's boots a couple of sizes too big to allow for growth, and no doubt the sloppy fit led to extra wear on both socks and shoe soles, exacerbated by the poor quality of wartime leather. Luckily dad was an excellent shoe mender – though he complained each time he was asked to work on them, so by the time I was twelve, he had taught me to do the job instead. I still regularly mended my own family's shoes until recently. This not only made me aware of the different standards of manufacture, it kept me abreast of changing materials. Hearing our members often discussing their footwear, and commenting: 'Boots are not made like they used to be!' set me thinking. The tops were constructed from thick ungiving hide, and the soles were three layers of even thicker leather, studded with three to six rows of hobnails, finished off with a steel toe plate and a horseshoe-like, steel heel plate. You knew you had been for a walk after an hour in those, and so did everyone else within half a mile when you were tramping down a gravelled road – but what lovely sparks you could strike after dark! I was given a splendid pair of my grandfather's boots – hardly used, size eleven, lovingly steeped in mutton fat, with nine rows of touching hobnails in each sole and weighing about two and a half kilos. I think we should be pleased that 'boots are not made like they used to be.' At least they tell us something about the stamina of yesterday's working man.

Another grumble is their cost today. I can remember my father, a farm manager in 1939, saying a pair had just cost him a third of his week's wages. A recent pair of Doc Martins, cost me one fifth of my week's wage as a Head Warden – a salary probably comparative to my father's. It appears we are now getting a bargain. But do we get fair wear? We certainly now have a wide choice. The first thing I needed to know, to forward this important research into Rangers footwear, was mileage. As it happened my wife had just bought me a pedometer for my birthday, however, that brought its own problems, forcing me into a second line of research, so I will get that out of the way first. This pedometer was of great interest to Wendy, she had often said I over-did the walking, and no doubt thought that this would settle the arguments. 'Ha, ha.' I strapped it to my belt on Saturday morning and by evening I had walked twenty-one and a half miles, and on Sunday thirty-five and a quarter miles! 'I jolly well haven't walked that far, the thing is faulty,' I insisted.

On our busiest path, I measured a mile with my 200 yard tape. I stepped that mile. I even counted my steps on my next pass – 1,840. But still that wretched Pedometer insisted on tallying each, at one and three quarter miles! So it was back to the sports shop. During the following weeks I test-marched all they had in the shop – they even sent away for models. At one stage I was wearing three at once and sounded like the crocodile in Peter Pan! The shop assistant was most impressed. He said he had not received a single complaint from the hundreds of university joggers who had bought them, and had certainly not realised they could tot up such high excesses. I said no, if I was a jogger, I too would want one that would let me get it over with as soon as possible! Anyway, the pedometer that I found the most accurate – one of his cheaper models – was called the 'Count A Step Electronic' and counted the steps in either your chosen walking, or jogging mode, and then you had to slide out a mini computer, to compute the mileage.

Armed now with a reasonably accurate way to tot up my yearly mileage, I could get down to working out how well my footwear has been holding up! I reckoned out my average weekly mileage over the last two years at 54 – I ignored my holidays of only one and a half weeks and the average three quarters of a day off each week, as we usually do just as much walking then anyway – and the total came to 5,616 miles. I reckoned I am not walking as much as I used to! I next estimated my footwear worn out during this time thus:

Work-boots.	3 pairs.
Wellingtons.	2 pairs.
Walking-boots.	1.25 pairs.
Chain saw-boots.	0.25 pairs.
Trainers.	0.5 pairs.
Shoes.	1.5 pairs.
House-slippers.	2 pairs.
Total.	10 pairs.

Average mileage per pair calculates out at 561. Is this satisfactory? I don't know! Looked at individually I was certainly disappointed with three pairs. The uppers came away from one pair of work-boots in under three months – a cheaper brand than my usual DMs. My first ever pair of 'plastic Dunlop's' only lasted three months of casual use – also giving me two corns! And my dog chewed up one pair of slippers. Adjusted to accommodate for what was my own carelessness, I have a true mileage approaching something like 750 miles per pair. This, I believe, is not at all bad!

My advice would be to always look carefully at a bargain shoe. Especially the stitching and gluing of upper to sole – it should be both, not one without the other and leather before even best quality plastic! I also look for composite soles, with a tread that doesn't look as if it traps every particle, to be dropped out the moment you step inside any door! And I always choose leather linings. One thing that this little bit of research has taught me, is that after sixteen years at this job, I am approaching the 45,000 mile mark. Am I in need of a service? Or can I go on to 50,000? (According to those calculations I finally approached 75,000, but as I later bought a mountain bike, shoe wear must have decreased – but 'hip' wear certainly escalated!)

22. Wendy and Fagus survey the woodland on the morning after the 1987 gale. The tall group of trees are all leaning dangerously - away from the camera.

23. Twenty minutes earlier I had yelled at a family to get off, as screaming with delight, they rocked up and down!

24. Iron Age skeletons brought to light after the 1976 storm. The County Archaeologist thought there may be as many as nine individuals.

25. A Bronze Age highlight of the University digs in the 1990's. The pot maker left his fingerprint in the indentation under the base.

26. *David Nash working on his sculpture with a chain saw. The (almost) upright butt of the big beech behind, shows how much wood has been removed.*

27. *One of the old hollow trees that I had to fight to keep. It later caused excitement among entomologists as being one of the few sites of breeding 'Golden Hoverflies' in East Anglia.*

254

28. A close up of the newly named Wendy's Gold, taken just before it was dug up and moved to safety in March 1985.

29. The Arable weed corner in Varley's Field in the 1990's.

13. Varley's Field Blooms, A Famous Sculptor and Falling out with a Ghost

Varley's Field Treasure

One accolade respecting Varley's field was a bit embarrassing. I was introduced to a lady, who said, 'I specialise in old meadows and wildflower recognition, the big field at the back of the Ring is rather special. I will be more than happy to spend a season or two listing all the flowers for you: I think the number of species will surprise you.' I felt so mean, but I had to tell her! However, I believe I made up for it the following Sunday. A lady was unlocking her car, loudly complaining to another standing by the passenger door, that, 'Cambridgeshire has been a complete let down.' Recognising Australian accents, I introduced myself and enquired as to what our County lacked. The driver explained that her mother had an incurable cancer, and she had decided to bring her on holiday to England, and during this last week, they had intended to walk in the beautiful Cambridgeshire flower meadows that their mother/grandmother had described to them. This was their last day, and they had not seen a single meadow fitting her description. 'You have not been looking in the right places, come with me,' I said. The young lady asked if it was far; I explained that I would take the shortest route to save her mother's energy. 'Oh Mother is quite fit for walking, it's just that we have a meal booked for one o'clock.' I promised we should have plenty of time, and led them to Varley's Field.

The 'Oohs' and the 'Aahs' said it all as we stepped inside. 'Oh Gran, you were so right,' cooed the daughter, as she proceeded to take photos of the meadow and her delighted mother, before crawling around taking close-up after close-up of the flowers. Her mother, also busy taking similar photos, explained that she was taking photos for the Family Albums, whilst her daughter was using transparency film, and would be giving a slide show back in Australia. I thought they should be left alone – and anyway I was dreading some visitor might call out – as they often did – 'This field is a credit to you Mr Clark; it's difficult to believe you planted it such a short time ago.' After lunch, I cycled around the top path. Glancing across Varley's I spied two familiar figures. I rushed over, 'It's past 2 O'clock,' I cried. They both turned to me with radiant faces as the daughter spoke, 'We decided that every moment in this meadow is so precious, that we shall drive straight to the airport!'

Digital Timing

For seven years my 'electric' watch had kept me to the second – until just weeks after arriving at Wandlebury, when I needed it most. Unable to find a similar model, it was back to a wind-up replacement. As long as I remembered to take it off when doing anything strenuous, it seldom gained more than five minutes in a day, or stopped. But of course, there was still the problem of getting immersed in my work. Most days – besides attending to jobs all over the estate – a student group or volunteer workers would arrive, expecting me to be on hand, or I would need to attend a committee meeting, give a talk, or just get home on time for meals! My life was organised chaos. Dear Wendy would come puffing along a path that I was scything the edge of, 'I have been looking for you everywhere! The coach party has arrived that you are due to speak too. You had better run! I'll carry your scythe back.'

Then one day I heard bleeping as I led Miss Green's class, a pupil glanced at her wristwatch, and took a pill out of her pocket. The digital watch era had arrived! I did a tour of the Cambridge jewellers, surprised to find digital watches in the majority of them. Most of the cases were constructed of a flimsy looking plastic, but I surmised that could be just the insulation 'my' watch needed. Many showed the time in digital form, one or two had simulated 'liquid crystal' hands, whilst others had real hands: all could be set for a daily alarm – which could be reset immediately for my next task or meeting – and some could also give an hourly beep. One very helpful assistant said he had got the 'bees knees' in memory watches. Out came a very garish card, advertising that the attached, large black plastic, digital wrist watch – for the sum of £14 – would play up to a dozen different tunes for at least two years before the battery needed replacing. Its attributes were speedily demonstrated. The 'Happy Birthday' tune could be set to mark every hour, on the birthdays of my nearest and dearest – up to five in number – and Jingle Bells during Christmas day! Various tunes or a simple beep could also herald the hour, as well as be used for two daily alarms and a reminder could be set for functions up to a year in advance. One could have 12 hour or 24 hour time, with or without, AM & PM showing; or replaced with simulated hands. There were functions for the date and day, elapsed time, a stop watch in hundredths of seconds and the time in most of the major cities in the world. It probably did things that I never discovered!

For the next six years, I seldom missed a date. Event organisers were impressed at how I finished a talk right on their allotted time – they seldom heard the couple of beeps two minutes before it was time for me to wrap up. I solved the problem of hearing the alarm whilst using a noisy chainsaw, by hanging the watch on a twig, and asking the volunteers to listen out for it – a bemused helper would touch my shoulder, and shout, 'Your watch is playing, Over the seas to Skye!' And off I would dash. But one afternoon I checked the time, to find myself looking at a bare wrist. I retraced my steps along a hedge I had trimmed, and searched the area where I had set a volunteer group at coppicing – to no avail – I was desolate. That evening, a spark of inspiration! The watch was in alarm mode for six am, and on the third morning, as I again retraced the route, I heard an exuberant, 'The Campbells Are Coming,' emanating from the heart of the trimmed hedge. Reunited, we stayed together for another couple of years – though in my pocket, for the strap attachment had broken – before the face went blank, and it refused to respond to another battery.

Bird Boxes and Nest Sites

One consequence of the loss of mature trees at Wandlebury has been a lack of nest sites for hole-nesting birds such as blue tits and great tits. So I have used up much 'spare' time constructing nest boxes, in order to have them ready whenever I noticed a need – taking care not to place too many for a single territorial species in close proximity; or they will only spend much time fighting one another off. This task eventually got beyond me – what with more gales and earlier boxes rotting or being destroyed by grey squirrels, a need for tens of boxes was not unusual. And so I spent pleasant hours instructing various groups in construction – one enthusiast was elderly 'Mr Raven! – supplying them with my own sawn planks from felled ash and elm trees. Some groups also placed them, but always with me in attendance, explaining which species of bird the box was for, their preferred locality, height, and direction it should face, etc. It is not at all helpful to place a box in full sun – the brood can be lost through heat suffocation – or on the edge of a flight line, helping the Sparrow Hawks to mop up the parents as they fly in and out.

The boxes are best put up in the autumn, for the birds often roost in them through the winter, then choose one for nesting quite early. The latest devastation and clear-up had left no time for nest box considerations, and mid-April was the soonest we could get to the job. In fact for the first time I had appealed for money to buy RSPB bird boxes, and one kind bird watcher had provided £250. A young lad doing 'Work Experience' had fixed the struts and squirrel-proof discs on the boxes, loading them on the trailer: before coming indoors to have his lunch with us. Suddenly – through our window – we saw a cock great tit dashing in and out of every suitable box, whilst his excited mate bounced around in the branches above, twittering fit to burst. We suspended lunch immediately, and fixed a box on the trunk of the tree – and even before our dessert was finished, moss was being taken in!

Later we drove off through the woods to a recently cleared area. I parked beneath the one remaining beech, and stepped into the centre of the clearing, proceeding to explain our strategy to my young companion. 'This glade is now ideal for our summer-visiting spotted flycatchers, so we will put up three open fronted boxes around the edge, the tree with a fork is just right for fixing a tawny owl box, and we can put a great tit box on the tree here, but on the east side, out of the afternoon sun.' Then, aware of increasing bird sound, I turned towards the trailer, and was astounded to see twenty or so birds chasing around in the branches just above it. A pair of blue tits were hanging on the end of a twig together – just a flap from the nearest box – obviously deciding, 'This one is ours.' 'We must get the ladder up quickly,' I remarked, and placed it against the nearest suitable tree. I asked for a great tit box, and climbed up whilst the lad steadied the ladder. In a moment the two nails were hammered home, but halfway down I felt the ladder shake, and an excited voice called, 'LOOK Mr Clark! LOOK!' His finger pointed to the top of my ladder, and I was just in time to see the tail of a great tit disappear inside the box. The rest of the afternoon followed in similar vein, with our following flock ever changing, some birds staying behind when boxes were chosen, and others joining as we entered new territories. Walt Disney would have loved to have been there with us that afternoon, but it was for our eyes only. 'We shall never see anything like this again,' I remarked, as we stood below the last box watching a pair of blue tits investigating, and then the cock bird sitting on the roof peering over the edge, as his mate disappeared inside.

David Nash – Sculptor

Just before the feller finished trimming out the last of the 1987 wind thrown trees, he brought in his huge old saw – it hadn't been used for years. 'If you can get this working, I'll cut up the big trunk at the top of the car park.' It took me all day, but it behaved perfectly the following morning, albeit with a grand plume of smoke. The top half of the trunk was soon cut through, but as he returned to his van for more fuel, the man who graded and numbered the trunks for loading, drove in. He stopped, and nodded towards the fresh cut, saying, 'What a shame, that's a good piece of timber, but I have not been able to place it, no one now has a big enough saw mill. Get it put out of your way; it will have to stay and rot.' The feller was pleased that he need not cut through the even larger base of the trunk, and willingly helped – he with his Bray, and me on the Drott – to stand it up again as a memorial,   laying the large sawn off section at the base – with misgivings on my part, as I wondered, 'How many children are going to fall off that during the coming years!'

The following week, a Fellow of Jesus College phoned to say he was setting up an event in the College grounds, and one of his sculptors needed a tree trunk suitable for carving. I said that there were some trunks that the timber merchants had rejected, one might be suitable. A few days later the Fellow, and sculptor David Nash, arrived, who showed me a photo of the clipped Irish Yews in the College garden, and said that he was working on the idea of carving a trunk into a similar shape with a chain saw. The finished sculpture would then be charred black with a propane burner and placed among the College yews for the exhibition. The trees that I thought might be suitable were scattered at some distance from the car park, and I hoped that by explaining the qualities of each as we walked, he might be able to make a choice, and save us having to visit them all. I was describing the first, when I realised that David Nash was no longer with us. I turned, to see him standing by the big sawn off log. It was love at first sight! 'Can I have it?' 'If you can do anything with it, it's yours.' I answered. He turned to the Fellow, 'I will start work in April.'

David arrived on the 7th, and paced around it deciding what to do. 'Can you roll it over, so that I can look at the underside?' I drove our tractor over, wrapped a chain around the log, rocking it only the slightest amount as the wheels spun, and drove home to fetch the Drott. By the time I arrived back, he had already cut some pieces from the top side – it looked like the start of a set of steps. He asked if I would mind leaving the machine and just look in from time to time. The trunk was gradually rolled around, until it resembled a set of discs, each some 30 centimetres thick, graduating from just over 2 metres in diameter at the base – once I stood it upright – to 60 centimetres at the top, and some 4 metres high. He finally decided not to smooth it or char it, but accentuate both the horizontal and vertical divisions, so making it look like a pile of blocks. The finished sculpture provided me with some amusement over the following days. Visitors continually asked why I had wasted time piling the logs like that – and were they safe? In fact so many lads climbed about on it, trying to kick off the blocks, that I had to move it to my house for their own safety.

Visitors, Ghosts and Gales

As the visitors returned, it was not unusual to hear the comment, 'It's nowhere near as bad as I expected.' If the clear up has been sympathetically carried out, and the replanting followed up quickly, many folk's memories of what stood before is quite poor. By buying pot grown trees after February, I was able to plant much later than we normally did: it is important to buy pot grown trees from a reputable nursery, too long in the pots, and they will never make good trees. One group of these metre high beech was planted in memory of an Essex policeman, whilst others were in memory of a Herts fireman – the donors happy to pay the extra sums involved. Another county's Tree Officer – after hearing one of my 'talks' – kindly gave us 2,500 tiny, 'Japanese paper pots' containing 50 mm (2 inch) high beech that he had personally grown, and these were planted in May, enabling us to dig up good bare root trees of our own for some years afterwards. By that July the woodlands once again looked a good mix of habitats. Flora and fauna abounded over the whole estate. Butterflies in particular swirled up as you walked through the Marjoram in Varley's Field. The mild winters seemed to be here to stay, with spring starting ever earlier; and although I preached at all my talks that we could expect more unreliable weather patterns because of it – especially gales – I secretly hoped that we would be spared them.

After years of vacillating by the Committee, the decision was taken to double the size of the car park, and in December 1989, as soon as my plan was passed by the authorities, a start was made. To save money, the job was being done entirely with the Drott, and I had been champing at the bit, wanting to enter it in a sale as soon as possible, for she was well beyond her sell by date – the rear sprockets were so worn, that great care was needed in turning, or the tracks were cast off. The plan was to use the excavated soil to make embankments either side to break up the area, and provide for tree, shrub and bulb planting; the surplus being trailered away to fill in the many tree holes. A deal had been made with a local contractor to bring in their surplus brick rubble for free – the spreading and crushing down would take place as and when it was delivered. Road planings – for the cost of transport only – would be spread and rolled down to a finished surface last of all. This was entirely dependent on the contractors work situation, consequently, although the excavation and the surrounding planting was finished by Christmas, only a little of the rubble had arrived.

In 1991 Wendy and I decided to celebrate the centenary of the New Year's dinner hosted by the Land Steward for the estate workers in 1891 – as reported in the Cambridge Chronicle. Dress code was to be of that era, but instead of a marquee we dressed up the school room. Everyone played their part to perfection, from the Duke and Duchess of Leeds, down to the scullery maid. The evening was a great success, though some found my home-made beers and wines strong enough. Luckily, as midnight struck, home was only a short walk for most. Then Caroline dashed in to say, 'Dad I think you should go after the coachman, he is walking in the middle of the road.' Running out with a torch, I was pleased to see the gentleman turn safely into the lower gates. But two motorists called in during the following days, to tell of a Victorian ghost who walks over the Gogs in the middle of the road at exactly midnight!

Unfortunately my prediction for more gales held true, as yet another assailed the woods. I inspected the damage, and gloomily arrived home to announce it would take some time to clear, but we might solve a puzzle. The tree was down that the Centurion supposedly frequented – a large pan of roots stood in the air, corresponding with an equal area of hole amounting to some 18 square metres, and all on the side he had 'appeared.' Early the next morning Wendy and I arrived there with broom, spade, pick and trowel. To our disappointment we cleared a pristine area of undisturbed chalk, with neither bone nor artefact up amongst the roots. Later on, when the feller had cleared the trunk away, I rolled out the stump with the Drott for us to search the other side – with the same result! The stump was then tipped back and we moved on. Unfortunately strong winds returned a few days later, and tipped the next beech tree against another, and we had to return.

A 'hung' tree, is the most dangerous to deal with, and the feller has to put a lot of reliance on the persons with him, to keep him safe. As I didn't want the tree it leaned on – or the dozen saplings around it – to be damaged, I would be guiding the tree with our Zetor tractor. We tied the hawser high in the tree and connected up to the tractor, the feller then cut out the 'jaw' at almost right angles to my direction of travel. That done, the two chaps cutting up the branches for firewood, moved well away, and the feller stepped into my view to signal 'start pulling' and 'stop' when the tree was upright. Then checking that no branches were hooked up, he stepping back under to start the felling cut, directed so that the 30 metre tree would fall to the right of my tractor only 20 metres distant. I was now holding the tree with the brakes and watching the top intently. The moment the tree started to fall I needed to reverse: too soon and it would crash back into the other tree; too late and the tight hawser could pull it on me and the tractor.

Out of the corner of my eye I saw a movement at the spot where the tree was about to fall – a man was standing there! I shouted 'Run you fool,' The tree was moving. I glanced back, still he stood there. I threw the tractor into 'creep' gear, leapt off, and head down raced towards him, shouting, 'Run. Run,' thinking my momentum would sweep us both out of harm's way. The topmost twigs raked my back as I realised I was alone. I ran round the fallen tree to the ashen faced men standing by the tractor they had just stopped. I demanded to know which way the intruder had run; and why they hadn't sent him off. 'What are you blathering about?' said one, 'I thought you was dead,' said the other. A tingle went down my spine as I remembered 'that stump,' now half hidden under the felled tree. The stump has now rotted away, and the new trees are taking over. Will the Centurion one day peer round the trunk of one of these? Only time – and the right visitor – will tell.

At day break on the 25th, of January the weather again looked ominous, and by the time Steve and a volunteer arrived, I deemed it too dangerous outside, and put them to 'Spring Clean' the schoolroom. It was Thursday, the day Wendy expected me to at least take her for the week's shopping! Inside the large Sainsbury's store, it was obvious a gale was blowing up, and I couldn't wait to get home. Once back, I donned my hard hat and left the house. Threading my way warily, I counted fifteen beech down in a short distance, but with my hand held anemometer climbing to 50 mph, I decided I had better return home. My radio crackled, and I smiled to myself, expecting it would be Wendy mentioning similar – and it was! 'I am on my way,' then I exclaimed, 'Wow, that gust was nearly 60 – two trees are falling at the top of the car park, I'll stay here in the meadow until it is safer.' Then I gasped, 'Oh no! The needle is hard against the stop. The big beech where we were planting yesterday has snapped like a carrot . . . its bringing the next one down . . . and the next . . . they are like skittles . . . nine are down . . . five more minutes and there'll not be a beech left!' But thankfully the needle dropped back to 40 mph, and I made my way home, to spend the rest of the afternoon servicing the chain saws.

Darkness was falling, when blue strobe lighting flashed in the workshop window. Outside, a policeman called, 'We need a chainsaw Mr Clark, and can you come too? A tree has fallen on a Doctor in his car!' I pointed to the saws and fuel cans, and ran into the house for my 'chainsaw' hat, then leapt in the car and we sped off. But in sight of the tree we were informed the emergency was over, a farmer had arrived with a JCB, and the tree was not actually on the Doctor's car anyway. As we turned in the road, a different voice asked if it was correct that a man with a chain saw was in the car. And off we sped towards Newmarket. A gardener was reported to be under a tree: as we raced through Six Mile Bottom, the radio announced that our help wasn't needed after all – and the poor man had been certified dead. As we slowed down a shadow loomed up ahead, a small tree lay on the road. I jumped out to cut the tree into manageable pieces – which proved to be difficult among moving shadows, made worse by the strobe lighting. We attended three more small trees, a huge flapping motorway sign, and an overturned lorry, before I was delivered back home. Using the road atlas to explain the adventure to the family, I was surprised to see that we had travelled almost a hundred miles – most of it I considered, 'bare knuckle' driving.

Again we had no electricity, but the phone line was intact, so things were easier to organise. I was determined to be open for the weekend, Steve and I sawing, and our familiar band of helpers clearing the pieces, we cleared a sign posted route to the buildings and open fields. Howbeit, strong winds returned, and we had go over the same ground three more times to keep the path safe. Then at midnight on the 12th of February, the howling sounded as bad as the 1987 storm. Out at first light, I almost walked into the end of the radio antenna. The triangular, 30 metre steel lattice mast, was bent double and both its shielding trees were down. Tony Sayers arrived to find out why he couldn't speak to me, and over the next couple of hours – using ropes, pulleys, the tractor and nearby trees, we pulled it back up into use.

Strong gusts felled further trees during the next two days, and I phoned the contractor – who had yet to set foot on Wandlebury – to tell him that his work load had tripled! He proved to be a most experienced feller, but with no machinery of his own. As the Drott had a very good all-round lighting system, I could do much of the work in the evenings, dragging the trunks into places that the self-loading lorries could reach, creating stump-heaps for badgers and such to live under, piling branches for small animal habitat and clearing up and burning ready for replanting – and wherever possible, lengthening the safe path network, often working until 10.00 or 11.00 pm.

Another 260 trees, 132 of them beech, had been lost. The one day each week that Wendy had insisted I take off, was now down to a two hour dash for the shopping. However, our reward – I confidently include Wendy too – was seeing Wandlebury get back off its knees, and start to flourish again. At last the old Drott was returned to the Cambridge Machinery Sale, where the original dealer bought it back for £1,600.

14. Ruffling Historians, Romancers and Police Superintendents – Wendy's Gold gets Upstaged by Bill Clark

Historical Arguments

1991 was also the year that past history would come back to haunt me! First, it was Tim O'Brien. It had taken five years after his arrival in 1973, before he published his paper, 'An Integrated Astronomical Complex of Earthworks at Wandlebury and Hatfield Forest from the Third Millennium BC.' From the moment he first went public in the Journal of Geomancy I became embroiled. The Cambridge Editor, Nigel Pennick, took him to heart, but I now had an additional problem! The CPS Secretary – Silvia Beamon – was a friend of Pennick, and had often had her previous work quoted in his journal, all excellent material, I hasten to add, and they both served on the Committee of Subterranea Britannica. I knew that there was no room for error in any challenges I made. I had long regarded O'Brien's field work as doubtful and had even procured a copy of his many pages of mathematics and knew that it had taken him two extra years of redefining the parameters to get it to all come together. I countered his claims in the Journal for, 'the important 5,000 year old indentations in the outer bank of the Ring Ditch'. 'They are Victorian pathways into the inner garden,' I wrote, and gave proof. I also opposed his claim:

'that an important hole on the north side of the Ring, pointed out to me by the Warden, is the site of a Monolith,' by writing that the hole was in fact on the south side. He came back with: 'The indentations are so accurate; they just have to be of astronomical importance – the gardeners just made use of what was there.' And the hole, he wrote, was certainly on the north side, but had been shown to him by 'another' Warden! In my last foray into the journal, I pointed out that not only could I still show him the hole – on the south side – but also that I was the only Warden employed during his time with us.

Our Secretary was now beginning to get apprehensive with the way things were going, and thought I should back off – but I had noticed two more issues, one with an important 'marker stone,' and another Victorian feature, that he had described as, 'an original Hill Fort entrance, hitherto ignored by previous archaeologists.' I investigated both, and for back up, asked Alison Taylor – County Archaeologist and our Secretary to take a look too. They agreed with my findings, and had probably hardly got back to their desks, when Rodney Tibbs of the Cambridge Evening News phoned me to ask if he could visit to talk about 'the latest finds' at Wandlebury. I intimated I was unhappy with the situation, and suggested he phoned Alison for her views first, and bring a photographer with him.

The following morning, our Secretary backed me to the hilt, and afterwards sportingly posed for photos, one at an obvious Victorian cutting, and the other by the 'marker stone' which O'Brien set great store by in his basic paper, but I said was a concrete plinth that had once supported a garden urn. Rodney then left, saying he would speak to O'Brien about our concerns, and get him to meet with us; however, he returned to say that O'Brien had refused to meet us, refuting all our concerns, saying that he had tested the stone himself – 'it was definitely shelly limestone.' At that – with I believe a little trepidation from Silvia – I brought out a large chisel and club hammer, and in front of them both, cut off one corner. Rodney's full page article,

272

ends; 'Sitting on my desk is what we found – a thin layer of concrete and the sharp, easily recognisable outline of a Burwell brick.'

O'Brien was next in the Telegraph Magazine's Sunday supplement – no less than seven pages – under the heading: 'Wandlebury Enigma Solved.' Only days before publication, he was back at a Cambridge University computer crunching numbers – information passed on to me by one of the operators, who had read in the Telegraph, of O'Brien's, 'formidable mathematical brain.' Except for a lot of harassment from visitors following up the Telegraph article, complaining that they couldn't find the 'circle of stones,' I had thought that would be the last we would hear of the Integrated Astronomical Complex. Now, all these years later, Anglia TV was advertising a half hour programme about, 'Mr O'Brien and his amazing discoveries.' I immediately rang the Producer, and gave him the low-down on the Wandlebury fiasco, suggesting some pertinent questions that could be asked. On the night, O'Brien came out with the same old stuff, all now transferred to Ireland! 'He is not going to mention Wandlebury,' I remarked to Wendy, however, towards the close, he was asked to comment about similar work he had done at Wandlebury Ring in Cambridge. He brushed the question aside with, 'Oh that was just some preliminary investigations with no relevance to this later work at all.' At least the Wandlebury battle was over.

Protecting the Bats

During the summer, youths broke down the door of the bat tower, so I bought a piece of metal fencing from a scrap yard, and constructed the present barred gate. Because they had also smashed all the thermometers, my assistant Steve, presented me with an old recording thermometer from a ship's hold. I converted the clock mechanism from turning the recording-drum once every 24 hours, to once in 14 days, and put a modern biro in place of the metal nib. Placed in a weather proof box, fitted with a plexiglass front, it allowed me and the visitors, to read the temperature of the thermometer placed way inside the tunnel – During my years of recording the temperature, I found it stayed close to 52°F for most of the time, only once going below 48°F and once above 56°F. Above the recorder I fixed a laminated notice, which included the suggestion that others could allow bats to use their cellars and redundant air raid shelters too. This caused much interest and requests for further information. Sadly, someone found a long metal stake to reach through, and that was the end of the recorder.

I was often asked to give my opinion as to whether a site was suitable for bats: on one occasion successfully stopping a war time 'Pillbox' from being demolished, by explaining how it could be made into bat hibernation quarters. Most enquiries though were still, 'Can you tell me how to get rid of bats? One lady was sobbing over the phone. If I couldn't get along, she said, she would have to move to a hotel for the night. Evidently she was saying good-bye to visitors on the doorstep, when one had glanced up and remarked, 'My goodness just look at all those bats flying out of your gable.' After clambering around for some time, it still took me until midnight to convince her that the bats had no access into her capacious loft – and definitely not her living quarters. My bat PR was such, that I received an annual update for some years – on the last occasion, she expressed disappointment that there were still less than a hundred streaming out on their nightly foray! Another time I spent until 1.00 am in a wealthy widow's bedroom, before locating her unwelcome visitor: I think Wendy believed my story. Numbers have since been declining further because of wet, cold, Junes, and on quite a few occasions I found dead young, and surmised that we might have lost the Noctules altogether. However, much to my surprise and delight, one autumn, no less than seven Noctules crawled out of a hole in a dead beech that I had just felled. I kept them under observation for the night, and happy with their healthiness, put them in another hollow tree the following day.

Re-burying Lost Troy

In September, the weird tale that Troy was really situated in England resurfaced with a bang! I had been sent the book "Troje lap in England" (Troy situated in England) by Dutchman, Ernst Gideon, back in 1980, 'Would I give it my appraisal?' A retired Dutch doctor living on the estate, kindly agreed to translate the section pertaining to Wandlebury – commenting later, 'I haven't bothered to read the rest; it is utter rubbish – as you will see when you read that Wandlebury was once the walled city of Troy!' Although I occasionally met Dutchmen with Gideon's book in hand, trying to pick out Trojan features – one stayed around for days, determined to find at least a part of the original stone wall that had once encircled the city of Troy, I deemed the story was long since dead and buried. Maybe it would not have happened at all, if I had been more observant with the original brochure I sent to Gideon! For it also contained a small map, showing the tree species to be found in the Ring, embellished by a stylised – crenelated – garden wall. Obviously enough for a researcher to grasp at, when looking for the slightest wisps of facts, to fit, or bend, to his theory!

Hence on a lovely sunny day, a group of vehicles swept into the car park, and a large man dressed in a leather tunic, and carrying a helmet and sword, strode around, posing for a photographer. I asked what was going on, and was told that he was Iman Wilkens, author of 'WHERE TROY ONCE STOOD.' The Mail on Sunday's 'YOU' magazine was doing a feature on him. They had visited the Little Chef at Four Went-ways – which was then a busy and popular watering hole on the A11 – and where he said one of the Trojan battles had taken place and now they were going to finish up at Wandlebury. He was not very pleased when I offered information to the reporter, and cut short his interview. As he got into his car he gave me a last petulant call: 'If you don't believe Troy was here, where do you think it was?'

Thankfully the published article made little mention of Wandlebury, mostly treating the subject humorously. The only photo showed him standing in front of the Little Chef signs, with the headline: 'THE PLACE THAT LAUNCHED A THOUSAND CHIPS.' It reported that he had been researching the story for thirty years, after reading that a Frenchman, Cailleux, first suggested it a hundred years earlier. Despite being word for word at times with Gideon, he makes no mention of him. They both believed many place names transcribe to the present day, the tomb of Ilos is Ely and Batieia is Bottisham; river names also come into it; Rhodios, Roding, Larisa, Lark, Temese, Thames, and so on. Except Wilkens makes no mention of our wall – giving due regard to the place names Wandlebury happens to be in the right place geographically! In 2002 I found the book on a second-hand stall for £2.50 – new price $24.95 (£12) – inside, beneath the title, the previous owner had written, 'When is a good read not a joy'!

Wendy's Gold gets Upstaged by Bill Clark

I had multiplied my Wendy's Gold snowdrops, passing two to the Cambridge Botanic Garden, and one to Anglesey Abbey. Meanwhile Joe Sharman had delivered one to Wisley, and was acquiring a name for himself as a snowdrop enthusiast. So by the spring of 1988 I thought it was time I enquired as to how things were progressing at Geest's. I was told the 'chipping' had been effortless and they now had over 800 bulbs, but it had been decided to go for another chipping. This spring I deemed it time to phone Geest's again. Consternation! The person answering said Geest's were no longer in the business, but followed up with, 'We are now the owners of their bulb concern.' Relieved, I

276

inquired after Wendy's Gold, and was asked, 'What are they?' After explaining, I was told that another firm had taken on the bulb development section, and was given their phone number. 'They have gone into liquidation, we have just taken over,' said the man who answered that phone. 'We have nothing called Wendy's Gold here; but I can give you the number of the Scottish firm who took some of their stuff before we came in.' That person had no knowledge of Wendy's Gold either, but volunteered yet another number: 'He will certainly know,' was his parting shot. I was beyond surprise, when the familiar voice of Geest's Procurement Manager answered! He began by being very friendly, but as I explained my quest to track down, what must by now, be thousands of Wendy's Gold, he became evasive. Not until I asked if something underhand had occurred, did he volunteer the truth. He was embarrassed to say, that they had lost the lot through a fungal infection during the second chipping!

Joe, now a partner in the Monksilver Nursery at Cottenham near Cambridge, usually visited Wandlebury each spring, when we walked through the snowdrops together. On one such occasion, he was accompanied by Matt Bishop co-author of 'Snowdrops' who was gathering the history of Wendy's Gold: as they left I presented them with one of my seedlings that had not yet flowered – a year later Matt phoned to say it was another good yellow, and asked for permission to name it 'Bill Clark.' Reputedly, single bulbs of Wendy's Gold changed hands for £70 in the early days, but an Australian lady was the only buyer I ever met – she had just paid £10 for one at the annual, 'Galanthus Gala' – saying she would have killed to get it! She was now taking the opportunity to visit, 'the place where it was discovered.' As Wendy and I had recently planted a group back on the exact spot of the originals, I offered to show her the, 'shrine'. Her excitement at realising she was meeting the actual man who named it, was only exceeded when – as I said farewell – Wendy walked round the corner. The Snowdrop book was published in 2001, so I took Wendy to Anglesey Abbey on her birthday, to purchase it. As we picnicked by the riverside, she searched the index: saying, 'I hope they used a bright yellow, it can be quite pale if it is not grown in full sun.' Disappointingly though, there was no illustration with the description on page 159, but as she turned the page, she chuckled at the snowdrop depicted, 'Well, would you believe it? I have been pushed off the page by Bill Clark!' To make up for it, hardly a spring now passes, without at least one magazine or newspaper illustrating Wendy's Gold. I have grown on many seedlings from it: Joe Sharman particularly liked the look of another one, and with the comment, 'Call it Wandlebury Ring,' I handed it to him – a description of it appeared in the 2010 RHS magazine, 'The Garden', where it was reported that one bulb had sold on eBay for £123!

Rampaging Romans

I was often asked to speak about the historical side of Wandlebury, so using book study – Wendy and I possess over 50 metres of books dating from 1764 on just about every subject – interlaced with the results of the 1956 University dig, and my own experiences with the skeletons uncovered by the 1976 gale, I developed an 'Iron-Age Walk and Talk.' This involved walking around the Hill Fort explaining its possible structure, pointing out various humps, bumps and hollows that I believed were archaeological features, whilst talking of Iron Age times, the Iceni and Queen Boadicea. I always tried to make it lively and interesting, gearing it to the respective audience. One early talk involved about 20 ten year olds having an end of term treat. Their enthusiastic teacher wanted their last day with her to be something for them to remember. They – dressed as Romans – were to meet me – in sack cloth, and brandishing a spear – on the site of the Iceni's circular, protective wall. I started with a fearsome act of keeping back the Roman horde! All went well, although I finished a

278

touch early, so taking the children back down into the bottom of the Ring Ditch, I stood at the front, and pointing my spear ahead, yelled, 'Now come on you Romans, show the Iceni what you are made of. CHARGE.' And the screaming children charged! Miss ran down the bank calling, 'Boys, boys. Stop, stop.' But they were already disappearing round the bend: she turned to me, 'Oh Mr Clark, what have you done!' All we had to do was stroll in the opposite direction to meet them.

A popular spot with the children was to sit or stand – according to the weather – to be told, 'Only a few centimetres below the surface here are the skeletons of people, who I believe died in battle.' And I would then explain the finding of them, followed by what I believe had happened there a couple of thousand years ago. I thought my first college group – especially with what they watch on film and TV – would find anything but the bloodiest truth rather tame, and went into gory detail. 'As the Archaeologist picked up the skull, face towards me, I knew he had died in battle.' I sliced my hand down the front of my face, 'His nose had been cut off with a sword.' 'Uuurh,' was the only sound one girl made, as she fell in a dead faint.

Looking back, I wonder how I managed to fit in all the school visits. In the last year before the Cambridgeshire County Council's cash-well started to dry up – one of the first to go was the enthusiastic Schools Advisor and his post – I hosted 51 educational visits, some of them entire schools, and most of them during May to mid-July. In that same season I also led 30 evening – youth and adult – tours round Wandlebury, and travelled to give 57 evening talks in Cambridgeshire and beyond – and still coped with the estate work and policing.

We remained popular with the private schools, for their usually small classes were easily delivered using a few parents' cars or their own mini buses. Miss Green stayed faithful even after changing schools: and fourteen years later, as I walked with her latest class along 'her' 250 metre hedge – the girls were counting the previous season's birds' nests –

she informed me that this would be her last visit as she was retiring at the end of term. Thinking of the wrench it must be, after a lifetime given to 'her girls,' I felt some commiseration was called for, and commented on what a loss it would be to the school and how sad she must be to leave. She stopped so quickly that two or three following girls bumped into us: turning to me, she cried 'SAD? SAD? I've a good mind to cartwheel the length of this hedge!' Something that I am sure would have stayed in her pupils' memories for ever, and would certainly have been a highlight in mine.

Disagreements up the Ranks

Generally I was on the most cordial of terms with the police – one summer alone my assistance led to the apprehension of three culprits causing fires in the area – but I found it best to be careful when dealing with those above the rank of sergeant! One instance concerned yet another stack fire. After hearing a lot of shouting, I was out in time to see figures crossing the road far ahead in the lights of a passing car, but then noticed a glow illuminating a stack in the farmer's field, and called up Wendy to do her familiar routine. Running to our car park, my torch beam revealed four cars, but as a police car had arrived at the stack, I ran back to that, breathlessly calling, 'I think I can help you.' 'Yes, yes, perhaps so, just wait there,' was the officer's brusque reply, as he walked over to another car that had just arrived. 'Just before the call came in, two likely looking car loads passed me by, get to Haverhill, and see what you can find out,' I heard him say. Trying to intervene, I said, 'Excuse me, I am the Warden here and....' 'I am well aware who you are, MR CLARK,' he interrupted, 'Please leave me to get on with my job,' and moved to the next car arriving. A fire engine also pulled in. 'Oh, hello Mr Clark,' said one fireman, 'I expect it was you that called us? Did you see the culprits this time?' 'I think so,' I said, 'In fact I believe they

280

are still here, but the man in charge, won't listen to me.' He looked across at the Superintendent and made some very uncomplimentary remarks! Then as he turned to his tasks, four cars drove out of the car park and turned towards Cambridge, whilst the 'Super' called: 'Right, Mr Clark, what was it you wanted to say?'

Another Superintendent who thought civilians should not stick their noses in only happened to be passing by! The driver of a broken down double decker bus parked on the Haverhill to Cambridge side of the dual carriageway, had used our phone to get assistance, and I walked over in the gathering dusk – his lighting had also failed – to place my traffic cones behind his bus. Round a bend just out of sight I placed a tripod sign with a reflecting arrow directing the traffic into the overtaking lane, and for the next three hundred paces, placed my cones – also reflective – to gradually widen out from the kerb. A car swung in as I placed the last one near the bus, on came a blue strobe, and out stepped a uniformed 'Super,' who busily brushed past to ask the driver if help was on the way. He then turned to me, 'Did you decide to place those cones?' 'Yes,' I replied. 'Far too many, but as I am here now, you can remove them.' I trudged back, placing the cones on the verge, picking them up on my return to plonk the stack by the bus. As I turned to go back for the arrow, the Super was placing the last of his three cones behind his car. There was a squeal of tyres as a car bore down on us: he in the most danger jumped for his life. Scattering the cones the car came to rest, one coat of paint short of the Super's car! I didn't wait to ask if I should replace my cones.

Flight of the Kestrel

From time to time folk brought us injured wild birds, but one midday meal was interrupted by a sweating jogger reporting a sick hawk sitting on the ground. After pointing out the position on my estate map, he went on his way, and I cycled off to look for it – only to see a Kestrel fly up as I approached. 'Good,' I thought, 'it must have only stunned itself.' Then I saw another in the grass, head drooping, eyes closed. Close to it lay a headless vole and a couple of field mice. The bird's mate had been bringing food – probably even trying to feed it! I put the almost lifeless creature in my bag and rushed home. I guessed rat poison was the problem. Plenty of water might be the solution. Whilst I held the bird, Wendy used a syringe to squirt water down its throat; the effort of swallowing seemed to bring back some life, only for it to droop down again when placed in a cage.

After lunch, more water, and finally pieces of liver. Back in the cage the poor thing flopped down again. During the afternoon I discovered a neighbouring farmer had put sachets of rat poison in a nearby pit where he dumped rubbish. There were a number of dead rats and one still crawling about – just the sort of animal that a hawk would pick up. I returned home in time for our next hourly 'drenching' session, and the following morning we were overjoyed to find the bird on its feet. We resumed our sessions, offering a little liver each time. On the third morning I put my hand in the cage, only to have it pinioned in a flash by a very fiery bird. Time for the leather gloves – for we still carried on with the water treatment, but put the pieces of liver in a dish.

The next morning a very lively Kestrel had eaten all the liver, and we decided it was time for our usual flight test for repaired birds. With me carrying the cage and Wendy a ball of string, we walked to the centre of the Ring meadow. Wendy unwound a few metres of the string and tied one end to the angry looking Kestrel's leg. For some seconds the bird clung to my glove, before gliding off and almost touching the ground before the wings started to flap. The wing beats got stronger; and finally, slowing my run behind, I guided it to a low branch. We walked back to the cage and Wendy untied the string, but instead of putting the bird inside, I again stood with arm outstretched! The bird clung to my glove for long seconds, before languidly floating off, to

282

perch back on the same branch. Wendy gave me a look that said, 'You shouldn't have done that!' Then with a strong beat of wings it flew out and off, but as if on an afterthought, turned in a wide arc, swooped in low over our heads and screeched, before soaring up and over the tree tops into the blue. We both had a catch in our voices, as we turned to leave.

15. Stirring up Wasps' Nests – The 'Min of Ag' Takes Note of the Orchard Reclamation and the Wild Flower Meadows – The University Archaeology Unit Takes us Back to Bronze Age Farming

Harvesting Wasp Venom for Medicine

1992 was the year I became involved in an entirely different scenario! My swarm calls, often turn out to be wasps, and after pointing out that they are part of the natural balance – one nest rids the countryside of thousands of flies and caterpillars – if it is necessary, I give the name of a reputable, pest control firm. However, my neighbours know that if they have a wasp problem, I can usually locate the nest, and deal with it. As a consequence, when I read in the Cambridge Evening News, that a Doctor at Addenbrookes Hospital was appealing for notification of nests, so that they could collect the venom, I got in touch. I had found twenty or so nests, by the time the doctor's young assistant cycled up to recce my finds, though only half of them were in a position to enable the venom collection box to be used – preferably, the entrance hole needs to be in level ground. The next day he was driven in by a young lady, who, after she had dressed up in her – almost – wasp proof suit, placed a small bottomless box over the entrance holes, and operated a switch to give the wasps electric shocks from a wire grill, infuriating them into stinging a bag of alcohol.

We have made progress over the years: I can now rearrange some nest entrances ahead of visits, so that the box can be used, and the young assistant has matured into a Doctor and Clinical Scientist. We both recognise different species, and we now know that the same species, from another nest, can act very differently and even pack a heftier venom shot! Until the doctor proved it in the lab, I had always believed that, as I am almost unaffected by most stings, the occasional wasp sting that caused a reaction, had either been previously used to sting a dirty maggot, or had penetrated directly into a vein. But in 1993, a bad year for wasps – in our vocabulary, that means there were very few nests – I was taught otherwise. I had found only three nests, and suggested we should not kill off the infuriated insects' nests afterwards. As they were well away from paths, we could leave them to settle down, and use them again the following week. All three nests were German Wasps, *Vespula germanica*, but the first nest we visited hardly reacted, and the second only a little more, we gloomily predicted that the dire weather was the cause.

However, at the third nest the occupants hit the wires with gusto. Even the incoming insects were infuriated by us standing in their flight path, and chased the Doctor and I – unclad in bee suits – some distance. The young lady assistant, finally satisfied with the amount of venom collected, moved off, and once free of attacking wasps, returned to their transport. The Doctor could now get back to helping that season's influx of allergy patients become de-sensitised. Meanwhile, there was a nest that folk definitely needed to be made aware of. I quickly drew a notice – DANGER WASP NEST, KEEP AWAY – and for the benefit of our foreign visitors, a large wasp too. After donning my bee suit, I returned to hammer the notice firmly a few metres in front, and placed a bright yellow flag right by the nest hole. With wasps hitting me from every angle!

The next time the Doctor arrived, I was told that there had been a bit of a hiatus. Patients had arrived for their first injections, and as the last one was being injected, the first one slumped forward; then during the following minutes, others followed suit. From thence onward, every venom sample is examined, in order for the strength to be standardised. Although the day was warm and sunny, the wasps all acted as they did the previous week, the only decent venom collection coming from the last nest. Later that evening, a group of children walking along the roadway, a good hundred paces from the nest, started to dance and shout, and I knew 'it' had to go! I stood guard until the last visitors left, before returning home for my insecticide powder and specially constructed long handled spoon. I cycled back in the dusk, heaped my spoon with powder, crept to the nest hole and tipped the powder in. What happened next I can only describe as a 'Vesuvius' of wasps! Covered in white powder, they were very visible in the dusk as I turned and sped past my bike into the nearest shrubs. Looking out, I could see a cloud of ghostly wasps attacking the bike saddle – I later found dozens of broken stings embedded in it.

Orchards and Archaeologists

One area of Wandlebury, the orchard, was overrun with everything that Mother Nature could throw at it. I had believed it was good habitat for our wildlife, and left it to its own devices. But when I read an article about the poor choice of apples available in supermarkets, my conscience was pricked a little, and when I later heard reports of wholesale grubbing out of orchards, felt positively guilty. Finally I decided that the remaining apple trees were important enough to warrant the removal of the unruly tangle of ivy, brambles, elderberry, elm and sycamore. The various varieties would be of interest to our visitors while nooks and crannies in the old branches, would still be available for the nesting blue tits, great tits, coal tits, tree-creepers, bats, etc. And without sprays, the caterpillars and aphids would provide their food, whilst our many species of bees and other insects would certainly enjoy the blossom. The bonus being, that any fruit out of reach of our visitors would remain for the blackbirds, thrushes and winter visiting fieldfares and redwings, mitigating a little, the loss of Cambridge hedgerows, which had once given them shelter and fruit.

When we applied to enter the meadows into the, 'Countryside Stewardship Agreement,' I discovered that grants were available for old orchard reclamation too: the Committee agreed that I should apply. In the summer of 1993, I made ready by cutting a young growth from each variety of tree – the buds of which, a local nurseryman grafted onto his rootstocks to grow them on for me: they would be duplicates to fill the gaps and take the orchard into the next century. By the autumn, all the grants were in place, and Steve and I started work. Our first task being to find the apple trees among all the other growth, and then individual branches among the mass of ivy! Whenever we had time from our other duties, we were in there hacking and sawing, pruning, logging, and digging out the weed tree roots. Each time the trash got to biblical proportions, Scouts, Guides, Work Experience, Community Service, Duke of Edinburgh Award toilers or just plain volunteers, were in there tugging, dragging and throwing the stuff onto our mobile incinerator.

One Sunday in that same autumn, I noticed two men wandering around, who were looking interestedly at the humps and hollows in the landscape – some of those that I had dowsed, but was unable to dig pilot-holes as the areas were protected. I asked what they thought they were seeing. They introduced themselves as, Charly French and Colin Shell of Cambridge University's Archaeology Unit, and said that they were looking for interesting sites close to the University: would the Cambridge Preservation Society allow any excavation? This was exciting news. I had already found a pit under a wind-blown tree in the corner of Varley's Field, and had privately disagreed with the archaeological assessment that it was a one off – probably a diseased person or criminal, made to live outside the hill fort. Upon showing them that area, they said it would be ideal for their students' summer excavation. I told them I would put the proposal to the CPS at our next Committee meeting – and by hook or by crook, get them to agree. In fact, the Committee were as interested as I was, and it only remained for the Unit to put in their request in writing.

By the spring of 1994 the orchard was cleared and ready for planting, and the Cambridge Beekeepers Association members arrived to help. Besides paying for the grafting of the apple whips, they also donated towards a further score or so of other old varieties, including plums and pears: all Steve and I then had to do, was put round the rabbit guards and attend to the usual watering and weed suppression. And it seemed no time at all before the Archaeologists arrived, to give a closer scrutiny to my chosen area in Varley's Field prior to their fortnight's work, with some geophysical surveying by magnetometer and resistivity meters. This intensified during the first two days of the training programme, before, on the second morning, an excavator also arrived and started stripping off the turf at the first of the pegged sites. As it moved to the next spot, eager students were in the hole being taught how to proceed – what to look for, and what to 'tag': whilst others were sieving a sample of the soil dug up by the machine and taking instruction on what to put in plastic bags. I initially surveyed the scene with some trepidation. How shall I explain this mass destruction of the lovely turf that I had been cosseting for so long if nothing interesting turns up? But I need not have worried. Feature after feature was revealed as the students scraped down to the chalk base, nine test stations and four trenches revealed post holes and other 'anomalies' and pits containing fragments of pottery and bones – enough for Dr French to suggest, 'Possibly a village, going back to the Bronze Age.' Only two stations drew a blank. All too soon the fortnight came to an end, and I was left to sprinkle grass seed over the replaced soil, and wonder at how much else was hidden there.

On Caring for Wildflower Meadows

The first MAFF inspection of our Countryside Stewardship Agreement work didn't go too well. The young lady and I, having met in front of the buildings, stood looking across at the short sward of white clover – humming with bumblebees – and she immediately asked why I was not keeping to the letter of the previous year's agreement? I said that it had been grazed earlier than recommended, to stop the coarse grasses taking over; once the flowers had finished, the sheep would be back, and just so long as we had no drought (effects of weather seemed absent from her knowledge) there would be further crops of summer flowers. On reaching Varley's Field, she needed to know why it was being grazed in sections. I pointed out the western corner had deeper soil and in consequence grew stronger grass, so needed extra grazing; the north corner was not quite so strong, but because it was the only area where the *Saxifraga granulata* grew, it was not being grazed until July. And the clouds of Meadow-brown butterflies we would soon see at the south end, would be there because I had not removed all their habitat when they were caterpillars the previous autumn. Also by grazing it in sections, there were always some flowers for the insects – especially the bumblebees – to visit. At the Picnic and Play areas I was accused of over grazing, but pointed out the many different species of rare, solitary wasp and bee nest holes; Insects that thrived on that kind of habitat. Although my reasons for the grazing and mowing regime were asked for in printed form, I doubt it went any further, for that was the last I saw of that young lady, for not only have the representatives changed with the seasons, the agency in charge has changed too.

Nation-wide, there seems to be confusion as to how wildflower meadows should be treated. Some of the finest wildflower meadows developed because of the way they were originally farmed, usually by livestock grazing – with the type of animal, soil, weather, and regularity of grazing, decreeing the overall plant life in each area. Now it seems that only folk possessing University degrees can be allowed to oversee such areas. Their common trait of late grazing or mowing to enable seeds to ripen and fall – which seems to be rolling out around the region – encourages all the rank grasses, and allows plants such as wild carrots, sheep parsley and ox-eye daisies to take over, thus losing the finer mix of grasses, and smothering the small flowering plants. This destroys the balance and continuation of flowering which is needed by the bumblebees and butterflies – many solitary bee species are geared up to catch certain 'flushes' of flower types. It is also much more difficult to mow the old dryer sward, needing sharper blades that get dulled exceedingly quickly, and the resulting hay being poor quality, is an encumbrance, rather than an asset! During my contracting period, when mowing similar grass for Stowe School, I regularly took six sharpened blades with me, but still often had to sharpen more on site, to enable me to mow 20 acres or so per day.

Last Community Service

The Community Service asked if I would be willing to take a regular, supervised group. I had provided the occasional task for groups in the past; they were supervised by mature, ex-police or service personal, and did a good job. However, the Unit was now only employing trained supervisors, and would probably be available midweek as well. My first contact with one of these groups was not good. The supervision was poor – allowing individuals to skive off, turning a blind eye to catcalling after our visitors, and leaving them to their own devices during tea breaks. Shortly

291

after I informed the Unit that this particular group was not welcome anymore, a regular Wandlebury visitor arrived in tears, and announced that her son was in the group, and implored me to, 'Get the Unit to let my son work with you alone.' She believed he was being led even further astray, and repeated lurid tales that the boy had told her, of what occurred during his work placements.

A while later, I arranged for a different group to dig a small trench around Bourn Windmill, in readiness for a lightning conductor to be installed by a specialist firm the next day. The lads all sat in the van smoking and chatting, whilst I in shirt sleeves, carried all my tools to the mill, and marked out the line of the trench. Still no one appeared! Looking up at the sky, the slightest rain specks could be discerned on my glasses, so returning to the van, I brightly said, 'OK lads, it's all ready for you.' 'You must be joking,' retorted one, 'you can't expect us to work in this weather.' There was a general murmur of assent. 'Look at me, standing here in shirtsleeves, do I look wet?' 'No, but you look stupid,' said another, to a ripple of laughter. I turned on my heel, and the young supervisor followed, remarking, 'You really can't expect them to work in these conditions Mr Clark, we'll wait a bit longer.' I started digging the trench, as it would soon be touch and go if we could get it finished in the time. Then a weak sun broke through, and I took a walk back to the car park to mention it, arriving just in time to see two lads, with the locked petrol cap off my car, dropping in a lit cigarette end! With that, the supervisor thought it best to return to base – luckily, as the kerfuffle ensued, three Cambridge students arrived on bikes to view the mill, and taking pity on me, stayed to help. What the Supervisor reported to the Unit I do not know, but they later called me to a meeting, and evinced sadness that I would not be wanting any more supervised groups, and informed me that their policy now forbid lads to be with untrained supervisors at all! And that was my last dealings with the Community Service.

Of the 70 orders put to me, five never arrived, three only did one or two visits, and one absconded from the area. Over the years, the occasional, 'Hello Bill,' tells me that one of the more successful is about to introduce his family, or at least tell me how he has never been in trouble since. A father of one lad, phoned the Cambridgeshire Radio Station during one of my broadcasts to thank me for helping his son. He had not known, until going through his son's belongings after his death, that it was me who had encouraged him to take up photography, which he had turned into a successful business. As the presenter – Richard Spendlove – commented, 'Bill, it doesn't get any better than that!'

Bronze Age Farming

On the 15th of June a JCB arrived, accompanied by its complement of hopeful young archaeologists. The aim was to enlarge some of the most promising stations of the previous year, and do trial pits over the rest of the field. Hopefully this would determine the extent of the village that predated the fort. As the excavator stripped off ever larger areas of turf, a multitude of features appeared: round pits and oval pits; with more post holes and trenches. I could hardly tear myself away to go about my own work, and returned as often as possible. As the students carefully deepened the holes, much speculation was bandied about between us all, especially over the larger round and oval pits – why so beautifully cut, and smoothly finished? The experts assured us that their first use would have been for grain storage. This raised doubts in my mind – surely, they would have been lucky to use a tenth of it – the significance of the post holes denoting a roof over them, eluded me at first!

Then one morning as I approached the largest pit, a young lady working out of sight in the depths, called out, 'Charly, I have found a lot of burnt grain.' Charly was in another pit, but still managed to get there before I did! He

293

stood up, trickling charred grains into my outstretched hands, and told me it was an early kind of wheat called, 'Emmer', mixed with what I could plainly see was barley. The shock of seeing for myself – and, what is more, holding grain that had been harvested sometime between three and five hundred BC, sent my heart pumping; this was as good as finding a gold chalice! Better, for I was allowed to keep some grain and Charly's explanation of past usage of pits will never again be questioned by me.

The final explanation for this particular pit indicates that the users had discovered heat sterilisation. The earlier pits were abandoned after one use, because grain moulds and mites would have permeated into the walls, making for fast – and heavy – inroads into any subsequent grain storage. Picture the empty pit after its first use, the thatched roof getting the worse for wear, and a layer of both mouldy and sprouted grain clinging to the sides and base, full of grain mites. Drop in the thatched roof – take away the supporting poles – throw in a burning ember, and sterilisation quickly follows. When cool, clear out the ash, then plaster the wall and floor with a thin coat of clay and rebuild the roof. A pristine pit now awaits the next crop, with the bonus that it is now more damp proof, so even less grain should be wasted around the outer edges! The evidence was, that this pit had been so treated three times, making four uses. And in so doing, they had preserved some grain for all time.

As I looked at the quality of it, I realised that my estimation of Bronze and Iron Age farming had been woefully inadequate. How did these primitive folk, grow such good grain so soon in their farming careers, then I realised that the pits were also explaining the reason. Although they were filled to the brim with rubbish, little of it was dark organic material. They must have been putting that on the land: how clever of them to understand the need for replacing nutrients, I thought. Then I recollected my explanation of manuring to young Caroline, showing her the large, healthy looking, fat-hen plants, and occasional wheat plants with massive dark green leaves, growing on the dung heap. They would not have needed a college education to notice that, or the taller, greener grass, growing around the animal droppings in the meadows. Not for them the huge wastage due to rodents, in stacks and sacks, that we suffered during the 1940s. It had taken another thirty generations: even in my own grandfather's youth, corn was still being sown by hand broadcasting, and harrowed in by oxen – before we also threshed our corn in the field and stored it in silos!

16. Lethbridge Chalk Figure – They say Dowsing, I say 'Dousing!'

Soon after I had tidied up after the third University dig – this one was inside the Ring area, again unearthing some marvellous archaeology, including the original fort entrance and a Roman track-way. I once again noticed someone taking what I deemed to be an educated look, at our humps and hollows – this time the site of Tom Lethbridge's 'Figure.' I introduced myself to the man, and he said that he was the editor of an antiquarian magazine, 'The Third Stone,' and was hoping to write an article about the Figure. I pointed out some of the salient features – quite difficult to recognise in the long grass and brambles – giving my reasons for my disbelief, and ended by lightly saying that I hoped it was not going to be the usual mishmash of nonsense. At that he answered, 'It seems I have met the very person to write it, could you possibly do it in four weeks?' And with that we exchanged addresses, he promising to send me a magazine, so that I was familiar with the format, and I promising to keep to his deadline. I had by this time accumulated a fair knowledge of Hill Figures in general and this one in particular! Much of my knowledge came from discussions with enthusiasts – and detractors – at the site, and I believed that I was at last winning my argument. Towards the end of an earlier discussion on the radio, one guest at odds with my explanation, grumped, 'It's all right for Bill, he insists on dealing in facts!' So, herewith, a slightly shortened version of my article in the August 1997 'The Third Stone' magazine.

Dowsing Gogmagog

The outline of the Goddess is still to be seen in the turf on the hillside opposite the cement lined pond, just above the woodland that hides the traffic on the A1307 below. Few of the visitors puzzling over the series of humps and hollows have any inkling of the ire that its formation caused. Or that all these years later, the controversy still lingers. Tom Lethbridge, a respected member of the Cambridge archaeology team investigating the origins of the Wandlebury Rings during 1955, decided he would rather do some surveying of his own. It concerned a chalk carving that was said to have once been in the vicinity, and could have some bearing on the name, Gog Magog Hills. It didn't take him long to decide that the only decent sized piece of turf left on the hill top, gave possibilities for finding this lost 'hill figure.'

He approached the Cambridge Preservation Society, the new owners of Wandlebury, for permission to search, and as this only involved thrusting an iron bar into the ground at intervals, to ascertain if the chalk subsoil was disturbed, or not, they agreed. Tom trudged back and forth across the hillside plunging his bar into the soil – small areas of artichoke stems thrust into the likely holes, were the only visible signs to the onlookers. Tom by now had recruited his own little band of helpers, and many comments were bandied across from the University group still working on the 'Iron Age dig' whenever they passed by. Things got heated at times: in one letter Tom speaks of the possibility that "My iron bar might land on A N Other's foot". There is no record of Tom's comments, when, upon his arrival one morning, he found, what Dr Bushnell (Curator of the Museum of Archaeology and Anthropology in Cambridge) later described to me as, 'a rather splendid steam train,

298

complete with smoke coming from the funnel, made out of string threaded around Tom's artichoke stems, by a group of students during the previous evening.

With the survey almost over Tom deemed it time for the next phase of bringing his 'God' to light, and he lodged a pencilled drawing of the likely formation with the CPS. (He might just as well have said , 'It will look like this,' for – after permission was given – months later it was exact in every detail, except for two tiny, but significant, last minute additions of female breasts!) There was the odd niggle from various people who didn't like Tom's uncompromising attitude, or the view of ever larger heaps of spoil. But it was not until he typically jumped the gun, by getting his half-finished, first figure, splashed across the pages of the Times as, 'this previously lost, three thousand year old hill figure,' that things really hotted up.

The first upset for the Society was when Terence Gray, who had gifted a considerable part of the estate, blamed the Society for allowing Tom to publish his account, especially his statement, that the previous owners had no interest in archaeology, and would never have allowed a dig! Various members of the Society inspected both the dig, and other chalk areas nearby, for comparison. Tom also called on his friends and acquaintances, but the most important kept their distance. If Tom had played things differently, he may have had more backing. Sir Cyril Fox had given a congratulatory reply to an early letter from Tom, but took care to keep well away once the storm broke. Except for Tom himself and his friend and helper C F Tebbutt, it is practically impossible to find an Archaeologist in agreement with either the way the dig was carried out, or that it could possibly be a chalk figure.

The Council for British Archaeology agreed to appoint a Committee of four to have a look at the diggings and give their opinion. On the day in February 1956 that had been chosen for the visit, one Oxford Professor was unable to attend, but the three gentlemen who did, were diligent, firm, but unswerving in their collective opinion.

'Tom had excavated a natural phenomenon of polygons, caused by periglacial conditions during the last ice age.' Finally the order was made to fill in, and turf over the 'Goddess',

Tom was no slouch when it came to getting into print, and his book, "GOGMAGOG", The Buried Gods", was ready for publishing. The Society Chairman, among the first to receive a copy, must have wondered if perhaps they were being a little hasty. But the order stayed, with the qualification that all care should be taken so that any future investigations could be made if necessary. Significantly, the contractor chosen for the task reported that the turf around the site was of no use. It was of such recent origin it would not hold together, turf would have to be bought at a cost of £48. The Society, very strapped for funds, decided that Tom should be approached to cover the cost. There is no record of any offer from Tom, but in his own inimitable fashion there was a reply; it took the form of a little publication put on sale in the local book shops. 'Gogmagog: The discovery and subsequent destruction of a great British antiquity'. Battle lines were drawn, and much sniping went on behind the scenes. Some were openly hostile to Tom; there was even talk of the Cambridge Antiquarian Society – for whom he had been Director of Excavations for thirty years – disowning him.

Then a further document arrived from the Council of British Archaeology. The Professor, absent from the February meeting – who happened to be an acquaintance of Tom's – had received a copy of his colleagues report from the CBA, closely followed by a copy of Gogmagog from Tom. He had since visited the site in the company of Tom, and was now insistent his views should be taken into account. He absolutely disagreed with his learned colleagues, and wanted his findings attached as a separate report. At this the Society seems to have lost its zeal for turfing over the site, although a last letter from Tom shows he thought 'She' had gone forever.

The Archaeologists may have abandoned Tom – so serious was the split that Tom left the area – but the group which Archaeologist, Glyn Daniel was to later call, 'the lunatic fringe of archaeology,' took him to their hearts. The site is still visited by, dowsers, ley liners, occultists, hippies, etc. Some look upon it as a fertility object, and bring various offerings to lay reverently in her breast and speak of the same benefits accruing to the childless, as those who couple on the celebrated anatomy of the Cerne Abbas Giant!

Having been the man in charge for twenty-five years, fielding the various inquiries from an inquisitive public, I have deemed it my responsibility to research the subject thoroughly. This was not only because I wanted to give informed answers, but it was also my job to look after Wandlebury in a responsible way, and that included the 'Hill Figure'. I have read all available literature on the subject, conversed with people around at the time, and watched over her, and those who have surveyed her since – one took some five days, by Magnetometer and Resistivity meters, and later, a 'high tech' survey with a Magnetometer coupled to a computer, was done by friends of Tom and the Goddess. The fact that no evidence whatsoever emerged from these surveys, has to my knowledge never been made public.

The Archaeology Committee mentioned plough marks through the figure area. Tom surmised these were Stone or Iron Age, with possible Napoleonic era, and 1941 ploughing too. I have spoken to old estate workers who remembered ploughing there in their youth, and the daughter of a servant, who was positive potatoes were grown there during the war years. Certainly, arable weeds and grasses were still dominant in the 1970s. During the last clean-up of the figure by volunteer enthusiasts, I took the opportunity to check the depth of the excavations. Fifteen percent is up in the plough depth of 217 mm, but all of this is the unique details of: goggle eyes, hair, face, arms, nipples, etc. Thirty five percent is the horse's legs, and rude appendage, still only 25 mm into the plough marks. Twenty percent is up to 75 mm below the plough, most of this comprises the body of the horse. A bare thirty percent, which makes up all of Gog's torso area, was the only piece a respectable 304 mm below the plough line. It would seem to me that only this area gives a true – findable – shape, below the plough: unfortunately, after looking in dozens of holes resulting from gale blown trees, I believe this is yet another! Even Tom said that detritus in the upper chalk proved that trees had anciently been on the site.

He also accused the Committee of ignoring the quantity of round pebbles found in the dig, left he said, from either Iron Age battles or practice; proof that the 'figure' was in situ at that time. The fact that they would have been a valuable resource, to be recovered by the participants, he either ignored, or didn't think of. At their riposte, that the stones were natural, he went into some detail that such pebbles did not occur at Wandlebury, and that there was no gravel capping to hold such stones. In fact, there is gravel capping at various sites all over Wandlebury, the pits that supplied gravel for the estate roads can still be seen. I have also watched as building foundations and pits were dug into virgin chalk, and picked out round pebbles there also.

In his book, Tom misconstrues John Layer's mention of a figure 'within the said trench' (which is circular) as being on the ditch banks, rather than in the centre. He makes no mention at all of Dr Dale who visited Cambridge, 1722-38, and clearly states, 'cut on the turf in the middle of the camp.' He gives full reign however to Cole's description when, as a boy – about 1724 – he remembered, 'that the road from Baberham still running through the camp,' and his father or mother always stopping to show him the giant carved in the turf. Tom of course again ignores the obvious conclusion that this mention too, means within the camp. He says it could be seen from Sawston as late as 1850, yet the 1810 map shows woodland in the way and my ring counts on fallen trees in 1976 show that trees were there in 1795 and would certainly have blocked any view by 1810.

302

In letters, Tom was very scathing about the polygon theory, yet during 1994, and 1995, the CUAU dig on the East side of the Ring – a few hundred metres from the Lethbridge site – uncovered similar configurations to his. A few marks were thought to be ancient weathering dating back to the last Ice Age, but most were unmistakably the result of farming and building operations during the Bronze and Iron ages. As I watched those features gain the light of day, I couldn't help thinking, 'What would Tom have made out of this lot!'

As late as Dec 1956 he was writing, 'It is anyone's guess who this chap is. Mine is that he is a Sun God.' The fact that only days later he made the only significant departure from his original pencilled sketch, and cut a couple of nipples into the outline and called it a Goddess; I think puts the whole thing into perspective. I am often asked for my opinion of Tom, and why I believe he got it so wrong? My theory, is that Tom finally let the academic backbiting, and collegiate jealousy get to him, and forced himself into a, 'Come hell or high water, I'll show em,' situation.

Addendum

The Cambridge University Archaeology Unit's final investigation of the series, was actually underway in 1997, when the Third Stone editor wrote to say that he was giving my article a second airing in a special edition, entitled, 'The best of issues 23 – 27. Unfortunately, the results of this dig were too late for his publishing deadline. Ten pits were dug across the 'Lethbridge' area. Two revealed the omnipresent grain/rubbish pits and most showed distinct plough marks breaking into the chalk surface. There was not the slightest hint of a, 'figure outline', showing in the four which purposely crossed the two further figures, which Tom had surveyed, mapped, but not been allowed to excavate. For me at least, the absolute final nail in the Goddess's coffin was the sight of gravel and stone deposits – over a metre thick – just above her head. Tom had been very caustic with the Society's experts, re his 'sling shot' stones in the figure outline. Did they think the stones were sucked off a Suffolk beach in an Ice Age storm? No Tom, they actually only had to be washed downhill for less than twenty metres.

A Little of My Book Study of the Hill Figure

Interestingly, no mention of a chalk figure was found in the private papers of the 2nd Earl of Godolphin's family, or the Dukes of Leeds.

Professor Grimes, Prof Piggott and Dr Cornwall, for the Council of British Archaeology, visited at the CPS's invitation, and all found against; the other member of the team, Prof Hawkes, was absent. After Tom got in touch – and sent him his book 'Gogmagog' – he did visit, and found for Tom, insisting that his report should be taken into account. Even at that late hour, it was then put forward as the, 'Minority Report'.

Dr Bushnell – curator at the 'Arc & Anth' in Cambridge, was also a CPS member and frequent visitor to Wandlebury. In conversation with him, at the site of the figure, he said that he knew Sparkes and Lewis, the experts on chalk deposits, and agreed with their findings in the 'Outside report' requested by the CPS. They wrote: 'Most of what we saw could not be man-made ....' Dr Bushnell then went on to relate how he visited one Sunday in 1956, and found Tom alone, 'digging like fury along this hair line.' He said Tom coloured up when he realised who it was standing behind him and muttered something to the effect that he couldn't leave the chaps alone for a minute without they moved off line. He then asked Dr Bushnell what he thought about the figure. Dr Bushnell – who had known Tom since their student days together – said he replied, 'Well Tom, I think this is your best jape so far!' Tom then stormed off, and never spoke to him again. He finished his conversation, by mentioning that Professor Hawkes – the author of the Minority Report – was also well known to him, and was a friend and acquaintance of Tom's too!

17. The Birds Talk to Me – I Become a TV 'Star'

It was a warm beginning to April and the birds made an early start to their nesting activities; in fact, as I went about my tasks on this Saturday, the song was more akin to mid-May. Then, during the afternoon, Wendy, caught up with me, 'What a lovely day! And what about all the bird song?' We walked along together. Two birds joined us at the next path junction and kept above us: Wendy laughed, 'I think these two are singing just for our benefit.' I stopped briefly. 'This happened when I passed earlier, it's not song, they are scolding us.' They kept pace with us for a while, and then fell back. I always carried my binoculars on patrol, and whilst Wendy headed homewards, I stayed nearby to watch events. A family walked into view. The birds flew towards them, but with hardly a twitter flew off again. A single man appeared from another direction, the same thing happened: and also when an elderly couple passed by.

It was time to test my preposterous theory! Our wild birds certainly recognised nest-boxes on a trailer, and a wheelbarrow piled high with food in the winter, but did they recognise the man who provided it all? I walked back into the area: two birds plunged into view, and keeping pace exactly, twittered and twittered, only falling back as I left their territory. I returned, back they came, getting very excited when I stopped in the centre of their patch. I tried to recollect exactly the tree that had fallen earlier and been cleared away. No! There had certainly been no box on it.

Then I remembered; it had sliced down the side of the next tree, breaking off two branches. Through my binoculars I picked out the two nail holes where a box had hung between them, and followed the possible trajectory as it was swept off. And there, deep in a blackberry bush it lay – still in one piece. In no time at all I was back with my long handled pitch fork, ladder and tools, and with two birds excitedly urging me on, I fished the box out of the bush and nailed it back in place. Would they still follow and scold me? Of course not, they were busy sorting out their nest.

In early May 1998, Bob Lemon, President of the CBKA, phoned to say that the BBC researchers for the cookery programme 'The Two Fat Ladies', had asked if it would be possible to film him opening a beehive to remove combs, spin out honey etc., with the two ladies in attendance. He wanted to know if I thought the orchard at Wandlebury would suit! I hurriedly painted one of my picturesque WBC hives, and set it up under an apple tree. The team liked what they saw, and arranged to film the following week. My final inspection of the bees revealed they still had no honey to speak of – and Graham, our CBKA Apiary Manager, who had his bees in an oilseed rape field – dashed in with a box of honey-filled combs, which we placed on top of the hive. For the bees, this was the equivalent of winning the lottery. They swarmed up among the combs in seconds, and would be very amenable by the following morning.

Just prior to the film crew's arrival, I placed all the equipment needed to spin out the honey and bottle it, next to the hive. The honey that the ladies spun out would need filtering and 24 hours of rest to settle out the air, before they could take away their full jar, so Graham brought some ready filtered honey, which we put into the bottling tank. With everything in place, I left Graham and Bob, gathered up a couple of our largest bee suits, and cycled to the Wandlebury entrance to meet the film unit. They planned to film the ladies driving down the hill on their motorcycle and sidecar; then next a shot of them driving into the Courtyard, meeting me, and asking to see some bees and buy some honey. The producer was keen that our meeting shouldn't look too contrived. I suggested that I could be sweeping the yard. She was quite pleased with this, but concerned that it would portray me, the Head Warden, doing a rather lowly task!

Twenty minutes was taken up with trying to drive through the opening and across the courtyard. At last the ladies stopped by me, before I had swept the whole yard! We each had to say our lines three times – to one another – and to camera. Even with very few words, saying exactly the same minutes apart, is quite difficult, and I was surprised that my unscripted comment, sending the ladies into titters and bringing forth a jocular answer, was left in. The film team then set up for a rear shot of the ladies driving across the grass to the 'Kissing Gate' by the orchard. Bob, who had now been ready for nearly two hours, was about to be introduced to the problems of filming, as he watched the now suitably clad stars, drive towards him time after time. The Producer was at last satisfied, and they could walk through the gates. My last role was to guard my recently constructed, 'noisy' iron gate, so the rest of the filming could go ahead smoothly.

The two formidable ladies were a delight to meet and work with, presenting me with a signed copy of their book, 'Two Fat Ladies Ride Again' at the end of the day. Despite rumours to the contrary, it is seldom that any money changes hands in these situations – although the unit did make a donation to the CPS on this occasion – profuse thanks and a few tapes, are the only mementoes I have of many radio and TV interviews; so I was surprised to find a photo of myself – complete with broom – in the ladies' next book, 'The Two Fat Ladies Full Throttle.'

The 'Stewardship' orchard plan was to keep as many of the original trees as possible, as these were considered important wildlife habitat. Two trees had hollow branches being used by Bats, and the old bark is host to a great variety of Mosses and Lichens – of the rarities listed in the excellent

'Nature in Cambridgeshire,' many have been found on old apple trees. The root stocks of the new trees were all specially chosen to be fairly vigorous, in order to replicate the original large trees and the habitat associated with them, for many years to come. The floor of the orchard is also a conservation habitat – first snowdrops and winter aconites and later dandelions, germander speedwell and wild white clover, all building up the solitary and bumblebee populations and sustaining them, before, and after, the short fruit tree flowering season – the end plan, being to sheep graze. So well was the orchard looking in fact, that no less than five more TV agencies asked to film bee related items there.

On the 16th of June, a lady – from an agency only needing a few seconds sequence – phoned to ask if I would be interested in half a day's filming, acting as a beekeeper in my apiary, for a TV commercial for Norwich Union. She made me an offer equal to one month of my usual salary. 'Come along and see the apiary.' I said with alacrity. During the evening I had calls from beekeeping friends, saying that they had also been asked to act in a commercial and asking for my opinion. I surmised that someone was, 'having us on'. The next evening, 'Sally' rang again, saying that she thought I was the ideal person, 'You just have to stand in front of the cameras wearing your bee suit and a pair of red braces, and "twang" them.' Later she called to ask if I could make myself available for location shots the next afternoon.

A cameraman duly presented himself. He filmed the location, and me doing a simulation of twanging my braces and posing in both serious and laughing mode, for profile shots with a still camera. Later that afternoon, Sally phoned to say she had passed the video and stills onto the commercial makers, Saachi and Saachi. At 5.30 pm, 'Sam' phoned from Saachi and Saachi. 'We are pleased with the video and the photos; can you get to a fax machine? We want you to sign up right away.' Sally then rang to say, 'You are going to be a TV star, best of luck with the filming.' She seemed surprised that I had already heard from Saachi and

Saachi. By the end of another half hour I was a fully signed up actor in the, 'Twang' commercial, to receive two months of my usual salary!

As I arrived home the phone rang again, Natasha from Cow Boy Films wanted to know when I could be available for the film unit to visit and discuss what was needed. Five minutes later, Jo from Cow Boy Films rang to say that she had received the contract confirmation from Saachi and Saachi, and that I would be hearing from her colleague Natasha, shortly! Half an hour later, Sam again rang from Saachi and Saachi, 'Can you stand by to receive some urgent calls from Jo of Cow Boy Films,' and hoped that I didn't mind taking calls so late in the evening. I was by now, hovering with my original theory, 'Is this an elaborate hoax!'

The production team from Cow Boy Films finally arrived to discuss exactly what they wanted – including the one thing I had already said I could not do – move occupied hives a short distance. They also required twelve hives at the location, and as I had only got nine of the WBC types that they wanted, they agreed to buy three themselves. (These must have cost in the region of £350, and coupled with their need for veils, overalls and gloves for most of the team, Thornes, the beekeeping appliance people, should have been glad that it was their catalogue that I had to hand!). I spent the next five evenings – late into the night – repairing and painting seven more hives – at least by filming day, only a handful of bees would remain at the original site of the hive I was having to move! The film unit phoned at just about every half hour or so with questions, instructions and requests.

Tuesday, 30th of June, the crew arrived somewhat late, but were soon busy setting up the staging, lights, and cameras. During the couple of hours this took, I was inside the, 'Star's' plush, air-conditioned, Winnebago caravan, with my two dressers, make-up girl and her assistant. I remarked that the pristine new bee suit that I was being fitted with (whilst my own gear lay in a heap by the door) made me look like an actor pretending to be a beekeeper. However, we eventually arrived on the set ready for some practice runs. The Director took one look, and bawled, 'I wanted him distressed. What is he doing looking like that? I want him distressed.' I remarked that I was now distressed, but got a look that would have frozen the proverbial brass monkey, and we scuttled off, with the Director's voice ringing out behind us, 'I want him back on set in eight minutes.' We raced back to the van, and I was dressed in my own bee suit!

Back on set, the Director looked on me more favourably, and we got down to some serious practice runs, using a high-speed camera with instant playback. The Director was not too happy with my co-ordination – my left hand continuously let go of the braces a fraction of a second before the right. On the 2,000 frames a second camera, this would look even worse. We finally decided it was sticky propolis – bee glue – on the gloves, made stickier by the heat from <u>seven arc lights</u>. Three of these lights were a metre across: not only could I hardly bear to open my eyes, but my hands were burning through the gloves. After another couple of dummy runs, the Director asked for the high speed camera to be loaded. During the wait I prepared the beehive for a fast lift up of two frames covered with bees, then retired to my 'director's chair', out of shot and the horrendous lights.

Even with all the lighting, the chief cameraman still waited, light meter in hand, for the sun. Suddenly there was a flurry of activity. The Director called, 'Three minutes Bill.' I dived for the hive, pulled out the most bee covered frame, shook it over my head, took out another and did the same. Frames back, roof back – because the hive was in shot – and stepped onto my mark, thumbs in extended braces. The Director called, 'Good Bill. Left hand out a bit more, right hand up a bit, a bit more tension, fine, a big smile, look into the camera, a bigger smile. Roll the camera.' A noise like a mini jet engine started up; 'Keep that smile Bill. Aaaaand action!' Two braces hit my chest at what felt like

312

togetherness. 'OK Bill, get out of the lights.' Everyone now crowded round the monitor of the slower camera, whilst I tried to remove bees inside my veil – one still got me on the end of the nose. I called my dressers! 'There must be a gap at the back.' Paola was unhappy with the state of my braces. So whilst her assistant struggled with my veil, and the make-up girl took advantage of the gap to put make-up on my reddening nose, Paola dived in through my fly buttons – literally – to make adjustments to both the front and rear of the harness. The girls were dressed in brand new, white bee suits, and this bizarre sight drew some ribald comments from the stage hands, who, at this juncture had nothing to do.

In no time at all, the Director called, 'Three minutes Bill,' and we again went through the actions. By the fifth time of asking, I was being met and stung – because of the expected heat I only had underwear beneath the thin overalls – by bees even from the nearby hives, and all the film crew were veiled up, whilst everyone else had moved well away. At last the Director called, 'Fine everyone, a short break now whilst the crew prepare for close-ups.' A tailors dummy was placed on my new mark, and the camera was moved to the front of the stage. I was pleased to see one of the big arc-lights and three of the small ones, had been switched off, but felt a bit apprehensive at how close the remainder were placed to the dummy. 'Take Six', went through with the inevitable call for more bees in shot. The rest is a blur through to 'Take Ten.' And nowhere was free from stings! At about this time the Director called for a lunch break, and I was quite surprised to find that it was one-o-clock. We had a most scrumptious dinner, served from the catering mobile, and all too soon it was time to be back on the set. Despite heavy cloud we eventually got in another couple of, 'Takes', and the Director decided that the first two sequences were, 'In the Can'. There was then a break of some three quarters of an hour whilst the set was rebuilt. I returned to the caravan to get much needed repairs to face and clothing, then we carried on with the last four or

313

five takes – bees flying off the comb, in close up. At last the Director called out, 'Thank you everyone. Thank you, Bill, well done, but I still wish we could have seen more bees!'

It took a couple of hours to repack all the equipment into the three lorries and two large vans. (Two lorries just contained huge diesel generators – no wonder there was so much heat from those horrendous arc-lights!) The catering van left after serving tea, and with it the double decker bus/diner, closely followed by the Winnebago, ten or so cars, and the mini bus, with <u>my</u> dressers and make-up girls on board, cheerily waving – did I see a blown kiss or two? The mobile toilet departed only as the last of the 62 crew wended their way back to London. Thankfully, and stiffly, I walked the few yards home, and in answer to Wendy's, 'How did it go then?' said, 'Just be sure and remind me. Never, ever, do another Commercial – whatever payment is offered!'

The next day Sam phoned at 10.30 am. Wendy took the call. Sam said she had seen the 'rushes', and that things looked good. However there was a problem: the high speed camera had malfunctioned; in fact all the film was unusable! This was relayed to me over my pocket radio, and I returned home to find Wendy coping with yet further calls from Sam, Jo, Doochy and Natasha. Each amazed that we already knew of the problem, and all continuing turn and turn about, changing times and dates, until it was finally agreed just before bedtime – that it could only be the following morning! 'What on earth am I going to do for bees,' I moaned to Wendy. I went outside with a torch to look in a small 'nucleus' hive, in which I had recently installed a swarm – many beekeepers can never find their queens in daylight – but after some trouble, and a little luck, I did, popping her into my special carrying-tube, and retired to bed – placing the tube under my pillow. Tomorrow could well be a very busy day.

On Friday 31st of June, the Unit arrived as before. This time all was in place much faster. I went to the Dresser's van. Paola was intrigued with my request for a small pocket, 'the size to accept this small tube on the back of my hat,' and nearly dropped it, when she learned that a queen bee was inside. (After I opened it to show them, a great concern developed, and her welfare took precedence over mine for the rest of the day!) The girls were about halfway through their work, when an urgent call came over the intercom for me to go to the orchard – 'there is a problem with the bees?' Trailing clothing and girls like some pantomime comic, I rushed along – expecting to see the bees vacating their queenless nucleus hive – only to be shown a huge swarm on the trunk of an apple tree, right next to where the camera platform was to be built. I was ecstatic. The Director was amazed that I was pleased about this. 'What about the crew's safety?' I called out to the stage hands. 'Put a tape round to keep folk away, but leave a small gap for me to walk through – and do not disturb them!'

Once we were ready, the sun behaved, and the Director soon called out our agreed 'One minute Bill.' Moving over to the swarm, I brushed my hands through it, dropping the bees over my hat and the hidden queen, turned and plunged my hands into a bowl of Fullers Earth, stepping onto my mark, just in time to hear the call, 'Roll the camera. Aaaaand action.' Two straps hit my chest with a satisfying thwack, and the Director gave an encouraging smile – the girls said he also liked the puffs of dust from the Fullers Earth. The filming went without a hitch, and the swarm of bees behaved beautifully, even so, it was lunch time before the Director called out, 'Well done Bill, that's those shots in the can. We'll film the bees on the comb after lunch.' As we all passed the swarm, I noticed a sudden 'shimmer', as the light reflected on thousands of quivering wings, and they took off as one, drifting up and away through the trees!

After another sumptuous meal we returned to the set where the stage hands had constructed a bee-proof cage in the hope of keeping more bees in shot. The rest of the afternoon was spent with me dashing back and forth into the cage, and on the call for "ACTION" jarring each bee covered comb – the stage hands, safely outside, tapping the sides of the netting to keep the bees flying. I was amused to see in the finished advert, just three of the twelve hives in shot, and only two bees flying past in the close-up. At least my payment doubled again for the second days filming, and Norwich Union later gave me an investment Bond, in the Property Trust we were advertising. The Film Unit also gave a £200 donation to Wandlebury – with the added perks for me, of three new WBC hive bodies, a new bee suit, a veil, and a much prized, boxed pair of red braces!

18. I Retire and Make a Nobel Prize Winner Envious

Retirement?

I was now working beyond my retirement date, both to enable Wendy to stay in our beloved Jarratts Cottage, with her pretty garden, as long as possible, and for me to round off my final 'Five Year Forestry Plan'. I informed the Forestry Commission that I would shortly be felling the last of the dying beech, in order to plant the replacements in the autumn. I was annoyed to receive a letter, informing me that I could not fell them, until my assumptions were proved correct! Some weeks later the young man who had signed the letter, finally arrived to give his opinion, and absolutely disagreed with mine? However, I told him that I required in writing – before he left the Estate – that he would take full responsibility for all damage caused to buildings or people by the dying trees. He then said he was not saying I could not fell them, but that their health was such, that I could only fell them after he had granted a felling licence. This procedure of course took some time, and I lost the chance to get them down before the winter: next, adding injury to my insult, only days before the licence arrived, a 30 mph wind took down three of my marked trees – the roots completely rotten – and branches out of four of the others – luckily the largest branch, only removed one brick from the garden wall!

Once my retirement date was announced, folk incessantly asked, 'What on earth are you going to do with yourself?' Various Chairmen and Committee Members had intimated Jarratts Cottage would be our home for as long as we needed, but I had lived too long in a commercial world not to be prepared for a complete change of heart, especially with an oft changing Committee, and so it proved – spurred on by the rules of the Charities Commission. Luckily, just when it seemed we had to leave Wandlebury for ever, the Admin Secretary – and long-time friend – Sally, informed us that she was about to relinquish the tenancy of the much improved flat we had turned down 25 years before. And we were allowed to move in as rent paying tenants, just days before John Woodward – my assistant for the previous two years took over. Even he voiced concern, and urged me to get started on a hobby, 'Why don't you take up painting or wood turning?' I remarked that I had enjoyed water colour painting during my school days. Little did I know that I had settled the main gift that the CPS Committee and Members were going to present to me at their planned farewell party in Christ's College – a most handsome set of everything that a 'Water Colourist' could ever need! After the CPS farewell party – which I found rather overwhelming, so many well-known people saying such kind words: and it being so final – we were invited to another for the Wandlebury residents, with the added purpose of greeting the new head warden and his wife. It was a splendid afternoon, hosted by Anka Owen in her recently finished Artist Studio – where I have since enjoyed many a Thursday afternoon in the company of the 'Greystoke' artists, trying hard to match my painting skills to my splendid accoutrements.

Soon after moving, two neighbours asked for help with plumbing problems, and John Woodward talked the CPS into allowing the beekeepers to build a large hut, which I was asked to help with – having to borrow my tools back, that I had donated to the CPS. I should have kept them all, for a short time later many of them were stolen during a

318

'break in'! I have since replaced most of mine, and they are still getting regular use. Wendy still wanted to be able to garden, and the piece of ground that went with the flat hadn't been attended to for some time. Although only the first of December, it would still be touch and go if she was going to be able to dig her first new potatoes in May as usual. There was a three metre high bramble bush, covering sixty square metres in the centre, ten metres of six metre high, four metre thick beech hedge to cut down to size, fifteen metres of garden wall covered in two metre thick ivy, and a collapsed brick shed to deal with. Next, Christopher South – on behalf of BBC Radio Cambridgeshire – phoned to say, 'Bill I have many times thought you have enough material to come in fortnightly instead of monthly, would that be possible?' I was not going to be at a loose end for a while!

One of the Wandlebury visitors put it all nicely into context later. I was asked if I could take over an evening 'Guided Tour', and as I stood at the top of the car park awaiting the last folk to get out of their cars I heard, 'Isn't that Mr Clark?' – and an elderly couple broke from the group and walked over. 'This is a bit of a Busman's holiday for you Mr Clark?' I remarked that I was in fact taking them round. The wife laughed. 'Of course how silly of us, we should have known, but you are retired aren't you?' 'Well, yes, although my wife might disagree,' I replied. She turned to her husband, 'Tell Mr Clark what you told the Bishop the other day.' The retired Reverend gave a rueful grin. 'The Bishop asked how I was enjoying my retirement. I said that I thought it was really designed for a much younger man!'

My contribution to the Millennium was to get the 17C clock in the cupola back into working order. Having only one hand confuses our visitors. I tell them, the clock is of a slower time, when minutes were not so important! The highlight was to ensure that it chimed the midnight hour right on the second, whilst Wendy held the phone so that Carolyn Gorwill – the Great, great, great, great, great, granddaughter of the land-steward who lived within its

319

hearing in the early 1800s, could hear the chimes in Canada – and enjoy two midnight hours! The piece of bow-saw blade that I fashioned into the pendulum hanger is still in place, and it would keep good time, if someone could keep an eye on the weather, and lengthen the iron pendulum during cold periods and shorten it when the sun beats down on the lead roof.

Nobel visitor

Dr Perutz, who won the Nobel Prize for Chemistry in 1962, was a regular visitor to Wandlebury, mostly walking alone, sometimes with his daughter: he usually took the same route around the perimeter. A quiet and pleasant man, looking deep in thought, yet always pausing to pass the time of day, or mention something he had noticed along the way. When I was cutting the young shoots off the old apple trees to use for grafting, he stopped to ask what I was doing. And after I explained, he said that he had an even older looking tree. 'Will it work for that too?' 'Of course,' I replied, 'you just need a young seedling – you could plant an apple seed yourself – about as thick as a pencil, and in July, all you have to do is take a bud from the apple tree; look I'll show you.' 'Oh, no, no!" he interrupted, 'You are far cleverer than I, you must come and do it for me.' The last time we met, was just after the Woodland Trust had planted up their 'Millennian Wood' at Wandlebury and named it Clarks' Corner, for Wendy and I. I espied Doctor Perutz frantically waving to me, and as we neared one another, I remarked, 'You are taking a shorter walk today Doctor.' 'Yes and I am so pleased. I have been reading the new notice-board – I didn't know! They have named the wood after you, aren't you lucky?' 'Yes, it was certainly a big surprise,' I answered, 'but you have a building named after you.' 'That is true, but I would much rather have had a field,' he replied.

19. Retirement Gives Time to Look Over Other 'Hedges' and Solve a 1970s Conundrum

Accidents on the A1307

After years of complaining to the authorities about the dangerousness of the road adjacent to Wandlebury, in December 2002 all residents received a Cambridgeshire CC letter, asking for comments on the enclosed map of a new road layout. Despite guessing this was just ticking boxes, for what the government now requires of them, we all got involved! I was by this time, reasonably proficient at deciding the cause of many of the accidents, for hardly an hour passed when the carriageway was in my view, that I didn't witness heart stopping moments – I was able to nearly double their list of accidents on the stretch, for starters – Collectively, we suggested quite a number of alterations to their improvements, including a speed limit and bringing the footpath from the Stapleford turn-off up to Wandlebury.

The first of the many accidents I had attended, involved a van skidding and knocking down the Footpath sign as I waited to cross to the post-box. I thanked my lucky stars that he had missed me, and after checking he was unhurt, grumbled at how stupid it was to drive so fast in such icy conditions. 'Ice had nothing to do with it mate, my steering's gone,' he snapped. I stepped onto the road, with the purpose of sliding my foot to show him, when he shouted, 'LOOK OUT,' and we both jumped for our lives, as a car slewed round and disappeared into the opposite hedge. With neither driver hurt, I could only smile, when I realised the wording on the van revealed the driver was a 'Refrigeration Engineer'!

Driving south over the sharp brow too fast, then being caught out by the adverse camber as the vehicle slams down, was quite common. One lovely sunny afternoon, a car rolled over once and was standing broadside on the verge with smoke pouring from the engine. I wrenched the door open, but the tubby driver was trapped by her feet; all I could do, was support her weight outside, and pray. A Magpas doctor soon arrived, followed by an ambulance. During the struggle to release her, it came as quite a shock to realise they all knew her, for she was a nurse in Addenbrookes A&E! On another sunny afternoon, I heard the familiar screech of tyres followed by a 'whumpf' and called Wendy from my radio to do the usual as I ran, but as I neared the road there was a second screech and 'whumpf.' Expecting carnage, I found the first car neatly at an angle, on its side and off the road, a lady just climbing down to the ground. Ten paces further on, a small van lay identically, with a male driver still clambering out.

Another time I woke with a start at 2.00 am – I sat up, straining my ears, but not a sound. Wendy woke as I opened the window, 'What's the matter,' she asked. 'Something woke me. I had better go and look.' Minutes later I was in the road: way down in the lay-by I could see rear lights, but as I switched on my powerful torch, the car drove off. Grumbling to myself, 'I bet he got out of control, I'll see his skid marks in the morning,' I turned to walk back. My light beam picked out the glistening white trunk of a lime tree in the central reservation – a large chunk of bark had been stripped off. As I ran, I could see bits of car strewn all around, and radioed Wendy, '999, all the services!' Next, I saw the shape of a car, half buried in the hedge on the far side of the service road. The driver sat slumped, but I could feel no pulse, and as the passenger seat belt hung loose and no windscreen, I searched in the hedge, but found no one. Back with the driver, I could still not feel a pulse, but as I took my hand away, I heard a faint gurgle, and with a shock, realised that the seat belt was tight across his throat; I immediately released it, struggling to stop him falling out onto his face.

For some minutes I lay against the car, holding him across my chest, for one foot looked to be trapped. The ambulance soon pulled to a halt, and within seconds, he was free, strapped to a stretcher and away. As I waited for the Police and the Fire Brigade, I surveyed the scene. It was extraordinary! The engine and gearbox was in small pieces spread down the roadside – even the flywheel and clutch plates lay separately, all the glass was shattered, the doors lay on either side of the tree, the two left hand wheels were in the hedge fifty metres further down – the right hand wheels were later found across the other carriageway, with one in the next field! Whilst the rear axle had managed to slide past the right side, the body shell had slid past the left of the tree, straightening up to the original line of travel and coming to a halt in the hedge. Both headlights – still in one piece – had shot out, to lay in front and on either side of the tree. Once the other services arrived, I returned home, showered off the blood, put my clothes to soak, and went back to a fitful sleep. When the police called for a statement the following morning, I was amazed to hear the driver was still alive: in fact, two years later he visited me!

I was not at all surprised, when we later received the Cambridgeshire County Council's completed plans for the new road layout – shortly before work was due to start – with not a single alteration to the original. Although I did feel we should have sent them a 'We Told you so,' letter, for not long after it was all finished in 2003 – after a few minor bumps, skids, etc. – workmen were back stripping off markings and making alterations. Some looked remarkably akin to our original suggestions – in fact with the 2011 building of the cycle way, and a fifty mile an hour speed limit on one section, many of our 'improvements' to that original plan, are now in place.

Intelligent Mowing Saves Wildlife

Since my retirement, I have seized the opportunity to look more closely at grass mowing. It is now over forty years since I conjectured that grass sward and invertebrate life, was being damaged with flail mowers. In the years since, these machines have grown in size, moved to larger tractors, and onto the ends of long, articulated arms – they can mash their way into almost any, out of the way place. Their versatility and speed has made them very popular with contractors, thus making them available to whoever desires even a day's cutting. Their ease of dealing with any type of growth has spawned a plethora of machines at the small end of the scale. If a gardener – of whatever age or gender – needs to trim a patch, however small, they are more likely to reach for an electric strimmer than a sickle! Nowhere is safe! I have searched wild flower areas on roadsides and nature reserves, directly after flail and rotary mowing has occurred, and found numbers of dead bumble bees, and in areas containing mining bee populations, as many as eight dead bees to the square metre, minced frogs, various members of the rodent family. And on one sad occasion, fledgling skylarks!

My 'Risk Assessment' for mowing over solitary bees homes, shows up the problems. The reciprocating 'finger' mower – depending on forward speed – makes about one cut per two cm of travel. Any bee flying up from a hole would be very unlucky to be caught by the blades: 0.0001% risk. The cylinder mower, little used on Nature Reserves, but popular on golf courses and private lawns – passes over with about two cuts per cm, but owing to the way it revolves, it can throw insects clear: 0.01% risk. Flail mowers make a minimum of four cuts per cm of travel, using a revolving cylinder of blades of variable diameter.

The material is severely mashed under a hood, before being thrown out at the rear: 20%+ risk. Strimmers and rotary mowers cover from a minimum 200 mm circle up to six or more square metres with a whirling set of whips or blades under a canopy. There can be in excess of a hundred cuts over every two cm: many are designed to suck up from the ground, so to present the grass upright to the blades. They all maintain a vortex of air and material, doing a varying amount of mashing according to the design: Minimum risk 20% up to 70%+. The swinging arc method of strimming possibly even pushes little hand-held machines towards the high end too.

It would certainly be prudent – to quote just two instances – to avoid mowing lakeside meadows during the period that froglets leave the water. And to avoid the two flight periods of the Brown Argus butterflies – May-June and August – in their perceived breeding areas. This could be crucial for these low flying insects. I have discovered one very good use for a flail mower though. Eradicating ragwort – *Senecio jacobaea*. It is a very nasty plant for any animal, human or otherwise, to eat – destroying the liver in no time – even the birds avoid eating caterpillars that feed on ragwort. Horse owners should definitely not allow it on their land – in fact, they and other agriculturalists, can apply for an, 'Enforcement notice' to be issued to neighbouring land owners, to eradicate it, and so remove the source of wind-blown seed. Common ragwort is mostly biennial, and Oxford ragwort mostly perennial, so no need to mow the year it appears – it will be below the blades anyway – but any plants that put up a flower spike should be cut before any petal colour shows; plants cut in full flower, can still make some viable seed, in fact, in wet weather, large plants in tight bud, can continue to make some seed. Hence my use of the flail mower, this mashes the flower heads ending any possibility of seed forming. If this is done each time shoots raise their heads, even the Oxford ragwort will eventually die.

As might be expected, eradicating all ragwort would not please me in the least! It has been recorded that 177 species of invertebrates feed on the nectar, and 77 species of insect herbivores, chew on the plant. The pretty Cinnabar Moth caterpillars, for instance, can trash a small patch of ragwort. And therein lies a problem for all 'Countryside Managers.' Whether to clear? When to clear? How much to clear? And what to clear it with! One summer's day, I saw two ladies setting up a 'transect' at the east end of a meadow shaded by trees, in readiness to count butterflies. In full sun, at the west end, a man was strimming all of the weeds growing among a plot of shrubs. This was the most ideal area in that field to find Peacock, Comma and Tortoiseshell butterflies; their eggs were probably already on the nettles being cut down, as too, the Speckled Wood and Orange Tip butterfly caterpillars, could already be feeding on the grass and garlic mustard also being strimmed! (I did champion mowing nettles, but in late June – first looking for any first brood pupae still hanging on the stems, and removing them to a safe place – the new growth providing the forage needed for the second brood of caterpillars). My own regime also made room for the thistle family – spear and woolly thistle, besides being spectacular plants, are heavy nectar yielders when in full sun, attracting bumblebees and butterflies, and later, yielding quality seed for such as the goldfinches. The carline and musk thistles are now quite rare, although there is usually a small group of musk each year in the far corner of the Gogs Trust land. (When going to check on them in 2009, the farm contractor had killed all but one whilst desiccating the oil seed rape. Hopefully there will be some viable seed to provide flowering plants from 2011 onward).

Bats and the Guided Busway

I hear that the numbers of bats hibernating in the tunnel each winter are still rising – although this makes me wonder if this means they are coming in from farther afield. Certainly cold June weather is of no help to those suckling young, but their biggest problem overall, must be the loss of the old trees, especially the elms, that used to provide hollows, holes and crevices for safe roosting, and a greater number and variety of insects. There are definitely fewer flying here on summer evenings now, than even ten years ago. My furthest call regarding these mammals was from Canada! Initially, family friend, Carolyn Gorwill, was requesting information to get rid of rats after finding droppings in her porch. A request for her to crush some droppings enabled me to give her the welcome news, that she didn't have rats scurrying below, but a bat hanging above! It was promptly named 'William'! And 2012, is his, or her, 10th seasonal visit.

Another task since my retirement, was to check the line of the projected route of the, 'Guided Bus,' in regard to its importance for bees. Julia Napier, the lady who requested it, already knew of a rare butterfly or two. 'What we really need, to stop this concrete track,' I said to Wendy, as we trudged along, 'is something exceedingly rare. Look in those empty snail shells and see if you can find Fabré's "Resin Bees;" they have never been found in Britain!' Then as she looked askance at the hundreds of small white shells, I added, 'Actually that is a good idea, not only do one or two of the bees that nest in holes and hollow twigs, use them, but *Osmia bicolour* uses them exclusively, and is uncommon enough to make folk sit up and take notice.' (It has been found there since the track was built) Suffice it to say, we did find a rare little bee using them, and I was able to say, that the numbers of *Hoplitis spinulosa,* we found along that section, were the most ever seen at any one site in Cambridgeshire! But of course we were still on a hiding to nothing. A County Council spending millions on barristers, were not going to allow a bunch of individuals with a few rare insects to stop their juggernaut!

Rare Bees and Losing the Beewolf

As it happened, the bee was unusual enough for me to have to order a more recent book for my collection – the R & S Report No. 35, A Review of the Scarce & Threatened Bees, Wasps and Ants of Great Britain by Stephen Falk – which caused some hilarity from the lady on the other phone! My address alone often brings forth comment, but coupled with my requested title! Unfortunately, our little bee wasn't in it, and I had to make other enquiries. Howbeit, there was a chapter about the Beewolf, *Philanthus triangulum* – the wasps that I and Caroline had seen digging in the paths on my first day at Wandlebury. The author lists them as 'Vulnerable' for England, but to my astonishment, gives no reference for Cambridgeshire. He then goes on to mention its liking for sandy heaths and cliffs, and confines it to those areas. (No wonder the Cambridge entomologists, had not bothered to look for it in the solid chalk of the Gog Magog Hills!)

From my first day at Wandlebury I had worked to keep those habitat areas – we also found species of mining bees too – by only repairing those path sections with a mix of sand and chalk, crushed lime-mortar and chalk, or chalk alone, depending on what was available when repairs where needed, the insects remained in situ. By removing unsuitable brick rubble, the areas were even extended. It was gratifying to see the steady rise in the numbers of holes being excavated. Always extremely busy, I had little time for observation, but with these numbers, I could watch 20 holes for ten minutes, and provide myself, with a 'Gallop Poll' on the Beewolf! On an average I would see one bee carried in during every third observation – only once did I see two bees in one session. This is equal to one bee per wasp for each 10 hours of activity, hardly making them a serious pest of honey bees, as some writers would have us believe. I believe *Philanthus* constructs an average fifteen cells, needing some four bees for each cell, so requiring around 60 bees for her seasons work. I also saw both males and females sipping nectar from flowers, which makes me think it is erroneous to say that they kill many bees just to imbibe their nectar, in fact Falk even says they eat them, which is certainly wrong – I doubt if any wasp species kills for their own sustenance.

In 1994 the CPS applied for grants to resurface some paths, to allow easier disabled access into certain areas – as parts of these paths were now wasp and bee habitat, I asked for the insects to be taken into account, with the result, that I and Committee member, Mike Francis – a retired architect – were given the task of designing the paths around them. The paths would be cambered, standing proud of the grassland and constructed entirely of soft carrstone, rolled firm to a minimum thickness of 150 mm, and furnished with plank edging. The idea being that the mining insects could still use it, although we recommended that one heavily drilled path should be avoided, just in case we were wrong. Though the returned tenders were priced on building to our design, the Committee considered that the Cambridge City's path contractor engaged for the job in 1995, had all the expertise needed, and he was allowed to build to his own design. Although the concept of using carrstone was adhered to, the thickness was 50 mm less, with little camber, and as the finished surface was level with, and in places, below the surrounding surface, the board edging was dispensed with. The consequence has been that although the wasps did use the path in good numbers, the areas have since either washed away or puddled.

Unfortunately, since my retirement, wet summers have also puddled some of the traditional sections, but the worst problem has been the continuous use of wood-chip surfacing – I was unable to find one P. *triangulum* hole in 2012. The present management of Wandlebury urgently needs to take its care into account!

Dating and Placing the Cupola

Also dating from the early 1970s, was my desire to satisfactorily date the Cupola on the stable block. I had found some serious rot in the main frame at that time, and whilst making my report at a Committee Meeting had said that the unused and out of alignment peg-holes in the framework, led me to believe that the Cupola was once on another building. My assumption was rejected, it being pointed out that such edifices were often constructed elsewhere, dismantled, and rebuilt in position. However I always felt uneasy with this explanation.

At that time, Wendy was already underway with collecting, researching and writing up the history of Wandlebury, and one print we discovered, and bought, was the, "NORTH-EAST VIEW OF CAMBRIDGE CASTLE" 1730, by Samuel & Nathaniel Buck – viewed from the site of the present Shire Hall. In the far distance, on the left-hand side at No1, is a minute building which the legend states is 'E of Godolphins House upon Gog-Magog Hill.' Even at this size, the cupola building can be seen to have a dip or flat area where the cupola should be. Wendy was of the opinion that this would most likely be a viewing platform.

I had to wait until 1978, during the Rattee and Kett reconstruction of the Cupola before I got a closer look at the framework – in addition to the names and dates scrawled by visitors and clock repairers on the inner surface, I was hoping to find hidden graffiti left by the original builders. Much of interest emerged, but only one date to do with the actual building: William Nutting had stamped his name and the date – 1848 – in the lead covering of the dome. A previous clock face, painted on the boards, was discovered when the lead was stripped off the sides, also the remains of fixtures for railings that had once surrounded the roof of the square lower storey. The uprights for the hexagonal bell chamber had been altered, and it was evident that the wooden louvres in the openings were later additions. This could still all be construed as repairs and alterations to better the weatherproofing at that date. My theory was still in the minority.

Around this time we saw in an Antique-shop window a 'wide view' print, entitled, 'THE NORTH-WEST PROSPECT of the UNIVERSITY and TOWN of CAMBRIDGE.' This view, taken from Trinity Conduit Head, was dated March 25th 1743 – again by the Bucks, and we purchased a hand tinted photocopy for £11. My reason for treating this as a 'must have', was that on the far right at Number 23, was 'Earl of Godolphins House upon Gogmagog-Hill.' Again minute, but plain to see, was that the cupola had been built in the intervening 13 years. At least we now had a time frame.

Eventually the rough proof of the first edition of 'Once Around Wandlebury' was in hand. Casting around for suitable illustrations for it, we went along to view a Relhan drawing – owned by the Antiquarian Society and deposited at the Fitzwilliam Museum. My first thought on seeing the 1801 Gogmagog drawing, was of great disappointment; the banks of the Ring Ditch were much enlarged in relation to the buildings, whilst the whole painting – I thought – was rather crude. However, there was no mistaking the cupola on the rear coach houses – I was correct, it was once on another building, but now I was also confronted with a confusing date and I resigned myself to the fact that I would probably never sort out the puzzle.

Fast forward to October 2009! Parish Magazine 'The Stapleford Messenger' ran an article, using an enlarged section of the Relhan drawing. After a pleasant read I casually glanced at the drawing then quickly took a closer look. There was something I had not noticed before! I snatched down Wendy's, Once Around Wandlebury – and yes, it is just discernible in the much smaller picture too. Relhan had drawn a second cupola in the spot it is in today. If only I had taken more interest, the answer was in front of me in 1985! Perhaps I shouldn't feel too badly about it, for most of that Committee also poured over 'Once Around

Wandlebury', looking for faults, and never picked it up either!

The skinny looking – probably taller – viewing cupola was drawn by both Messrs Buck – the clock cupola was not in the Bucks view – and Relhan! Relhan's drawing faithfully shows taller openings and a slightly bell shaped dome minus a weather vane, in comparison to the coach house clock with a rounded dome complete with weathervane. By the 1840s the desire to add a storey to the coach house block, meant the cupola would have to be dismantled, so why not move what was a top heavy looking structure on the small building, to the large stable block? It would not be so easy to see out of its lower openings, nevertheless by fixing railings in place, intrepid viewers could clamber outside. By then, tree planting was fast obscuring the distant views – just as now the golf course planting is about to obscure most of the views from Post 7 – and as the trees grew taller still, the desire to visit the cupola diminished, until the final closing of the openings with the louvres – to keep out the wind-blown rain – blocked off the views completely.

30. Detail taken from North-East view of Cambridge Castle 1730 by Samuel and Nathaniel Buck, seen from the site of the present Shire Hall. The Stable Block has a distinct flat centre to the roof.

31. Detail taken from The North-West prospect of the University and town of Cambridge, 1743, also by Samuel and Nathaniel Buck. Viewed from Trinity Conduit Head. The viewing tower is now built.

32. Detail taken from Reylan's drawing. The viewing tower can just be seen close to the tree branches. The cupola is in plain view, but low down on the rear coach house - before the coach house was both lengthened and made higher.

33. Wendy's picture of the Cupola taken from the garden in 2011.

20. What Does the Future Hold?

In common with many others, I fear for the future of our countryside. From the top of this hill, since my retirement, I have observed the faster than ever spread of housing, and new roads marching towards us from the north and west, which will inevitably mean a heavier footfall in such as Wandlebury. The springing up of a wind farm on the south side has brought industry, suddenly, intrudingly close. During my 'school' walks I always avoided 'delicate' areas – the emphasis was always on teaching care of the environment. When I gave my reasons for giving a certain bush or corner of a field, a wide berth, because a bird was sitting on eggs, or a leveret was in hiding, it never failed to impress – as did my reasons for putting rotting wood, ivy and brambles, so high up the conservation scale.

Latterly – not just in Wandlebury – folk expect to walk and play wherever they please, it is just too bad if a skylark is nesting where their dog wants to run. Also the falling off of grants and charity donations has placed an emphasis on bringing in the fee paying public, no matter what! From twenty or thirty people on mountain bikes to a hundred or so enjoying a theatre production or thousands with a pop concert. Stuff that was once for town parks, now regularly gets set up – night or day and even permanently – in the most out of the way places.

Large amounts of cash from the Lottery Fund, worries me too. Look at the hard surfacing, bridges and such like, that now encourage folk into parts of the Fens almost 'twenty four seven'. Only the hares and the plovers reached such places a short time ago. This sort of 'customer' encouragement and improvement of 'services' will certainly not help the really wild habitat or bring back species that have been lost.

Many farmers are at last realising that it is in their interests to farm sustainably, for example, my friends the Towlers, earning a good living, yet still entertaining wildlife on their Scald End Farm, whilst others are even actively encouraging wildlife. Visiting my old employer, Jim Dutton, in Wivenhoe last year, I counted yellow hammers and corn buntings in dozens along their conservation strips. Later, on the screen of the computer in their sitting room, I saw how the barn owl and tawny owl chicks were coming along in the nest boxes out in the trees, that they had laboriously entrenched cables to. A week or two later his son David – a keen ornithologist – excitedly phoned to say they had seen both a water rail and a bittern in their reed bed. Farmers like these, lift my spirits considerably.

We need to keep a link to the past. Without me, Caroline would not have known that it was once possible to play in fields yellow with cowslips. (And later share that joy with her sons – Eden and Roman.) Today's Rangers won't have a bench mark to refer to, believing the fifty or so butterflies in Varley's is good, when as a youth mowing hay, I would have seen thousands! – Or that their 'Dawn Chorus' walk is not only missing a lot of decibels, but at least half a dozen species. That brambles are the chosen nest sites for yellowhammers, corn buntings and whitethroats. Old growth elder is a much loved nest site for goldfinches, and if you want to keep a hawthorn shrub growing for nearly ever, it needs to be cut down to <u>ground level</u> every once in a while.

However, despite complaining about deteriorating joints, it is still a joy to walk in the dappled shade of the planted trees, and wander over the now permanent meadows, perhaps passing the time of day with the present, dedicated Ranger-carers at Wandlebury, who like all the others at the 'sharp end,' continue to do all they can.

Appendix

Some earlier references to a 'Chalk Figure' at Wandlebury

Babington. Ancient Cambridgeshire.   1853-83
Carter E. The History of the County of Cambridge. 1753
Conybeare E. A History of Cambridge.   1906
Gardner R. History, gazette and directory of Cambridgeshire. 1851
Gooch. 'Cambridge'   1811
Highways and Byways in Cambridge & Ely   1837
Lysons History of Cambridge.   1808
Porter Enid. Cambs Customs and Folklore. Page 186 – 8 1969
Teversham T F. A History of the Village of Sawston. 1942

Photocopy of unknown publication, posted through my letter box in 1976, read:
Page 202 EAST ANGLIA AND THE FENS. WANDLEBURY CAMP, STAPLEFORD, CAMBRIDGESHIRE.   Sheet 154 TL4953. The author quotes: "Camden's silence is the most potent – for he had been there. One wonders if the cutting of the giant could even have been prompted by his visit and the subsequent appearance of the Britannia, the first Latin edition of which was published in 1586?   The earliest

reference we have to the giant comes from Mundus alter et idem (1605), by Joseph Hall, a Cambridge graduate; and in 1640 John Layer.".......etc. – End of quote.

L Elvin, a researcher for Gogmagog Golf Club wrote: "GOG MAGOG HILLS. From Brayley, E W. & Britton J. Cambs or original delineation's of that county, Lond. J, Harris, 1818." Elvin further quotes the usual stuff from Layer, Gervase Camden etc – and follows it with a mention of a Dr Gale thinking there is a Roman connection because of Roman coins being found whilst digging a cellar in 1685 – and a Mr Gough observes that "Vandlebury is the fourth of the chain of which begins at the large camp on the hill where the hunting tower once stood opposite to Audley Inn," etc.

In 'Gods and Graven Images' 1987 by Paul Newman. Page 122:
The first published reference to the Wandlebury Giant is found in a work by Bishop Joseph Hall appearing in Frankfurt in 1605 but quickly followed by an English edition: "A Giant called All Paunch, who was of incredible height of body, not like him whose picture the Schollers of Cambridge got to see at Hogmagog Hills, but rather like him that ought the two Apple Teeth which were digged out of a well in Cambridge, that were little less than a man's head." Newman also repeats this verbatim in his update to Gods and Graven Images, entitled, 'Lost Gods of Albion', 1997, on page 115. (Including quite a bit of my, "Dowsing Gogmagog", published in the Third Stone Magazine!)

Heichelheim,E.M. 'Antiquity' March 1939:
Under the heading 'THE GOGMAGOG GIANT OF CAMBRIDGE'. "...........but John Layer, a comparatively modern antiquary, cannot be cited as reliable evidence for this fact, because the figure was already known to an Elizabethan author, Joseph Hall, who matriculated at Cambridge in 1589 and mentioned the giant in a book which he wrote in his younger days before c. 1605. Cp. Mercurius Britannicus (Bishop Joseph Hall), Mundus alter et idem (ed. Frankfurt, c. 1605) lib. 1, chap 11 – then

338

follows sentence in Latin – next – Cp. in addition the contemporary translation of Bishop Hall's book by John Healey, another Cambridge scholar : 'The Discovery of a New World, Written Originally in the Latin by Joseph Hall, c. 1605; Englished by John Healey, c. 1609; edited by Huntington Brown (Cambridge Mass. 1937) .... etc" – then – "For the biography of Bishop Hall and John Healey see the introduction to Brown's edition." Further research reveals this was on page 44. The book was entitled 'Discovery of a New World or a Description of the South Indies, printed by Edward Blunt & William Barrett.

William Cole of Milton also quotes Bishop Hall's work and then goes on to write about his own boyhood visits to Cambridge via the Gogmagog Hills – see my quote under 'A giant within the Ring'.

T C Lethbridge in a letter to the Times 12th June 1936, wrote:
'Gogmagog or Gourmaillan, was undoubtedly responsible for the name of these hills – his figure cut in the downland turf, either inside Wandlebury Camp itself or on the hillside close beside it, was still inside in the mid 18th cent .....'

Antiquaries who make no mention of a Wandlbury Hill Figure are:
Camden.
Cobbett 'Rural Rides' 1821. (I found no mention of any chalk figures.)
Defoe. 1724. (He makes no mention although he visited Wandlebury.)
Gervase.
Eliot, 'Orthoepia Gallica' or 'Fruits for the French' 1593. who says that the hills were made by – Atlas, cousin-germane to Gogmagog – and that we can see an image of Gogmagog's rival Corineus at the London Guild Hall.

The following, are snippets from various Lethbridge letters sent to the CPS Chairman – the Rt Hon, H U Willink, Master of Magdalene College. One, asking for permission to dig, suggests what could be found, and attached to it – with now very rusty pins – a pencil drawing of the possible figure.

Extremely close in detail to the figure that was eventually excavated, though without the nipples! Senses tell me, this drawing always accompanied that letter, but of course Tom's backers, would say it was attached later.
Dec 1954.

'. . . well this is as far as I can get with a steel bar. It was perfectly easy to find – no   problem at all, but hard work following it up.'
May 11th 1955.

'. . . now all this is really sport to me, I have had all the fun of finding the things.   I know all about political tricks.'
May 12th 1955.

'. . . the last little man that bumped into me like this spent a long time in a bug house   afterwards.'
May 15th 1955.

'I have no intention of being drawn into a row unless I am deliberately insulted. To me this is only a sport and I have no ambition to be an archaeological pope!'
March 24th 1956. (Writing about a professor who partly disagrees)

'He may be right, but I could never get past seeing the whole of his breakfast spread   out on his waistcoat.'
Dec 1956.

'It is any ones guess who this chap is. Mine is that he is a sun god.

In an "Outside report", requested by the CPS, Mr Sparkes and Mr Lewis – experts on chalk deposits wrote: '. . Most of what we saw could not be man-made. .'

Illustrations

on Wandlebury. I took this photo on a Friday afternoon before placing a notice by them, 'Please leave these flowers for others to enjoy.' By Sunday evening, not one was left! 115

Index

Cambridge Water Company, 155
Cambridgeshire
  BBC Radio Cambridgeshire, 234, 293, 319
  Cambient, 128
  Cambridge Evening News, 53, 121, 153, 154, 171, 200, 233, 272
  Cambridge Machinery Sale, 244, 269
  Cambridgeshire County Council, 145, 159, 169, 171, 236, 279, 321
  South Cambs DC, 144, 242
Christ's College, 318
Clacton, 98
Clarks' Corner, 320
Colchester docks, 97
Colchester Natural History Society, 107
Colmworth, 1, 4, 7, 8
Community service, 167
Community Service, 160, 169, 291
Coombe, 77, 83
Cottenham, 277
Country Park, 129
Countryside Commission, 129, 248
Crime, 162, 172, 195, 197, 225, 248, 273, 280
Deer, 247
Divining, 131, 134
Dogs, 2, 73, 74, 78, 86, 104, 110, 138, 197, 214, 223
Dormouse, 126
Downham Market, 170
Dowsing, 133, 134, 301
Drains, 130, 135
Driving test, 61
Drought, 154, 155, 159, 169
Duxford Hire, 233, 234
East of England Show, 186, 210
Education
  School, 4, 5, 7, 10, 17, 26, 27, 28, 29, 38, 41, 52, 54, 59, 148

School visits, 147, 169, 171, 173, 176, 195, 204, 246, 278
Schools, 236
Electricity cables, 235
Epping Forest, 114
Essex
  Colchester Machinery Club, 113
  Essex County Council, 114
  Essex Naturalist Trust, 114
  Essex Naturalists Trust, 106, 107
  Essex River Authority, 107
  Essex River Board, 114
  Tendring, 97
Farm buildings, 32
Farmers Weekly, 146
Farming
  Bulls, 32, 34, 57, 69
  Chickens, 72
  Conservation, 52, 336
  Cows, 18, 31, 34, 57, 59, 62, 63, 67, 73
  Crops, 12, 19, 82, 84, 98
  Foot and Mouth, 59
  Harvest, 23
  Herbicide, 29
  Horses, 24
  Insecticides, 121
  Ploughing, 29, 51, 101
  Potato picking leave, 41
  Slaughter, 20
  stacks, 23
  Sugar beet, 239
  Tractors, 25, 39, 42, 49, 51, 101, 108, 112, 206
  Vermin, 12, 137
Fenland Country Fair, 210
Fires, 151, 155
Forestry Commission, 146, 154, 317
Fungus, 165
Gamekeepers, 79, 80, 86